PURSUING

GOD

A DAILY
ENCOUNTER

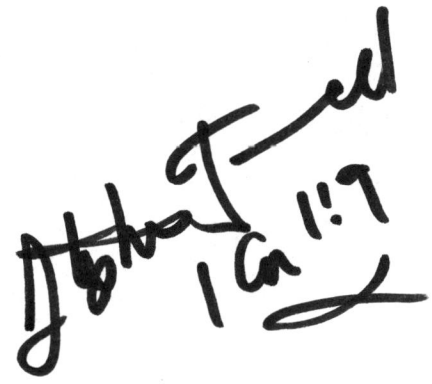

DR. STEPHEN TRAMMELL

PURSUING GOD

A DAILY ENCOUNTER

DR. STEPHEN TRAMMELL

Published in the United States by Champion Forest Baptist Church, Houston, TX
www.championforest.org

Scripture taken from the Holy Bible, New International Version®, NIV®

Copyright© 1973, 1978, 1984 by Biblica, Inc.™

Used by permission of Zondervan. All rights reserved worldwide.
WWW.ZONDERVAN.COM

The "NIV" and "New International Version" are trademarks registered in the United States Patent and Trademark Offices by Biblica, Inc.

Book design by Jacque Sellers

Cataloging-in-Publication Data

Trammell, Stephen.

Pursuing God : a daily encounter/by Stephen Trammell.

384 p. 22 cm.

Summary: 365-day devotional designed to enhance the reader's daily walk with God.

Includes index.

ISBN 978-0-982-6630-0-4 (pbk.)

ISBN 978-0-9826630-1-1 (Spanish Ed.)

1. Devotional Calendars. 2. Devotions, Daily.
3. Devotional Literature. 4. Spiritual Growth. 5. Meditations.
6. God-Meditations. 7. Discipleship. 8. Prayer Books and Devotions.
I. Title.

242.2 –dc22

PURSUING GOD
INTRODUCTION

Life is a journey. The scenery changes and the terrain fluctuates, but the one constant in this life is the abiding Presence of God. To think that God would take the initiative to come to our rescue and to make Himself known to us in Jesus is still awesome to behold. God also chooses to invite us into His redemptive story. We get to participate with Him in His master plan.

A significant part of God's plan is doing life with others. For over nineteen years, I have been married to Tonya and experienced the beauty of two becoming one flesh. She has believed in me from day one and encouraged me to reach my God-given potential. Tonya taught me how to study when we met in college and has selflessly placed her "yes" on the altar to go wherever God leads us.

God has brought some wonderful people into my life along the way to introduce me to Jesus, to help me grow in my relationship to Christ, and to help me understand and fulfill God's calling on my life. These include family members, pastors, Sunday School teachers, professors, coaches, and fellow followers of Christ. I am grateful to God for the individuals He has sprinkled along my path to help build me into the man of God He has created me to be. Growing up with such a godly mother, being married to such a godly wife, and gleaning from so many fully devoted followers of Christ have immeasurably influenced my walk with God and enabled me to stay on mission with God.

For the past three years, I have had the delightful privilege of serving with my best friend and my pastor, Dr. David Fleming. Almost twenty years ago, he and I pastored within five miles of each other for six years during our seminary days and commuted to school together. That forged a friendship that has prepared us for the collaborative journey God has called us to with our amazing Champion Forest Baptist Church family.

As John Maxwell says, "Teamwork makes the dream work." I am so blessed to have such a catalytic and innovative team to serve with. My special thanks goes to my gifted and attentive Administrative Assistant, Mary Shemroske, for keeping our office in such impeccable order and for creating an environment of effectiveness and efficiency. I want to thank Chris Todd, Jacque Sellers, and Andrew Maddox for your perpetual commitment to excellence in this project. Thank you for investing practically, artistically, technologically, and spiritually to make this book a reality.

I am grateful to the entire staff, deacons, and members of Champion Forest Baptist Church for your friendship and faithfulness in ministry. You guys are amazing. I also want to express my appreciation to Heather Garza for her journalistic touch in proofreading and editing the manuscript.

My prayer is that God will use this book to help you encounter His Presence each day and to help you grow in your love relationship with Him.

EXTENDING GOD'S GRACE

Grace, Life, Peace

"Grace and peace to you from God our Father and the Lord Jesus Christ."
Phil 1:2 (NIV)

Do something great by extending God's grace and peace.

You cannot give what you do not have. On this first day of the year, reflect on your salvation event, but also remember, salvation is an event followed by a process. Where were you when you responded to God's offer of salvation? Think about the moment you confessed your sin and invited Jesus to take over your life. In that moment, you became a recipient of God's grace.

Grace is something you cannot earn, nor is it something you deserve. Grace is a gift from God based on the atoning work of Jesus on the cross. You received God's riches at Christ's expense. In God's grace, you received the gift of eternal life. Your eternal destination is secure. Yet, there's more.

The result of receiving God's grace gift is peace. You are now in a right relationship with God in that Jesus took on the full wrath of God for your sin. The righteousness of Christ has been imputed to your account. Peace is the fruit of your love relationship with God made possible by Christ's death, burial, and resurrection.

Peace is not connected to circumstances. You can be in the midst of a trying situation and yet have the peace of God in your life. You can be facing adversity in your daily living and still have the peace of God.

Now that you have the grace and peace of God, are you willing to share that eternal gift with others? Is there anyone in your sphere of influence who is in need of God's grace and peace? Begin praying for them by name, and allow God to use you in the process.

January 2
PARTNERING WITH OTHERS
Dream, Life, Partnership

"In all my prayers for all of you, I always pray with joy because of your partnership in the gospel from the first day until now, being confident of this, that he who began a good work in you will carry it on to completion until the day of Christ Jesus."
Phil 1:4-6 (NIV)

Do something great by partnering with others.

Has God given you a dream that cannot be accomplished without others? As you study the Old Testament and the New Testament, seek to identify the partnerships that God blessed. From the Old Testament, I immediately think of Moses and Aaron, Joshua and Caleb, David and Jonathan, Naomi and Ruth, Elijah and Elisha. From the New Testament, I immediately think of Peter, James, and John, Paul and Barnabas, Paul and Silas, Paul and Titus, and of course, Paul and Timothy.

As John Maxwell says, "Teamwork makes the dream work!" Paul understood the power of partnership. Writing from his imprisonment in Rome, Paul affirms his partnership with the church at Philippi. His relationship with the church family brought him great joy. Paul needed them and they needed him.

Do you sense the value of being connected to a small group of Christ followers? Consider taking your partnerships to a new level this year by participating in a short term mission trip somewhere to spread the fragrance of Christ.

KEEPING AN ETERNAL PERSPECTIVE

Heaven, Something Great, Perspective, Eternity

"For to me, to live is Christ and to die is gain." Phil 1:21 (NIV)

Do something great by keeping an eternal perspective.

Imagine flying at an altitude of thirty-thousand feet and scanning the colorful blocks of land on the earth's surface. There is something about the view that gives you such a unique perspective on life. You begin to realize how small you are and how big the earth is.

How do you view your life? Are you just breathing oxygen and taking up space, or are you living on purpose by keeping an eternal perspective? God's story is both massive and eternal. His plan includes you. You are an integral part of God's redemptive story. God saved you, filled you with His Spirit, and gifted you to fulfill His purposes in your lifetime.

Paul embraced an eternal perspective. He never lost sight of his win-win situation. If he lived, Christ lived with him. If Paul died, then he would live with Christ. Paul allowed his eternal perspective to fuel his courage and boldness for the Lord.

- *"But our citizenship is in heaven. And we eagerly await a Savior from there, the Lord Jesus Christ, who, by the power that enables him to bring everything under his control, will transform our lowly bodies so that they will be like his glorious body."*
  Phil 3:20-21 (NIV)

Will you choose to live this year with eternity in mind? Remember, there's more to this life than what you see. There is life beyond the grave!

January 4
SERVING OTHERS
Something Great, Selflessness, Serving

"Each of you should look not only to your own interests, but also to the interests of others." Phil 2:4 (NIV)

Do something great by serving others.

Analyze your family tree for a moment. Think about those in your family tree who have consistently proven themselves as tender, compassionate, thoughtful, and generous. You may want to pause right now and pray a prayer of thanksgiving for them and their impact in your life. Now think about those in your family tree who have consistently exhibited selfish behavior. They are always looking to see how people can benefit them and satisfy them.

Selfishness is our natural propensity. We are by nature selfish and self-centered. Until we allow Jesus to take full control of our lives, we will be self-absorbed. Once we allow Jesus to be the Lord of our lives, His life will be lived in us and through us. Jesus is the ultimate example and model of selflessness.

- *"For the Son of Man came to seek and to save what was lost."*
  Luke 19:10 (NIV)
- *"For even the Son of Man did not come to be served, but to serve, and to give his life as a ransom for many." Mark 10:45 (NIV)*

You are never more like Jesus than when you are serving.

RELEASING THE PAST

Forgiveness, Solitude, Memory, Redemption, Something Great

"Brothers, I do not consider myself yet to have taken hold of it. But one thing I do: Forgetting what is behind and straining toward what is ahead, I press on toward the goal to win the prize for which God has called me heavenward in Christ Jesus."
Phil 3:13-14 (NIV)

Do something great by releasing the past.

Don't allow your past to prevent you from doing something great for God in the future. Everyone has a past. Everybody has pollution at some level in their past. We have made decisions we regret, said hurtful words we regret, and have had impure thoughts. We have caused pain in the lives of others, and we have also been the recipient of pain from others. Living in a fallen world becomes evident by looking into the rearview mirror.

Paul enjoyed the favor of God. While participating with God in the redemptive process, Paul also encountered the trauma of severe persecution. His rearview mirror included scenes of immense failures and tremendous successes. Paul understood the vital importance of releasing the past and embracing the future.

Memory has power. Satan uses memory to immobilize us. God uses memory to remind us of the depth of His love. God wants to do something great through your life in spite of your past. God factored in your sin before you were even born. God made provision for your sin and your success by allowing Jesus to pay your sin debt in full.

Find a private place of solitude. Take out a notepad and ask God to reveal unconfessed sin in your life. In the quietness of the moment, begin to write down what God reveals to you. Specifically confess each sin by agreeing with God that you have broken His heart and missed the mark. Now receive God's cleansing for your sin and release the past.

January 6
PRAYING IT THROUGH
Prayer, Something Great, Persistence

"Do not be anxious about anything, but in everything, by prayer and petition, with thanksgiving, present your requests to God. And the peace of God, which transcends all understanding, will guard your hearts and your minds in Christ Jesus."
Phil 4:6-7 (NIV)

Do something great by praying it through.

What are you anxious about right now? Is there anything keeping you up at night? It sounds like you are in need of the peace of God. How do you get to the place of peace? Pray everything through.

Notice the process that Paul establishes. Instead of being anxious, be thankful as you present your requests to God. Replace anxiety with gratitude for what God is going to do in and through your situation. Take every item and pray it through.

Before Jesus chose His twelve disciples, He spent the entire night praying it through. Read carefully and discern the process Jesus embraced.

> • *"One of those days Jesus went out to a mountainside to pray, and spent the night praying to God. When morning came, he called his disciples to him and chose twelve of them, whom he also designated apostles: Simon (whom he named Peter), his brother Andrew, James, John, Philip, Bartholomew, Matthew, Thomas, James son of Alphaeus, Simon who was called the Zealot, Judas son of James, and Judas Iscariot, who became a traitor." Luke 6:12-16 (NIV)*

Jesus took everything to God in prayer. If Jesus, being God's Son, valued prayer at that level, what about us? Do something great by praying it through.

RELYING ON CHRIST'S STRENGTH
Obedience, Reliance, Something Great, Dependency

"I can do everything through him who gives me strength." Phil 4:13 (NIV)

Do something great by relying on Christ's strength.

Jesus has saved us to represent Him on the earth. He has instructed us to love our enemies, to pray for those who persecute us, to forgive our debtors, to judge not, to go the extra mile, and to fulfill the Great Commandment and the Great Commission.

- *"Love the Lord your God with all your heart and with all your soul and with all your mind and with all your strength.' The second is this: 'Love your neighbor as yourself.' There is no commandment greater than these." Mark 12:30-31 (NIV)*
- *"Therefore go and make disciples of all nations, baptizing them in the name of the Father and of the Son and of the Holy Spirit, and teaching them to obey everything I have commanded you. And surely I am with you always, to the very end of the age." Matt 28:19-20 (NIV)*

It is impossible to obey Christ's instructions without His power. Jesus does not expect us to obey Him without His enablement. The Christian life is a life of total dependency upon Jesus and His provision.

How did Paul accomplish so much in the Lord's service? Paul lived in full surrender to Christ and in total dependency upon Christ's strength.

Are you relying on Christ's strength? You can do everything Christ calls you to do in the strength He provides. God can accomplish more through your life in six minutes than you can accomplish on your own in sixty years. Will you be found faithful? Rely on the strength Christ provides.

January 8
HUMILITY

Christ-Centered Living, Bankrupt, Humility

"Blessed are the poor in spirit, for theirs is the kingdom of heaven." Matt 5:3 (NIV)

Christ-centered living involves humility. Recognizing your spiritual bankruptcy apart from God is imperative for the follower of Christ. You cannot come into the Kingdom of God without acknowledging your utter hopelessness outside of God's provision. To be poor in spirit is to identify your true condition of lostness and separation from God apart from His divine initiative of salvation. In other words, don't ever lose sight of where you would be had God not come to your rescue in Christ.

To be poor in spirit is to continually recognize your dependency upon God. It is embracing the attitude opposite of self-sufficiency. Our culture rewards those who come across as independent and self-sufficient. In God's Kingdom economy, He rewards those who place their sufficiency in Christ. Operating in daily dependency upon God is a true mark of the Christ-centered life.

As Rick Warren says, "Humility is not thinking less of yourself; it is thinking of yourself less." The standard that Jesus raises in the Beatitudes is that of being selfless. That attitude does not come naturally. To be selfless is to place the needs of others before your own. Selflessness is a fruit of Christ-centered living.

Center your life on Christ, and embrace His way of living the victorious life.

BROKENNESS

Broken, Christ-Centered Living

"Blessed are those who mourn, for they will be comforted." Matt 5:4 (NIV)

Are you constantly broken over your sinfulness? Christ-centered living involves brokenness. In the language of the New Testament, there are nine different words used to describe sorrow. The Greek word Jesus uses here is the strongest of the nine. This level of mourning is equated with grieving over the death of a loved one. Mourning over your sin is a prerequisite for receiving comfort. Brokenness over sin leads to confession of sin which leads to forgiveness of sin. Thus, brokenness precedes blessing.

One cannot come into the Kingdom of God without being broken over sin. Without true repentance, there is no salvation. Once a person becomes a child of God, he or she must be continually broken over his or her sinfulness. We must love what God loves and hate what God hates. Those who are continually mourning will be continually comforted by God.

- *"For I know my transgressions, and my sin is always before me. Against you, you only, have I sinned and done what is evil in your sight, so that you are proved right when you speak and justified when you judge." Psalm 51:3-4 (NIV)*
- *"Godly sorrow brings repentance that leads to salvation and leaves no regret, but worldly sorrow brings death." 2 Cor 7:10 (NIV)*

Step 1: Demonstrate godly sorrow for your sin.
Step 2: Confess and repent of your sin.
Step 3: Receive God's forgiveness and comfort.

Don't ever get numb towards sin. Allow God to keep you sensitive to sin. Sin should break your heart just like it breaks the heart of God. Now walk in the freedom you have in Christ.

January 10
MEEKNESS
Christ-Centered Living, Bridled, Meek

"Blessed are the meek, for they will inherit the earth." Matt 5:5 (NIV)

Christ-centered living involves being bridled. Meekness is not weakness; it is power under control. You have the capacity to live a sinful lifestyle that will bring disrepute to Christianity and disdain to the character of Christ. The world, Satan, and your flesh have agendas to disintegrate your Christian witness. You have everything you need to embrace a sinful lifestyle unbridled. You can choose to walk in the flesh right now and commit the most heinous of sinful acts.

The Christ-centered life, however, is one of decisive restraint. The Christ-centered life is submitting to the full control of Christ in your life. It is consciously choosing to give Jesus the reigns to your life. Instead of trying to live the Christian life in your own strength, you allow Jesus to live His life in you and through you. Your fleshly desires and carnal propensities are brought under the rule and reign of Christ.

- *"I have been crucified with Christ and I no longer live, but Christ lives in me. The life I live in the body, I live by faith in the Son of God, who loved me and gave himself for me." Gal 2:20 (NIV)*
- *"So I say, live by the Spirit, and you will not gratify the desires of the sinful nature." Gal 5:16 (NIV)*

Be gentle in how you treat others. Surrender to the Spirit's control in your life. Center your life on Christ.

HOLY AMBITION
Righteousness, Christ-Centered Living,
Maturing, Hunger, Thirst, Holy Ambition

"Blessed are those who hunger and thirst for righteousness, for they will be filled."
Matt 5:6 (NIV)

Christ-centered living involves holy ambition. There is nothing more appealing to a starving person than food. For the follower of Christ, the spiritual appetite is a craving for righteousness. At salvation, you receive the righteousness of Christ and a resulting passion for righteous living.

- *"This righteousness from God comes through faith in Jesus Christ to all who believe. There is no difference, for all have sinned and fall short of the glory of God, and are justified freely by his grace through the redemption that came by Christ Jesus."*
  Romans 3:22-24 (NIV)
- *"God made him who had no sin to be sin for us, so that in him we might become the righteousness of God." 2 Cor 5:21 (NIV)*

As you seek the Lord and His righteousness, He satisfies your soul. You cannot pursue worldliness and godliness at the same time. The paths are in opposition. To grow in Christ-likeness is to daily pursue Jesus and His agenda for your life. Continual prayer and consistent intake of God's Word will feed your passion for His righteousness.

Remember, whatever you feed grows; whatever you starve dies.

January 12
BEING MERCIFUL
Mercy, Christ-Centered Living

"Blessed are the merciful, for they will be shown mercy." Matt 5:7 (NIV)

Christ-centered living involves being merciful. Has the Lord been merciful to you? Capture a snapshot of what shape you would be in right now had you not been a personal recipient of God's mercy. God is not asking you to do anything He has not already done for you.

- *"But because of his great love for us, God, who is rich in mercy, made us alive with Christ even when we were dead in transgressions--it is by grace you have been saved."* Eph 2:4-5 (NIV)
- *"Let us then approach the throne of grace with confidence, so that we may receive mercy and find grace to help us in our time of need."* Heb 4:16 (NIV)

You need God's mercy for salvation and in sanctification. You need God's mercy day by day in order to live the Christ-centered life. His mercy is both inward and outward. You receive God's mercy inwardly and express God's mercy outwardly.

Sing with me, "Mercy there was great and grace was free; pardon there was multiplied to me; there my burdened soul found liberty, at Calvary." God, in His mercy, did not give you what you deserved. God placed on Jesus the iniquity of us all. Shouldn't that transform how you view others? Shouldn't your treatment of others flow out of the mercy you have received from God?

The most merciful act you will ever employ is sharing the Good News of Jesus with others.

PURITY

Christ-Centered Living, Purity

"Blessed are the pure in heart, for they will see God." Matt 5:8 (NIV)

Christ-centered living involves purity. God's standard of perfection is Christ. The purity of Christ is the bull's-eye for the believer. To be pure in heart is to be right with God. You cannot have a right relationship with God without having a right relationship with others. You cannot have a right relationship with others without having a right relationship with God.

Purity is impossible without the righteousness of Christ being imparted. The impartation and imputation of the righteousness of Christ takes place at the moment of conversion.

- *"In him we have redemption through his blood, the forgiveness of sins, in accordance with the riches of God's grace that he lavished on us with all wisdom and understanding." Eph 1:7-8 (NIV)*
- *"In the same way, count yourselves dead to sin but alive to God in Christ Jesus. Therefore do not let sin reign in your mortal body so that you obey its evil desires." Romans 6:11-12 (NIV)*

The righteousness of Christ is a grace gift from God. God is holy and demands His followers to be holy. Live in light of your position in Christ. Pursue holiness in private and in public. Stay in God's will by staying in God's Word.

"But you, man of God, flee from all this, and pursue righteousness, godliness, faith, love, endurance and gentleness." 1 Tim 6:11 (NIV)

January 14
PEACEMAKING
Christ-Centered Living, Peacemaking

"Blessed are the peacemakers, for they will be called sons of God." Matt 5:9 (NIV)

The Bible opens with peace in the Garden of Eden and was interrupted when man sinned. Jesus made peace a reality again by sacrificing His life upon the cross to destroy the penalty of sin and death. In eternity, peace will be fully restored. As long as there is the presence of sin upon the earth, peace will be challenged.

Christ-centered living involves peacemaking. As a follower of Christ, you have the privilege and responsibility to be a peacemaker. Being a peacemaker is the result of a holy life and the willingness to confront the culture with the claims of Christ. To be a peacemaker is to build bridges to broken and sinful people in order to show them the love of Christ and the way of Christ.

God raised up Nathan to confront King David concerning his sinful indulgence with Bathsheba. Nathan announced to David, "You are the man!" As a result, David repented and wrote Psalm 51. Nathan was a peacemaker in that he built a bridge to David in order to help David make peace with God.

You have to be willing to get close enough to people to impact their lives. Sometimes that means looking beyond yourself and your circle in order to be used of God to be a peacemaker.

Are you at peace with God? Are you at peace with others? Will you help others make peace with God? Remember, we are just fellow beggars who have found bread...the Bread of Life.

"Blessed are those who are persecuted because of righteousness, for theirs is the kingdom of heaven." Matt 5:10 (NIV)

It has been estimated that as many as 160,000 Christians are martyred each year worldwide. Godliness generates hostility. To live for Christ is to live in constant opposition to Satan and his crafty agenda to undermine God's agenda. You cannot wholeheartedly follow Christ and never anticipate opposition. If you are a threat to Satan, then you can expect to encounter persecution at some level. Christ-centered living involves being persecuted.

You may not face martyrdom as a result of your Christianity, but, you may be harassed for your faith in Christ in a culture that is anti-God and anti-Christian. Our culture is not Christ-centered, and thus, as a child of God, you will never be completely accepted and understood.

The level of persecution for you may be that of trying to live out your faith in a home environment that does not honor Christ. Maybe for you it is a work environment that tempts you to compromise your convictions. Persecution may come in the form of an unhealthy relationship that stretches your faith and pushes your patience to the limit.

Jesus says that you can be blessed in the midst of the persecution. You can know His abiding peace even in the darkest places and most difficult situations. Jesus promises to give you the ultimate relief from persecution by allowing you to experience the abundant life He gives on earth and eternal life in heaven. It is a win-win situation.

There's no one who can comfort you more than Jesus. He knows persecution first hand.

January 16
GOD IS OMNIPRESENT
Omnipresence

"Where can I go from your Spirit? Where can I flee from your presence? If I go up to the heavens, you are there; if I make my bed in the depths, you are there. If I rise on the wings of the dawn, if I settle on the far side of the sea, even there your hand will guide me, your right hand will hold me fast." Psalm 139:7-10 (NIV)

There is nowhere that God is not! God is everywhere all the time! Whether you are 100 feet beneath the ocean's surface scanning coral reef in the Caribbean on a scuba excursion or reclining in the cabin of a 747 jet traveling internationally, God is there. You cannot escape God's presence. God is omnipresent.

God's hand will guide you. God's right hand will hold you fast. You are never in a safer place than in the hand that formed you and fashioned you. God is bigger than your circumstances. God is stronger than your enemies.

Are you worrying about anyone right now? Is there a family member or a friend that you are burdened for right now? Do you have someone in your life that you want to be with, but you just can't be with them at this time? Allow the reality that God's presence is not limited by your limitations to minister to you. God is both present with you and with the person whom you are concerned about. You can't be at two places at one time, but God can.

Place your confidence in God's ability to be your sufficiency and your source of strength. Trust God to make His presence known to you and the person for whom you are burdened.

GOD IS OMNISCIENT

Omniscient, All Knowing,
Attributes of God, Omniscience

"O LORD, you have searched me and you know me. You know when I sit and when I rise; you perceive my thoughts from afar. You discern my going out and my lying down; you are familiar with all my ways. Before a word is on my tongue you know it completely, O LORD." Psalm 139:1-4 (NIV)

God is all-knowing. There is nothing that God does not know. Has it ever occurred to you that nothing ever occurs to God? Even when you pray, you are not bringing God up on your situation or circumstances. In His teaching on prayer, Jesus said, "Do not be like them, for your Father knows what you need before you ask him" (Matt 6:8 NIV). God knows everything you have faced, everything you are facing, and everything you will face.

God knew you before you were conceived by your parents. "The word of the LORD came to me, saying, 'Before I formed you in the womb I knew you, before you were born I set you apart; I appointed you as a prophet to the nations'" (Jer 1:4-5 NIV). God knew exactly what He wanted to do in you and through you to fulfill His purposes during your lifetime on planet earth. It is hard to fathom, but God even knew the choices you would make up to this point and knows what choices you will make today.

The beauty of God's love is that in His omniscience, knowing everything about us and our decisions, He chooses to love us and to use us for His glory.

January 18
GOD IS OMNIPOTENT

Omnipotence, God's Nature, Character of God, Attributes of God

"I have seen you in the sanctuary and beheld your power and your glory."
Psalm 63:2 (NIV)

God is all-powerful. There is nothing God cannot do. Someone once asked me, "Can God make a rock so large that even He cannot lift it?" My response is that God would not make a rock that He could not lift because that would go against God's nature and character. Weigh this reality, God is omnipotent. There is nothing God cannot handle. There is nothing God cannot solve. There is nothing God cannot remedy.

- *"You are the God who performs miracles; you display your power among the peoples." Psalm 77:14 (NIV)*
- *"Yet he did not waver through unbelief regarding the promise of God, but was strengthened in his faith and gave glory to God, being fully persuaded that God had power to do what he had promised." Romans 4:20-21 (NIV)*

What giant are you facing? Do you believe that God is more powerful than your giant? Moses placed his trust in the power of God as he stood between the approaching Egyptian Army and the Red Sea. David placed his trust in God's power as he stood before the towering giant, Goliath. Daniel rested in God's power as he "read between the lions." You can trust in God's power to sustain you in seasons of uncertainty and deliver through seasons of adversity.

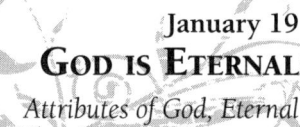

GOD IS ETERNAL
Attributes of God, Eternal

"Trust in the LORD forever, for the LORD, the LORD, is the Rock eternal."
Isaiah 26:4 (NIV)

God is eternal. God was not born and will not die. God will not become something; He is. God is above time. He is not limited by our space and time constraints. God is perpetual and everlasting. God has been and will always be.

- *"Abraham planted a tamarisk tree in Beersheba, and there he called upon the name of the LORD, the Eternal God."* Gen 21:33 (NIV)
- *"Now to him who is able to establish you by my gospel and the proclamation of Jesus Christ, according to the revelation of the mystery hidden for long ages past, but now revealed and made known through the prophetic writings by the command of the eternal God, so that all nations might believe and obey him--to the only wise God be glory forever through Jesus Christ! Amen."* Romans 16:25-27 (NIV)

You were born, and you will one day die if the Lord tarries His coming. You have a specific birthday to celebrate. Your days upon the earth are temporal, yet our Eternal God created you for relationship. You were made by God to bring Him pleasure and to fulfill His purposes in your lifetime. Though you are finite, our infinite God has prepared the way for you to know Him personally, intimately, and eternally.

Has God invited you to join Him in a God-sized assignment? Are you facing any decisions that require looking beyond your own strength and personal ability? If so, you are in a wonderful position to experience God as the Rock eternal. Where God guides, He always provides.

January 20
BEING A MODEL TO FOLLOW
Model, Example

"You became imitators of us and of the Lord; in spite of severe suffering, you welcomed the message with the joy given by the Holy Spirit. And so you became a model to all the believers in Macedonia and Achaia." 1 Thess 1:6-7 (NIV)

Are you a model for others to follow? Think about the godly people God has placed in your life. Take note of their daily conversation and conduct. Do you see Jesus in them?

I grew up in a single-parent family after my parents divorced when I was seven. Each Sunday, my mother would consistently bring my brother and me with her to church. God used my Sunday School teachers, pastors, and other godly men and women to model Christ before me. On March 28, 1979, I gave my heart to Jesus and received His gift of eternal life. Jesus became the Father who would never let me down.

As a follower of Christ, I am to model Christ before others. By allowing His life to shine through me, I am simply the conduit through which Jesus makes Himself known to others. Jesus is the ultimate model to follow. He has called us to imitate Him and to become a model for others to follow.

Pause for just a moment. Close your eyes and begin to visualize the godly examples that have influenced your life. Thank God for each one of them.

THE MOVEMENT OF GOD
Turn, Serve, Wait, Movement

"The Lord's message rang out from you not only in Macedonia and Achaia--your faith in God has become known everywhere. Therefore we do not need to say anything about it, for they themselves report what kind of reception you gave us. They tell how you turned to God from idols to serve the living and true God, and to wait for his Son from heaven, whom he raised from the dead--Jesus, who rescues us from the coming wrath." 1 Thess 1:8-10 (NIV)

Martin Luther King, Jr. was a man used of God as a pastor and civil rights leader to bring unity in the midst of diversity in America. He poetically and eloquently magnified the value God places on human beings. Dr. King mobilized our nation to look beyond the color of our skin and to embrace the content of our character.

The movement of God is discernable when people turn to God and away from idols. An idol is anything that takes the place of God in your life. When people turn turn away from idols to serve the living and true God, it's called a movement of God. In my lifetime, I have seen people who were far from God at one point and then have witnessed the redemptive activity of God bring them to full surrender to the Lordship of Christ. You just cannot explain that in human terms. When a life is transformed by God, He deserves all the glory.

Have you turned to God from idols? Are you serving the living and true God? Are you waiting for and anticipating the return of Jesus? Are you ready to join God in His redemptive activity to bring others into a saving relationship with Jesus?

Join the movement of God!

January 22
FEEDING ON GOD'S WORD
Accept, Receive, Word of God

"And we also thank God continually because, when you received the word of God, which you heard from us, you accepted it not as the word of men, but as it actually is, the word of God, which is at work in you who believe."
1 Thess 2:13 (NIV)

How do you view the Bible? Have you developed an appetite for God's Word? In order to grow spiritually, you must have a daily intake of God's Word. We have so many opportunities to hear, receive, and accept God's Word. You can read it. You can hear it on the radio, on a CD player, or on an ipod. You can hear God's Word being preached on television and in church. The more you feed on God's Word, the more you develop an appetite for daily intake.

- *"For the word of God is living and active. Sharper than any double-edged sword, it penetrates even to dividing soul and spirit, joints and marrow; it judges the thoughts and attitudes of the heart."*
  Heb 4:12 (NIV)
- *"All Scripture is God-breathed and is useful for teaching, rebuking, correcting and training in righteousness, so that the man of God may be thoroughly equipped for every good work."*
  2 Tim 3:16-17 (NIV)

Commit to read four chapters of the Bible each day. For example, read chapters one through four in the book of First John. Select one verse from each chapter that God uses to speak into your life. Write an action statement for each of the four verses that you identify. Accept God's Word by receiving it into your heart and putting it into action.

VALUING OTHERS
Increase, Overflow

"May the Lord make your love increase and overflow for each other and for everyone else, just as ours does for you." 1 Thess 3:12 (NIV)

How do you make your love for others grow? You place the same value on others that God does. If we could ever fully embrace God's perspective on people, our love for others would increase. Our tendency is to judge people based on externals while God evaluates the heart. We tend to overemphasize the outside and underestimate the inside. God has planted unlimited potential in every human being. The key that unlocks potential is an abiding relationship with Jesus Christ.

- *"'I am the vine; you are the branches. If a man remains in me and I in him, he will bear much fruit; apart from me you can do nothing.'" John 15:5 (NIV)*
- *"We ought always to thank God for you, brothers, and rightly so, because your faith is growing more and more, and the love every one of you has for each other is increasing." 2 Thess 1:3 (NIV)*

Increase your love for others by serving them, praying for them, and viewing them from God's perspective. Sometimes our expression of love for others is inhibited by busyness. Often our love for others is stifled by our self-centeredness. It's difficult to increase our love for others when we become consumed with ourselves.

Read through the Gospels and notice how Jesus balanced His love relationship with the Father and meeting the needs of people. As your love relationship with your Heavenly Father grows, your love for others will increase proportionately.

January 24

ORDERING YOUR LIFE

Priorities, Ambition, Order

"Make it your ambition to lead a quiet life, to mind your own business and to work with your hands, just as we told you, so that your daily life may win the respect of outsiders and so that you will not be dependent on anybody."
1 Thess 4:11-12 (NIV)

Where there is order, there is fruitfulness. Strive earnestly to live a disciplined life. What does that look like? It looks like a life that is orderly and balanced. It is a life that is disciplined and focused. Allow these words to be absorbed in your spirit: order, balance, discipline, and focus. Lead a quiet life. Mind your own business. Work with your hands. Maximize your potential and do not be dependent on anybody. That is not to say that you don't need others. You need others, but your dependency is not to be a result of laziness or passive neglect.

What is the goal of a balanced life? Is it to produce personal happiness? Is it to minimize stress? Those are certainly by-products of a balanced life. The goal, however, of a balanced life is to be an irresistible influence for Christ in our culture. Your life is to be lived in such a way as to win the respect of outsiders. Those who are outside of the family of God should be able to view your life and be drawn to Christ. Your life should be magnetic and convincing.

Do you lack order, balance, discipline, and focus? Maybe you have too many plates spinning. Maybe it is time to simplify your life. Identify and remove the clutter from your life. Create some space. It may be the most spiritual thing you do this week.

STEPPING STONE OR STUMBLING BLOCK
Stumbling Block

"Jesus turned and said to Peter, 'Get behind me, Satan! You are a stumbling block to me; you do not have in mind the things of God, but the things of men.'"
Matt 16:23 (NIV)

Peter deeply cared for Jesus. Peter had just spoken the powerful words given by God to affirm that Jesus was truly the Christ, the Son of the Living God. Jesus then shared with His disciples that He would be killed and, on the third day, be raised to life. Peter had the audacity to rebuke Jesus.

As one commentator observed, Peter "could hardly have understood that, by his attempt to dissuade Jesus from the cross, he was placing arrows in the bow of Satan to be shot at his beloved Savior." In the language of the New Testament, a stumbling block, or *skandalon*, refers to an animal trap where food is strategically placed to lure the animal into harm's way. Satan was using Peter to set a trap for Jesus. Satan had already tempted Jesus to take a shortcut to God's plan. Now, Satan is using Peter to seek to get Jesus to bypass the way of the cross.

We become a stumbling block when we think that our way is better than God's way. We become a stumbling block when we fail to consider the way of God. Be careful not to oppose the plan of God. Be on guard not to become an instrument in the hands of the enemy.

Let's commit to becoming a stepping stone for others to come to know Christ. Let's eliminate our proclivity to becoming stumbling blocks. God's way is always the best way. Let's embrace the way of the cross.

January 26
MAKING SENSE OUT OF LIFE
Fully Devoted, Follower of Christ, Cross, Making Sense

"Then Jesus said to his disciples, 'If anyone would come after me, he must deny himself and take up his cross and follow me.'" Matt 16:24 (NIV)

Does life make sense to you? Are you clear about why you exist and why God has placed you right where you are? Do you understand where you fit in God's story?

It all begins with God and His invitation for you to join Him. The first step is to respond to God's invitation as stated by Jesus in Matthew 16:24. Discipleship is both initial and perpetual. You make an initial commitment to Christ by confessing your sin and receiving God's provision for the forgiveness of your sin. Your old life of sin is exchanged for the new life Christ provides. Your commitment to Christ is perpetual in that following Christ is an ongoing moment by moment conscious decision to continue following Christ.

Long before you decided what to do with God, God decided what to do with you. "If" you choose to become a follower of Jesus Christ, you come into alignment with God's purpose and plan. God's redemptive story includes you. Life will never make sense until you come to the place of turning your life completely over to Jesus. Allow Him to be the Lord of your life. Bring Jesus to the center of your destiny and your daily decisions.

EMBRACING GOD'S AGENDA
Humility, Making Sense, Self-denial

"Then Jesus said to his disciples, 'If anyone would come after me, he must deny himself and take up his cross and follow me.'" Matt 16:24 (NIV)

While driving down the interstate, I discovered a billboard advertisement that had this phrase in large gold letters with a dark background: "It's all about you." That phrase captures the ebb and flow of Christianity in the twenty-first century. Consumerism has captivated the local church. Christians are choosing churches based on the mentality of, "What have you done for me, lately?" We have fostered a culture of spectators. Let's watch the show and be entertained.

Embracing that self-centered and me-istic lifestyle will not help you make sense out of life. In fact, life will become muddy and unclear. Jesus explained the Christ-centered life as the one where self-denial is a prerequisite. Jesus clarifies that life is not about you. Life is about God's agenda.

To come after Jesus, you must deny yourself. It does not mean to neglect your needs or to embrace passivity. Self-denial on God's terms is for you to utterly disown yourself. To deny yourself is to come to the place of total abandonment to God and His will for your life. Self-denial is essential in saving faith and in living out your faith before a watching world.

Arthur Pink wrote, "Growth in grace is growth downward; it is the forming of a lower estimate of ourselves; it is a deepening realization of our nothingness; it is a heartfelt recognition that we are not worthy of the least of God's mercies."

It's not about you. It's all about Him

January 28
OBEDIENCE AND DILIGENCE
Making Sense, Obedience, Surrender

"Then Jesus said to his disciples, 'If anyone would come after me, he must deny himself and take up his cross and follow me.'" Matt 16:24 (NIV)

Life without Jesus doesn't make sense. You can spend your life succumbing to the current of busyness and end up weary and depleted. You can slither down the fast lane of materialism and land on the island of emptiness. Life just won't make sense without Jesus.

Jesus says that in order to come after Him, you must first deny yourself and take up His cross. To take up His cross is to identify with Jesus in His shame, suffering, and death. The cross was a horrific means of capital punishment. The Romans reserved this method of death for their enemies.

- *"And being found in appearance as a man, he humbled himself and became obedient to death--even death on a cross!" Phil 2:8 (NIV)*
- *"Therefore, since Christ suffered in his body, arm yourselves also with the same attitude, because he who has suffered in his body is done with sin. As a result, he does not live the rest of his earthly life for evil human desires, but rather for the will of God."*
  1 Peter 4:1-2 (NIV)

For you to take up His cross daily is to willingly surrender your life to Jesus in every area of your life. Choose to identify with Jesus through your obedience to God's Word and through your diligence in serving others. Even in the hard seasons of life, choose to identify with Christ.

BEING FULLY DEVOTED
Obedience, Making Sense

"Then Jesus said to his disciples, 'If anyone would come after me, he must deny himself and take up his cross and follow me.'" Matt 16:24 (NIV)

Are you a fully devoted follower of Christ? Do you obey what you already know? To follow Jesus is to obey His commands. Obedience is a true mark of being a fully devoted follower of Christ. Being a follower implies that you are on a journey. Jesus is the leader. Jesus is the One whom you follow. Wherever He leads, you go!

- *"Whoever claims to live in him must walk as Jesus did."* 1 John 2:6 (NIV)
- *"To the Jews who had believed him, Jesus said, 'If you hold to my teaching, you are really my disciples. Then you will know the truth, and the truth will set you free.'"* John 8:31-32 (NIV)

Obeying Jesus requires submission to His Lordship. In order to truly follow Jesus, you must fully surrender to His leadership. Allow Jesus to have full control of your life. Allow Jesus to live His life in you and to shine His light through you. As a follower of Jesus Christ, your part is to obey Him. Your obedience to Christ will illuminate your proximity to Christ. Stay close to Jesus. Obey what you know!

January 30
ALIGNING YOUR LIFE
Finding Life, Making Sense

"For whoever wants to save his life will lose it, but whoever loses his life for me will find it." Matt 16:25 (NIV)

Jim Elliot served in the mission field of Ecuador trying to reach the Aucas for Christ. He and his missionary partners were killed by the ones they were seeking to reach. As a young, modern martyr, Jim Elliot's quote takes on new meaning: "He is no fool who gives what he cannot keep to gain that which he cannot lose."

Your life will never make sense until you give your life to something bigger than your personal dreams and ambitions. When you align your life with God's world redemption plan, your life will begin to make sense. Christ-centered living involves loving what God loves and hating what God hates. Christ-centered living involves being willing to forsake personal aspirations in order to fulfill the desires of God's heart.

What is your life focused on now? Are you living for yourself, for personal happiness, for personal fulfillment? Have you come to the place of releasing your personal agenda in order to embrace God's agenda? Are you willing to set aside personal preferences in order to surrender to God's way?

LIVING WITH ETERNITY IN MIND
Body and Soul, Making Sense

"'What good will it be for a man if he gains the whole world, yet forfeits his soul? Or what can a man give in exchange for his soul?'" Matt 16:26 (NIV)

Jesus establishes the value of a soul. On one side of the scale is the world including achievements, acquisitions, and accolades. On the other side of the scale is eternal life. The bumper sticker which advertises, "He who dies with the most toys wins," is wrong.

Life is not measured by how much you attain on this side of the grave. As one of my precious members from my seminary church would say, "I've never seen a hearse pulling a U-haul." There's more to this life than ascribing to an incessant materialism. Gaining wealth, status, and prestige while losing your soul, is fatal.

- *"For this very reason, make every effort to add to your faith goodness; and to goodness, knowledge; and to knowledge, self-control; and to self-control, perseverance; and to perseverance, godliness; and to godliness, brotherly kindness; and to brotherly kindness, love. For if you possess these qualities in increasing measure, they will keep you from being ineffective and unproductive in your knowledge of our Lord Jesus Christ."* 2 Peter 1:5-8 (NIV)
- *"Therefore, my brothers, be all the more eager to make your calling and election sure. For if you do these things, you will never fall, and you will receive a rich welcome into the eternal kingdom of our Lord and Savior Jesus Christ."* 2 Peter 1:10-11 (NIV)

Making sense out of life involves living with eternity in mind. Allow Christ to be the center of your life. Make Him the number one priority of your life. Eternity is at stake!

February 1
MORE THAN ENOUGH
Jesus, More Than

"Do not think that I have come to abolish the Law or the Prophets; I have not come to abolish them but to fulfill them." Matt 5:17 (NIV)

Jesus is more than enough. In His earthly ministry, Jesus brought clarity to the Law and the Prophets. He was more than the summation of the Law and the Prophets. His life bore witness to the reality to which they pointed. Jesus demonstrated that He was more than sufficient to bear the sins of the world.

- *"Now to him who is able to do immeasurably more than all we ask or imagine, according to his power that is at work within us, to him be glory in the church and in Christ Jesus throughout all generations, for ever and ever! Amen." Eph 3:20-21 (NIV)*
- *"For I know the plans I have for you," declares the LORD, "plans to prosper you and not to harm you, plans to give you hope and a future." Jer 29:11 (NIV)*

What are you facing right now that has you fearful of the future? Are there any perplexing situations that you are wrestling with that keep you up late at night? Are you in a season of uncertainty?

Jesus is more than enough. You can trust Him with your life and your eternity.

MORE THAN EXPECTED

More Than, Jesus

"'And if someone wants to sue you and take your tunic, let him have your cloak as well. If someone forces you to go one mile, go with him two miles. Give to the one who asks you, and do not turn away from the one who wants to borrow from you.'" Matt 5:40-42 (NIV)

Imagine going to a restaurant that came highly recommended and after your dining experience you said, "Wow! That was more than I expected!" Imagine returning from a vacation and marveling over the memories that were made and the unique experiences that were fashioned. Reflecting on your vacation, you affirm that it was more than you ever dreamed it would be.

Jesus wants us to embrace His "more than" way of life. In other words, Jesus wants us to be willing to live our life in such a way as to demonstrate a "more than" attitude. Are you willing to do more than your family members expect? Are you willing to love more than you thought possible? Are you willing to forgive more than you thought you could? Are you willing to benefit others more than yourself?

- *"Do not repay anyone evil for evil. Be careful to do what is right in the eyes of everybody. If it is possible, as far as it depends on you, live at peace with everyone." Romans 12:17-18 (NIV)*
- *"Do not repay evil with evil or insult with insult, but with blessing, because to this you were called so that you may inherit a blessing." 1 Peter 3:9 (NIV)*

Commit to do more than God expects of you. Give God your very best. Don't give God the leftovers. Allow Him to receive the first fruits of your life. Live a more than life in order to honor God and to bless others.

MORE THAN YOU EVER IMAGINED

More Than, Jesus

*"'You have heard that it was said, "Love your neighbor and hate your enemy."
But I tell you: Love your enemies and pray for those who persecute you, that you
may be sons of your Father in heaven. He causes his sun to rise on the evil and
the good, and sends rain on the righteous and the unrighteous. If you love those
who love you, what reward will you get? Are not even the tax collectors doing
that?'" Matt 5:43-46 (NIV)*

In my walk with God, I have discovered that God will cultivate the fruit
of the Spirit that is lacking in me. If I am lacking in the area of patience,
God will provide me with opportunities to develop patience. If I am giving
little evidence of the fruit of the Spirit known as joy, God will test my level
of joy through trying circumstances to cultivate that particular fruit of the
Spirit.

God is love. God's passion for the world is that all may know His love
through a personal love relationship with Jesus. We are to make God's love
known to the world. When you fail to demonstrate God's love to others,
He will cultivate that fruit of the Spirit by creating environments that give
opportunity for you to show His love. Often, it comes by way of difficult
people that God allows to come into your path. How will you respond to
the opportunity?

Are you willing to do more than love your neighbor? Are you willing to
love your enemies and to pray for those who persecute you? Jesus is not
asking you to do more than He did. In the darkest moments of His trial
and crucifixion, Jesus simply entrusted Himself to the Father. It doesn't
matter how dark your circumstances become. You can entrust your life
to our Heavenly Father. God can do more than you ever imagined! Your
Heavenly Father loves you more than you know!

MAKING AN ETERNAL IMPACT

Impact

"Now to him who is able to do immeasurably more than all we ask or imagine, according to his power that is at work within us, to him be glory in the church and in Christ Jesus throughout all generations, for ever and ever! Amen."
Eph 3:20-21 (NIV)

What kind of impact will you make with the time, energy, and resources God has given you? How much is God able to do through a life totally yielded to Him?

There's room for you to do something great for God. He wants to do more than you could ever ask or imagine. God's plan for your life is much larger than what you can accomplish on your own. In order to make an eternal impact with your life, you will need to move into the realm of faith. Begin operating your life on the basis of what God can do. How much is God able to do?

- *"If we are thrown into the blazing furnace, the God we serve is able to save us from it, and he will rescue us from your hand, O king."*
  Dan 3:17 (NIV)
- *"Yet he did not waver through unbelief regarding the promise of God, but was strengthened in his faith and gave glory to God, being fully persuaded that God had power to do what he had promised."*
  Romans 4:20-21 (NIV)

The level of your faith will determine the level of your impact in God's kingdom. Faith is the currency of heaven. Earnestly seek the Lord and ask Him to increase your faith and to enable you to put your faith into action. Are you ready for God to do more than you have experienced up to this point? There's more!

February 5
RESISTING THE STATUS QUO
Impact, Status Quo

"That night all the people of the community raised their voices and wept aloud. All the Israelites grumbled against Moses and Aaron, and the whole assembly said to them, 'If only we had died in Egypt! Or in this desert! Why is the LORD bringing us to this land only to let us fall by the sword? Our wives and children will be taken as plunder. Wouldn't it be better for us to go back to Egypt?'" Num 14:1-3 (NIV)

There is a consistent gravitational pull on our lives to go back to our old patterns. The children of Israel were satisfied with the status quo. They did not want to pursue all that God had in store for them. They wanted to bypass the miracles of God and His abiding presence in order to return to the familiarity of Egypt. Even though they were in bondage as slaves in Egypt, they desired to settle with the status quo and not do something great for God's glory.

- *"Jesus replied, 'No one who puts his hand to the plow and looks back is fit for service in the kingdom of God.'"* Luke 9:62 (NIV)
- *"Brothers, I do not consider myself yet to have taken hold of it. But one thing I do: Forgetting what is behind and straining toward what is ahead, I press on toward the goal to win the prize for which God has called me heavenward in Christ Jesus."* Phil 3:13-14 (NIV)

Don't allow the status quo to keep you from doing something great for God's glory. Push through the gravitational pull that seeks to lure you back into your comfort zone. Fix your gaze straight ahead. Focus your life on God's agenda.

OBTAINING GOD'S PERSPECTIVE

Impact, Holy Discontent

"Then Moses and Aaron fell facedown in front of the whole Israelite assembly gathered there. Joshua son of Nun and Caleb son of Jephunneh, who were among those who had explored the land, tore their clothes and said to the entire Israelite assembly, 'The land we passed through and explored is exceedingly good. If the LORD is pleased with us, he will lead us into that land, a land flowing with milk and honey, and will give it to us. Only do not rebel against the LORD. And do not be afraid of the people of the land, because we will swallow them up. Their protection is gone, but the LORD is with us. Do not be afraid of them.'"
Num 14:5-9 (NIV)

You always find what you are looking for. If you are looking for giants in the land, you will find them. If you are looking for the milk and honey, you will find it. If you are looking for the activity of God, you will find it. God is always at work.

Joshua and Caleb embraced God's perspective on their situation. They were not satisfied with what they had already experienced with God. They lived with a heart of holy discontent which caused them to crave more. They wanted a fresh encounter of God's presence and provision.

What are you looking for? Are you searching for the activity of God so that you can join Him? Can you affirm the reality that the Lord is with you? Don't be satisfied with the God-moments of years gone by. Seek to join God in His activity now. God is at work now. Are you willing to make an eternal impact by aligning your life with God's activity? Live with a heart of holy discontent.

February 7
MOTIVE MATTERS

Impact, Motive

"'Be careful not to do your "acts of righteousness" before men, to be seen by them. If you do, you will have no reward from your Father in heaven.'" Matt 6:1 (NIV)

You will make no Kingdom impact if you are serving yourself. If you are displaying acts of kindness to be applauded by others, you will limit the Kingdom impact available to you. God rewards your conversation and your conduct based on your motives. Motives matter to God. The world is enamored by the externals. God is not impressed. The heart of God is moved when a child of God is serving, giving, and living to bring glory to God.

- *"But the LORD said to Samuel, 'Do not consider his appearance or his height, for I have rejected him. The LORD does not look at the things man looks at. Man looks at the outward appearance, but the LORD looks at the heart.'" 1 Sam 16:7 (NIV)*
- *"'And you, my son Solomon, acknowledge the God of your father, and serve him with wholehearted devotion and with a willing mind, for the LORD searches every heart and understands every motive behind the thoughts. If you seek him, he will be found by you; but if you forsake him, he will reject you forever.'" 1 Chron 28:9 (NIV)*

Evaluate your motives. Why do you do what you do? Who are you trying to please? Is your heart pure? Pour your life out to bring glory to God. He alone is worthy!

Turning Interruptions into Opportunities
Interruptions, Impact, Opportunities

"As Jesus was on his way, the crowds almost crushed him. And a woman was there who had been subject to bleeding for twelve years, but no one could heal her. She came up behind him and touched the edge of his cloak, and immediately her bleeding stopped." Luke 8:42-44 (NIV)

Often, God makes His greatest impact through you when you are on your way to do something unrelated. Jesus was on His way to heal Jairus' twelve year old daughter who was dying. On His way, Jesus was interrupted by the touch of a woman who had been subject to bleeding for twelve years. Jesus turned the interruption into an opportunity to make an eternal impact. She was healed.

- *"Be very careful, then, how you live--not as unwise but as wise, making the most of every opportunity, because the days are evil." Eph 5:15-16 (NIV)*
- *"Be wise in the way you act toward outsiders; make the most of every opportunity." Col 4:5 (NIV)*

Be attentive to the interruptions that you encounter as you are doing life. When you face an interruption, look to see what God might be inviting you to do in order to make an eternal impact. Often the interruption is the invitation to join God in His activity. Pardon the interruption; it may have eternity written all over it!

February 9
PRAYING FOR OTHERS
Impact, Intercession

"I urge, then, first of all, that requests, prayers, intercession and thanksgiving be made for everyone--for kings and all those in authority, that we may live peaceful and quiet lives in all godliness and holiness. This is good, and pleases God our Savior, who wants all men to be saved and to come to a knowledge of the truth." 1 Tim 2:1-4 (NIV)

You can make an eternal impact through intercessory prayer. Intercession is simply speaking to God on behalf of another person. If I were to tell you that I am praying for you, it means that I am going to be speaking to God on your behalf. I am going to intercede for you. Intercession is building a bridge for others through prayer. As you pray for individuals, seek to get in their skin to identify what they need and what they are experiencing. The Holy Spirit will prompt you to pray specifically for the needs of those individuals.

I am deeply moved by the reality of intercessory prayer. As I pray for others, I am joining the Holy Spirit in His intercessory prayer ministry. I am also joining Jesus, who is at the right hand of the Father, in His intercessory prayer ministry.

> • *"Who is he that condemns? Christ Jesus, who died--more than that, who was raised to life--is at the right hand of God and is also interceding for us." Romans 8:34 (NIV)*

Let's commit to make an eternal impact through embracing intercessory prayer. Who is God placing on your heart right now? Speak to God on their behalf.

BEING AN IRRESISTIBLE INFLUENCE

Impact, Irresistible Influence, Invite

"The first thing Andrew did was to find his brother Simon and tell him, 'We have found the Messiah' (that is, the Christ). And he brought him to Jesus." John 1:41-42 (NIV)

Be an irresistible influence for the glory of God.

You were made by God to make an impact for His glory. God has impacted you by providing the gift of eternal life through the atoning work of Jesus upon the cross. God has impacted you by filling you with His Holy Spirit. Now it is time for you to make an impact for Him.

To be an irresistible influence is to allow Jesus to shine His light and to share His love through you. Living a life that draws others to Christ requires being intentional about the opportunities God provides. Andrew was an irresistible influence for God's glory. He intentionally brought others to Jesus.

> • *"Another of his disciples, Andrew, Simon Peter's brother, spoke up, 'Here is a boy with five small barley loaves and two small fish, but how far will they go among so many?'"* John 6:8-9 (NIV)

Will you seek to be an irresistible influence for God's glory each day? Seize the opportunities God places before you to draw others to Christ. Invite others to become followers of Christ.

February 11
THINKING BIG
Availability, Something Great, Think Big

"Then King David said to the whole assembly: 'My son Solomon, the one whom God has chosen, is young and inexperienced. The task is great, because this palatial structure is not for man but for the LORD God.'" 1 Chron 29:1 (NIV)

Think big...because God is a big God.

Have you ever been invited to participate in a God-sized task? Maybe you are facing something right now that is God-sized. God enjoys bringing us into His story. He is not limited by our limitations. We spend so much time evaluating ourselves in relation to others. We feel inadequate or unqualified and wonder if God could really use us. God specializes in using those deemed useless by the world's standards. We bring pleasure to God when we simply say, "Lord, I'm Yours! Use me!"

God doesn't need you to do something great for Him. Actually, He is big enough to fulfill His plan with or without you. The beauty of God's love is that He chooses to enable you to do something great for Him. Will you make yourself available for God's use?

I would have never dreamed that God wanted me to surrender to preach. Yet, on February 23, 1986, God allowed me to get involved in a Jet Ski accident that almost took my life. While struggling to stay alive in the intensive care unit, God called me to preach. I was only sixteen years old.

Think big...because God is a big God. He can do something great through you regardless of your age or life stage. Are you willing to make yourself available to God for His glory?

GIVING GOD YOUR BEST

Something Great, God's Worth, Best

"With all my resources I have provided for the temple of my God--gold for the gold work, silver for the silver, bronze for the bronze, iron for the iron and wood for the wood, as well as onyx for the settings, turquoise, stones of various colors, and all kinds of fine stone and marble--all of these in large quantities." 1 Chron 29:2 (NIV)

Do your best...God is worth it.

David was willing to give God his best for the preparation of the construction of the temple. Though David would not be the one to build the temple, David gave his best in order for Solomon to carry on the work. David made an investment that would outlive him and outlast him.

Is God worth your best? Do you value your relationship with God in a tangible way? Are you giving evidence of your love relationship with God through giving Him your best?

- *"And this is my prayer: that your love may abound more and more in knowledge and depth of insight, so that you may be able to discern what is best and may be pure and blameless until the day of Christ, filled with the fruit of righteousness that comes through Jesus Christ--to the glory and praise of God." Phil 1:9-11 (NIV)*
- *"Do your best to present yourself to God as one approved, a workman who does not need to be ashamed and who correctly handles the word of truth." 2 Tim 2:15 (NIV)*

God deserves your best in conversation, in conduct, and in contemplation. God deserves your best even when your actions go unnoticed. Make a commitment to do something great for God by giving Him your best. God is worthy!

February 13

DEVOTED TO GOD

Heart, Something Great, Omniscience, Passion

"Besides, in my devotion to the temple of my God I now give my personal treasures of gold and silver for the temple of my God, over and above everything I have provided for this holy temple..." 1 Chron 29:3 (NIV)

Put your heart into it...because God knows.

What are you passionate about? What makes you come alive? Whatever you are passionate about will determine how you allocate your time, energy, and focus. Your passion follows your devotion.

David was fully devoted to God. As a result, David was passionate about loving what God loved and hating what God hated. In his devotion to God, David expressed his passion by giving generously to the Lord's work. He willingly gave his personal treasures to provide for the building of the temple.

- *"For where your treasure is, there your heart will be also.'"*
  Matt 6:21 (NIV)
- *"So we fix our eyes not on what is seen, but on what is unseen. For what is seen is temporary, but what is unseen is eternal."*
  2 Cor 4:18 (NIV)

Is your heart right with God? God knows what makes you come alive. God knows what you are passionate about. Being all-knowing and all-seeing, God knows the level of your devotion to Him. What changes do you need to make in your priorities to reflect full devotion to God? God will do something great with a life fully devoted to Him.

ENERGIZED BY GOD'S LOVE
Provision, Faith, Something Great

"Besides, in my devotion to the temple of my God I now give my personal treasures of gold and silver for the temple of my God, over and above everything I have provided for this holy temple: three thousand talents of gold (gold of Ophir) and seven thousand talents of refined silver, for the overlaying of the walls of the buildings, for the gold work and the silver work, and for all the work to be done by the craftsmen. Now, who is willing to consecrate himself today to the LORD?"
1 Chron 29:3-5 (NIV)

Stretch...God will help you.

Love has an amazing influence. We know that God is love. God has demonstrated His love for us in that while we were still sinners, Christ died for us (Rom. 5:8). God gave us His best by allowing Jesus to die on the cross to pay the penalty of our sin and to provide eternal life. Love is an attribute of God's character that is clearly expressed in the redemptive process.

You will never stretch beyond the capacity of God's love. David was willing to give God his best and to consecrate himself before the Lord in response to God's love. God's love in us and for us energizes us to do something great for God. God's love compels us to sacrifice in order to benefit others. God's love mobilizes us to look beyond ourselves.

Has God allowed you to come into a situation that has caused your love to be tested? Do you sense that God is stretching you in order to demonstrate that He is more than enough to sustain you in the situation and to deliver you through the situation? Trust in God's abundant provision. Respond to God's love by giving your best and consecrating yourself and your service to Him.

February 15
GIVING WHOLEHEARTEDLY
Something Great, Rejoice, Blessing

"The people rejoiced at the willing response of their leaders, for they had given freely and wholeheartedly to the LORD. David the king also rejoiced greatly."
1 Chron 29:9 (NIV)

Rejoice...God will bless you.

God blesses obedience. Nothing brings more joy to the heart of God and to the child of God than obedience. When you give freely and wholeheartedly to the Lord, you expand your capacity to rejoice. Joy overflows as you align your life with God's plan.

David and the people rejoiced. David had a reason to rejoice; he gave freely and wholeheartedly. The people rejoiced because of the willing response of their leaders. God blessed their obedience.

Are you that kind of leader? Do those in your sphere of influence rejoice because of your faithfulness to God? God has demonstrated His gracious generosity by building the ultimate bridge to you and me. If you ever need a reason to rejoice, simply look up to your Heavenly Father and realize how blessed you are to have a loving Heavenly Father, who freely and wholeheartedly gave His Son to be your Savior.

TRUTHFUL EVALUATION
If, Deception, Integrity

"If we claim to be without sin, we deceive ourselves and the truth is not in us."
1 John 1:8 (NIV)

Accuracy promotes intimacy.

If you want to have an intimate love relationship with God, you must have an accurate estimation of yourself. Taking personal inventory can be helpful. Have you ever stopped long enough to really get down to your current reality? You can live at such a fast pace in this life that you neglect the need for introspection. Looking within to capture the truth of your spiritual status is vitally important.

An accurate estimation of yourself requires truthfulness. Being honest about your thought-life, being honest about your motives, and being honest about your inner desires, are marks of spiritual maturity. The tendency is to evaluate others under a microscope and to evaluate ourselves with binoculars. Everyone looks good from a distance. Take a close look at your life.

Don't live in deception. Don't gloss over the things that break the heart of God. *"So, if you think you are standing firm, be careful that you don't fall!"* (1 Cor 10:12 NIV).

February 17
CONFESSING SIN
Forgiveness, If, Confession, Cleansing

"If we confess our sins, he is faithful and just and will forgive us our sins and purify us from all unrighteousness." 1 John 1:9 (NIV)

God keeps His promises.

If you confess your sins, God will forgive you and purify you. God's forgiveness and cleansing is not based on your consistency, rather on His faithfulness. God is holy and demands holy living.

At salvation, you received the imputed righteousness of Christ. You are a child of God and positioned in Christ as rightly related to God. However, daily cleansing from sin is needed. Living in a fallen world perpetuates the sin that can contaminate your life.

- *"Since we have these promises, dear friends, let us purify ourselves from everything that contaminates body and spirit, perfecting holiness out of reverence for God." 2 Cor 7:1 (NIV)*
- *"Come near to God and he will come near to you. Wash your hands, you sinners, and purify your hearts, you double-minded." James 4:8 (NIV)*

To confess your sin is to say the same thing about your sin that God says about it. Don't neutralize your sin by overlooking it and ignoring it. Instead, confess your sin specifically, and receive God's forgiveness and cleansing. Walk in light of the cleansing you have received.

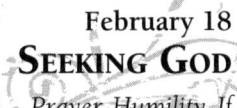

February 18
SEEKING GOD
Prayer, Humility, If

"If my people, who are called by my name, will humble themselves and pray and seek my face and turn from their wicked ways, then will I hear from heaven and will forgive their sin and will heal their land." II Chronicles 7:14

Your impact for God will never rise above your prayer life.

God honors those who seek Him. God took the initiative to bring us into a right relationship with Himself. His heart is for you to know Him intimately. God has done everything needed to enable you to have an intimate love relationship with Him. Will you respond to God's invitation?

If you will humble yourself, pray, and seek God's face and turn from the path of evil, God will respond with blessing from heaven. God promises to hear, forgive, and heal. Are you in need of God's heavenly touch? As you seek God, He responds to your pursuit.

Can you imagine where you would be had God not pursued you long before you ever thought about Him? Can you visualize where you would be had God not built the ultimate bridge to come to where you were?

You are armed with an opportunity to take your relationship with the Creator of the universe to a whole new level. Will you seize the opportunity by taking God at His Word? Will you capture the awesome privilege of connecting with Almighty God through prayer?

February 19
THE GOSPEL ACCORDING TO YOUR LIFE
Bridger Generation, Legacy, Evil

"After that whole generation had been gathered to their fathers, another generation grew up, who knew neither the LORD nor what he had done for Israel. Then the Israelites did evil in the eyes of the LORD and served the Baals."
Judges 2:10-11 (NIV)

All it takes is one generation.

It is difficult to fathom how one generation can witness the mighty works of God, such as water from a rock, manna from heaven, and crossing the Red Sea on dry ground, and fail to pass down the faith. From generation to generation, the faith of our fathers can erode or explode, evaporate or emanate. All it takes is one generation.

In our modern context, the younger generation known as the Bridger generation, are those born between 1984 and 2002. They comprise 27 percent of the United States population. They are also known as Mosaics, Millennials, and Generation 9-11. The Bridger generation has a desire for authentic faith and acceptance of others. Will the faith be handed down to them?

> • *"Keep my commands and you will live; guard my teachings as the apple of your eye." Prov 7:2 (NIV)*
> • *"We must pay more careful attention, therefore, to what we have heard, so that we do not drift away." Heb 2:1 (NIV)*

God has called us to reach and disciple every generation for His glory. Will you live in such a way that those who know you, but don't know God, will come to know God because they know you? As Dr. Johnny Hunt says, "The people in your community may not read the Bible, but they will read the gospel according to your life."

ORIENTING YOUR LIFE

Obedience, Jesus, Bridger Generation, Focus

"'Why were you searching for me?' he asked. 'Didn't you know I had to be in my Father's house?' But they did not understand what he was saying to them."
Luke 2:49-50 (NIV)

The secret to concentration is elimination.

Our life on planet earth is full of distractions. It can be very difficult to focus on what really matters in this life. There are so many tugs and so many allurements. How do you get children to focus on things of eternal value when they are saturated with external impulses?

In the Bible, we get a glimpse of Jesus at the age of twelve. While Joseph and Mary were in the caravan headed home, Jesus was in the temple sitting among the teachers listening to them and asking them questions. Three days later, Joseph and Mary return to Jerusalem in search of Jesus. You can imagine their consternation and relief when they found Him. Jesus responded to them by clarifying that He had to be in His Father's house being about His Father's business.

- *"Then he went down to Nazareth with them and was obedient to them. But his mother treasured all these things in her heart. And Jesus grew in wisdom and stature, and in favor with God and men."* Luke 2:51-52 (NIV)
- *"'My food,' said Jesus, 'is to do the will of him who sent me and to finish his work.'"* John 4:34 (NIV)

Jesus oriented His life around His Heavenly Father's agenda. Are you investing in the next generation at that level of intensity? Are you passionately giving your life to our Heavenly Father's agenda? There's an entire generation to reach for God's glory. Are you in?

February 21
DEPENDENCY UPON GOD
Jesus, Bridger Generation, Death, Miracle

"Now when Jesus returned, a crowd welcomed him, for they were all expecting him. Then a man named Jairus, a ruler of the synagogue, came and fell at Jesus' feet, pleading with him to come to his house because his only daughter, a girl of about twelve, was dying." Luke 8:40-42 (NIV)

Have you ever been desperate? Our natural tendency is to be strong and independent and seek to figure things out on our own. God has a way of reminding us of our dependency upon Him. Sometimes the reminder comes in the package of suffering.

The ruler of the synagogue, Jairus, was suffering as a parent as he watched his only daughter, at the tender age of twelve, lay dying. Jairus sought Jesus and fell at His feet. Jairus was in a season of desperation and pleaded with Jesus to come to his house to rescue his dying daughter. On His way, Jesus was interrupted by the woman with the issue of blood. Jesus healed this woman, and then the report came that Jairus' daughter had died.

- *"When he arrived at the house of Jairus, he did not let anyone go in with him except Peter, John and James, and the child's father and mother. Meanwhile, all the people were wailing and mourning for her. 'Stop wailing,' Jesus said. 'She is not dead but asleep.'"* Luke 8:51-52 (NIV)
- *"They laughed at him, knowing that she was dead. But he took her by the hand and said, 'My child, get up!' Her spirit returned, and at once she stood up. Then Jesus told them to give her something to eat." Luke 8:53-55 (NIV)*

Jesus is the answer for every generation. Will you be available to share Jesus with the next generation? Those in desperation need a demonstration of the love that Jesus provides.

Paved with Humility
Children, Jesus, Bridger Generation

"At that time the disciples came to Jesus and asked, 'Who is the greatest in the kingdom of heaven?' He called a little child and had him stand among them. And he said: 'I tell you the truth, unless you change and become like little children, you will never enter the kingdom of heaven. Therefore, whoever humbles himself like this child is the greatest in the kingdom of heaven.'" Matt 18:1-4 (NIV)

Every generation can only enter the kingdom of heaven one way. Through repentance and childlike faith, a person from any generation can enter the kingdom of heaven. Jesus not only solidifies the method of entry, but He also identifies the measure of greatness in the kingdom of heaven. The road to greatness is paved in humility.

Children have the wonderful capacity to believe. They want to believe that anything is possible and they can dream some amazing dreams. Being around children has a contagious factor of faith. The simplicity of their faith can also be very convicting for those who have become too familiar with the cognitive realm. Children have the refreshing quality of demonstrating humility in their willingness to acknowledge their need for comfort, love, and acceptance.

What will the next generation see in you? Will the Bridger generation be convinced that repentance and childlike faith in Jesus is the answer by simply observing the way you live? Your conversation and conduct immersed in humility for God's glory will demonstrate to a watching world the reality of kingdom citizenship.

February 23
PRIVILEGED RESPONSIBILITY
Faith, Children, Jesus, Bridger Generation

"And whoever welcomes a little child like this in my name welcomes me. But if anyone causes one of these little ones who believe in me to sin, it would be better for him to have a large millstone hung around his neck and to be drowned in the depths of the sea." Matt 18:5-6 (NIV)

Jesus loves the little children.

As you read these powerful words of Christ, you may be offended by the strong language used. Jesus does not water down His conviction about the vitality and vulnerability of children. Jesus confronts us with the reality that the children are our responsibility. If we choose to mislead them, we will suffer the consequences. If we choose to guide them in the way of the Lord, we will be blessed.

The vast majority of those who come to place their faith in Christ alone for salvation do so before the age of twelve. Children exhibit tenderness toward the things of God. They are so open to what God wants to do in their lives and through their lives. Children are like tender clay in the hands of a potter. God has given us the responsibility to help mold them and shape them into fully devoted followers of Christ.

With this awesome privilege comes tremendous responsibility. Jesus wants us to take our responsibility of influencing children toward Him seriously. Think of what is at stake when children are misled. Not only is their immediate future jeopardized, but also their eternal destiny.

I am so grateful for the godly men and women that God placed in my life during my formative years to point me to Jesus. They faithfully modeled the Christ-centered life. Every generation deserves to be led to the foot of the cross and introduced to a saving relationship with Jesus.

Usefulness to God

Example, Bridger Generation, Youth

"Don't let anyone look down on you because you are young, but set an example for the believers in speech, in life, in love, in faith and in purity."
1 Tim 4:12 (NIV)

After being involved in a life altering Jet Ski accident and surrendering to preach at age sixteen, I remember officiating one of my first weddings. I was standing near the altar steps just before the wedding rehearsal was to begin when the mother of the bride asked, "Where's the minister?"

When I announced that I was the minister, you should have seen her face fall. She reacted by darting out the words of surprise that, in her estimation, I was just a kid. Those were the "good old days."

Paul's words of encouragement and instruction to his young son in the ministry have been a life-line over the years of my ministry. Every generation has the honor of participation in God's redemptive activity. Regardless of your current life stage, whether you are in the Bridger, Buster, Boomer, or Builder generation, you have the wonderful invitation from God for participation in God's world redemption story.

Don't allow your inadequacies and insufficiencies to barricade you from joining God in His activity. Your usefulness to God is not based on your particular generational identification. Your usefulness to God is based on your identity in Christ and your availability to Christ.

Surrender to the Lordship of Christ and be an example to others in your conversation, your convictions, and your conduct. Every person in every generation will one day stand before God to give an account for the deeds done while in the body. Set a Christ-honoring example for others. Be a model to follow!

February 25
HANDING DOWN THE FAITH
Influence, Bridger Generation, Legacy, Scripture

"I have been reminded of your sincere faith, which first lived in your grandmother Lois and in your mother Eunice and, I am persuaded, now lives in you also."
2 Tim 1:5 (NIV)

Today is my dad's birthday. He is now on the spiritual path to finish well. However, when I was a child, my dad became an alcoholic which led to my parents' divorce and ultimately to his imprisonment. As a result, my dad was not an integral part of my upbringing. When I look over my childhood, the one constant in my life was church. My mother and my mamaw made certain that I went to church with them each Sunday morning, Sunday evening, and Wednesday night. My mother played the piano and my mamaw played the organ.

God used that consistency in my life to allow me to be under the influence of the gospel each week in Sunday School, in worship, and in my church's basketball league. God brought godly men into my life at church that would take me fishing, camping, and hunting. I watched those men closely to see how they treated their wives and their children. On March 28, 1979, I gave my heart to the Father who would never let me down. Jesus became the Lord of my life, and He also became my Heavenly Daddy!

Paul identified the sincere faith that Timothy's mother and grandmother exhibited before him consistently. Timothy became a follower of Christ and devoted his life to teaching and preaching God's Word. I love how Paul affirms the sincere faith that first lived in Timothy's grandmother and mother.

Are you handing down the faith? Is your faith sincere? Will the next generation be able to look at your life and see the reality of Jesus and His Lordship?

GOD HAS THE FINAL SAY

Forgiveness, Joseph, Life Changing Experience, Sovereignty

"You intended to harm me, but God intended it for good to accomplish what is now being done, the saving of many lives." Gen 50:20 (NIV)

The sixty-six books of the Bible provide us with a string of pearls that demonstrates God's redemptive activity. Long before we were born, God took the initiative to rescue us from our fallen condition. God factors in our poor choices and even the decisions others make that affect our lives. How refreshing to know that God has the final say. Your past, present, and future circumstances will never circumvent the mighty acts of God.

Joseph had a life changing experience through the gateway of betrayal. Joseph's brothers sold him into slavery and tried to cover up their sin through deception. God elevated Joseph to Potipher's house where he was later falsely accused by Potipher's wife. Joseph went from the pit to the palace and then to prison. His life's circumstances appeared to be most unfortunate. Yet, God knew right where Joseph was and what Joseph needed most. God was with Joseph and delivered him from prison to second in command over Egypt in preparation for the upcoming famine. When Joseph's path intersected that of his brothers, he demonstrated the life-giving grace of God. Instead of having them pay for their sin, Joseph forgave them and acknowledged God's sovereignty.

Have you had the ultimate life changing experience by placing your faith in the completed work of Jesus on the cross? Are you living out the reality of God's transforming power? Have you experienced God's forgiveness at the level of being able to forgive others in the same measure?

February 27
PREPARING FOR YOUR NEXT ASSIGNMENT
Life Changing Experience, Moses, Burning Bush

"But Moses said to God, 'Who am I, that I should go to Pharaoh and bring the Israelites out of Egypt?'" Ex 3:11 (NIV)

Who am I? Why am I here? These two basic questions are innate in every human being. We long to know who we are, and we strive to discover why we are placed on this planet called earth. Our security is proportionate to our understanding of our identity.

God allowed Moses to experience forty years in the palace and then forty years in the desert. God wanted Moses to learn some things about his personal identity through a desert experience that he could not learn in the palace. God was preparing Moses for the purpose of delivering the children of Israel from Egyptian bondage. The burning bush encounter was a life changing experience for Moses. The encounter enabled Moses to come to know God in a personal way. God revealed His holiness to Moses and then unveiled His plan for Moses to embrace.

As you can imagine, Moses could not visualize himself as the deliverer of the children of Israel. They had been slaves for over 400 years. Moses began making excuses and tried to deny his usefulness to God. Moses began to focus on what he lacked and missed the reality of God's ability to do the extraordinary through ordinary people.

Have you ever doubted your usefulness to God? Have you ever tried to convince God that you are not fit for His plan? God is not impressed with our abilities or our inabilities. God is not limited by our limitations. Are you willing to yield to God's control and allow Him to have His way in your life? God is willing to take you through a desert experience to prepare you for His assignment.

OBEYING GOD INSTANTLY

Obedience, Availability, Life Changing Experience, Isaiah

"Then I heard the voice of the Lord saying, 'Whom shall I send? And who will go for us?' And I said, 'Here am I. Send me!'" Isaiah 6:8 (NIV)

Isaiah had a life changing experience. He looked up and saw the Lord in all of His holiness. Isaiah looked inward and recognized his own sinfulness in light of God's holiness. Isaiah then looked outward and detected the sinful condition of others. In this life changing experience, Isaiah heard God's call and responded with instant obedience. Isaiah said, "Here am I. Send me!"

Will you make an impact upon every generation? Are you willing to allow God to call you to a new level of living? God's grace always matches His assignment for your life. Where God guides, He always provides. There is never a better moment than now to obey God instantly and make yourself totally available for His use. God can do more in you and through you in the next six months than all the previous years of your life combined.

God values the work He does in you more than the work He does through you. Before God used Isaiah to make an eternal impact, God had to do an internal work in Isaiah's life. The internal work always impacts the eternal work. Don't bypass what God wants to do in you. Isaiah came face to face with the holiness of God in worship. Isaiah's worship led to a personal assessment of his morality and then the morality of those around him. After God did this great work in Isaiah, He invited Isaiah to join His world redemptive activity.

You have a chance to make an eternal impact for every generation. Are you available? Look upward! Look inward! Look outward!

March 1
READING BETWEEN THE LIONS
Daniel, Faithfulness, Loyalty

"So the king gave the order, and they brought Daniel and threw him into the lions' den. The king said to Daniel, 'May your God, whom you serve continually, rescue you!'" Dan 6:16 (NIV)

Daniel had a track record of faithfulness to God. His loyalty to God was unwavering. After the king signed a decree forbidding Daniel to pray to God, Daniel allowed his devotion to God to supersede his devotion to the king. Daniel was not willing to disobey God in order to obey the king. Instead, Daniel honored God at the expense of the king's retribution. Daniel paid a hefty price for his obedience. He was thrown into the lions' den.

Your devotion and faithfulness to God may not ever lead you to be thrown into a literal lions' den. However, your lions' den may simply be having others misunderstand you or criticize you for your devotion to God. Your family members may not support you in your walk with God. Your co-workers or neighbors may not fully understand your commitment to serving God. Your lions' den may be when your peers fail to comprehend your level of loyalty to God.

Serve continually! Trust God completely! God can shut the mouths of the lions. God can redeem the hurt you endure. Allow God to use you to make an impact for His glory for every generation. Be comforted by the fact that God is all-knowing and nothing escapes His attention. God knows right where you are, and He knows exactly what you need to accomplish His plan.

THE POTTER'S HOUSE

Surrender, Life Changing Experience, Jeremiah

"So I went down to the potter's house, and I saw him working at the wheel. But the pot he was shaping from the clay was marred in his hands; so the potter formed it into another pot, shaping it as seemed best to him." Jer 18:3-4 (NIV)

The safest place for you to be is in the center of God's will. The most dangerous place for you to be is in the center of God's will. When you are living in the center of God's will, you experience His provision and protection. However, you are the greatest threat to Satan when you are living in the center of God's will. When you think about it, being on Satan's radar is an indication of being a threat to his kingdom. You cannot walk in the center of God's will unopposed.

One of my Sunday School teachers who flew an A-10 fighter jet in the Air Force used to say, "The closer you get to the enemy, the greater the conflict." Motion causes friction. When you are living to please God, be ready for that spiritual motion to cause friction and spiritual warfare.

Jeremiah, known as the weeping prophet, experienced the painful reality of being on the potter's wheel. God placed Jeremiah on the potter's wheel to demonstrate His loving and corrective touch. God demonstrated the value He places on purity, holiness, and full surrender. God expects that of every generation and every nation.

Don't resist those seasons of being placed on the potter's wheel. Remember that God is the Potter and you are the clay. God tenderly and lovingly molds you and shapes you for His glory. God removes the impediments in your life that restrict His flow through you. Be still! Rest! Give God access to every area of your life. Allow God to shape you for His eternal significance.

March 3
PRAYING THROUGH THE SEAWEED
Prayer, Life Changing Experience, Jonah

"From inside the fish Jonah prayed to the LORD his God." Jonah 2:1 (NIV)

If you spent three days and three nights inside a great fish that God provided, you would probably place that in the category of a life changing experience. Your entire life would be marked by that one experience with God. You would never be the same. Your view of God and your reverence for God would be catapulted to a new level.

- *"The engulfing waters threatened me, the deep surrounded me; seaweed was wrapped around my head." Jonah 2:5 (NIV)*
- *"To the roots of the mountains I sank down; the earth beneath barred me in forever. But you brought my life up from the pit, O LORD my God." Jonah 2:6 (NIV)*

Can you imagine Jonah, with seaweed wrapped around his head, praying to God from inside this large fish that God provided? I wonder if Jonah was kneeling, standing, floating, or treading water while he was praying. It clearly illustrates that God is willing to go to extreme measures to rescue us from ourselves and from our sin.

You don't have to wait for God to bring you to a place of desperation to call out to Him in prayer. You have the perpetual invitation to nurture your love relationship with God in moment by moment prayer and surrender. Remove the seaweed that tends to cling to your mind, and embrace the opportunity to commune with the Creator of the universe. Your life changing experience can continue as you faithfully seek God's face in prayer.

Whether you are in the tumultuous waters within the large fish called life or on the tranquil dry ground of daily life, pray to our Living God. God loves you and His heart beats for you. You are the apple of His eye!

FORSAKING YOUR FIRST LOVE

Priorities, First, Devotion

"Yet I hold this against you: You have forsaken your first love." Rev 2:4 (NIV)

When I was a teenager, I raced motocross. One afternoon, I was on a track with my brother and some friends practicing in the heat of the day. At this point, I was in the lead and throttling through a sandy turn when my dirt bike slid out from under me at a high speed which slammed my body to the ground. The pain was so immense and the heat was so intense that I began to see stars. I was nauseated and just knew that I had broken my wrist. My brother came to my rescue and said, "Come on man! Ride it out! Let's keep riding!"

After my visit to the emergency room and a cast secured to my right arm, I proudly walked up to my brother and confirmed my suspicion that my wrist was broken. The X-ray enabled the physician to see what we could not see. The X-ray provided information that was not attainable from an external view of my arm.

Jesus has the unique ability to X-ray the church and to X-ray our heart. Jesus detects the internal workings. Jesus weighs motives and our current reality. Jesus knows the reality of our priorities.

> • *"Remember the height from which you have fallen! Repent and do the things you did at first. If you do not repent, I will come to you and remove your lampstand from its place." Rev 2:5 (NIV)*

Remember, repent, and return. Remember the former intensity of your love relationship with Jesus. Repent of those things that have caused you to drift from your first love. Turn away from those things that have robbed you of your devotion to the Lord. Return to daily surrender and full devotion to Jesus as your first love.

March 5
RECONCILING RELATIONSHIPS
Reconciliation, Forgiveness, Relationships

"Therefore, if you are offering your gift at the altar and there remember that your brother has something against you, leave your gift there in front of the altar. First go and be reconciled to your brother; then come and offer your gift."
Matt 5:23-24 (NIV)

In yielded worship before the Lord, your sensitivity to the things of God is heightened. Your awareness of God's holiness and your personal sin becomes elevated when you are consecrated before the Lord in worship. If during the act of offering your gift at the altar of worship, God brings to your mind the reality of a strained relationship, leave your gift and diligently go and be reconciled.

God values unity in the body. God expects us to protect the vitality of our relationships with others. You cannot have a right relationship with God, even in worship, if you are not in a right relationship with others. Living in a fallen world perpetuates the litter of strained relationships. Make reconciliation your "first" response to God in worship. You have been reconciled to God through the finished work of Jesus upon the cross so that you can be an intentional reconciler on this broken planet.

> • *"If you have been trapped by what you said, ensnared by the words of your mouth, then do this, my son, to free yourself, since you have fallen into your neighbor's hands: Go and humble yourself; press your plea with your neighbor!" Prov 6:2-3 (NIV)*

Your gift becomes acceptable to God at the level of your relational purity with God and with others. Guard your relationships. Seek immediate reconciliation! Exhibit humility and brokenness! Ask for forgiveness! Extend forgiveness! Do whatever it takes to make things right between you and God. Do whatever it takes to make things right with others.

FORTIFYING FIRST PLACE
Priorities, Integrity, Discipline

"But seek first his kingdom and his righteousness, and all these things will be given to you as well.'" Matt 6:33 (NIV)

What is competing for "first" in your life? What gets the majority of your time, energy, and attention? Maybe you feel like you have too many plates spinning and several wobbling. Maybe you are overwhelmed with the tugs on your life, and you wonder how you are going to pull it all off before each deadline.

Jesus understands the allurements and tugs of life. He had to say "no" to the wrong things so that He could say "yes" to the right things. Jesus had to say "no" to the good opportunities so that He could say "yes" to the best opportunities. Jesus had to guard His mornings so that He could have unbroken fellowship and communion with our Heavenly Father. Jesus had to strategically carve out time to simply rest and be away from the crowds and the demands on His life.

There is only so much of you to allocate. You cannot please everyone and you cannot satisfy every request. Some of your spinning plates will have to crash. The wonderful news is that God's Will can be accomplished within the 24 hours that He has given you each day.

Make room in your life for Jesus to occupy "first" place. Guard your daily intimacy with Him. Create margins in your life to foster balance. No one can do this for you. Only you can enthrone Jesus to the "first" position of prominence in your life. What adjustments do you need to make right now?

March 7
JUDGING OTHERS
Confession, First, Introspection

"Why do you look at the speck of sawdust in your brother's eye and pay no attention to the plank in your own eye? How can you say to your brother, "Let me take the speck out of your eye," when all the time there is a plank in your own eye? You hypocrite, first take the plank out of your own eye, and then you will see clearly to remove the speck from your brother's eye." Matt 7:3-5 (NIV)

We tend to judge others by a different standard than we judge ourselves. When we look at ourselves, we tend to use a filtered lens that makes us look pretty good. When we look at others, we tend to utilize the most powerful microscope to examine their lives. We can be rather selective by choosing someone who will make us look good.

The truth is, everyone looks good from a distance. Proximity affects accuracy. Jesus is giving us a new lens to view ourselves and others. Instead of bypassing the reality of a massive plank in our own eye in order to identify the speck of sawdust in our brother's eye, Jesus wants us to examine our own life first.

- *"For I know my transgressions, and my sin is always before me."* Psalm 51:3 (NIV)
- *"'Woe to me!' I cried. 'I am ruined! For I am a man of unclean lips...'"* Isaiah 6:5 (NIV)
- *"If we claim to be without sin, we deceive ourselves and the truth is not in us."* 1 John 1:8 (NIV)

Introspection paves the way for realization of God's impartation of grace in which we live and breathe. God already knows about the plank. Be quick to remove it, and be slow to critique the speck in your brother's eye.

PUTTING OTHERS BEFORE YOURSELF
Humility, First, Servanthood

"Sitting down, Jesus called the Twelve and said, 'If anyone wants to be first, he must be the very last, and the servant of all.'" Mark 9:35 (NIV)

Our culture thrives on being the best at whatever you do. Reality television shows have magnified the surge of cynicism and critical evaluation. You're too tall or you're too short or your vocal pitch is too high or too low. Everyone is striving to win. Everyone is clamoring for the top spot. In our culture, being "first" is the epitome of success.

Jesus redefines success. To be first, you must be last. Being at the top is all about being at the bottom. Instead of being first, success is about letting others be first. It is putting others before yourself. The portrait of success that Jesus paints is that of being selfless. The way of Jesus is counter-culture. The current of the Christ-centered life goes against the flow of culture.

Descending into greatness requires placing the needs of others before your own. Jesus was willing to serve His disciples by washing their feet and ultimately washing their sins away through His shed blood upon the cross. Are you willing to serve others? Are you willing to put others first? That does not come naturally. It requires being fully surrendered to the Spirit's control in your life.

Do you qualify as "servant of all" in your sphere of influence? Look to Jesus! He is the model to follow!

March 9
GOING GLOBAL
Missions, First, Gospel, Evangelism

"And the gospel must first be preached to all nations." Mark 13:10 (NIV)

There are over 12,000 people groups among the nations of the earth. Jesus died on the cross so that every person who calls upon His Name will be saved. Jesus is the hope of the world. There is no other payment for the penalty of our sin. Jesus is the only way.

- *"'Salvation is found in no one else, for there is no other name under heaven given to men by which we must be saved.'" Acts 4:12 (NIV)*
- *"Jesus answered, 'I am the way and the truth and the life. No one comes to the Father except through me.'" John 14:6 (NIV)*
- *"That if you confess with your mouth, 'Jesus is Lord,' and believe in your heart that God raised him from the dead, you will be saved. For it is with your heart that you believe and are justified, and it is with your mouth that you confess and are saved."*
  Romans 10:9-10 (NIV)

What will you do to ensure that the message of the gospel gets to every people group on earth? How will you participate in the redemptive process? How many people will be in heaven because of your witness?

Shine the light of Jesus and share the love of Jesus every moment of every day. Seize every opportunity that God gives you to make Jesus known. Pray for the lost. Share your salvation story, and lead others to come to know Jesus. We are not waiting on Jesus to come. Jesus has commissioned us and empowered us to get the gospel to all nations.

BEARING HIS NAME
Suffering, Persecution, First

"'If the world hates you, keep in mind that it hated me first.'" John 15:18 (NIV)

One of our deepest needs is to be accepted by others. As a result, we invest so much of our time and energy seeking to please others. We do not like anyone to reject us or to think less of us. We strive to be admired and affirmed by others. Often our pursuit winds up streaming us into a performance trap.

Satan plays into the equation in that he fuels our desire to be liked by others. He seeks to get us to neglect our daily intimacy with the Lord in order to neutralize our effectiveness as followers of Christ. Satan's opposition is in proportion to our mobilization in God's army.

Jesus reminds us that He endured opposition for God's glory. Jesus was hated and despised. Jesus suffered persecution and ultimately death for God's glory.

- *"To this you were called, because Christ suffered for you, leaving you an example, that you should follow in his steps." 1 Peter 2:21 (NIV)*
- *"However, if you suffer as a Christian, do not be ashamed, but praise God that you bear that name." 1 Peter 4:16 (NIV)*

If the world hates you, remember that it hated Jesus first. If the world despises you, remember that it despised Jesus first. Walk in the honor of bearing the name of Jesus. Continue to give Jesus "first" place in your life, and remember that Jesus went first, for you.

March 11

RELYING UPON GOD

Trust

"Some trust in chariots and some in horses, but we trust in the name of the LORD our God." Psalm 20:7 (NIV)

This verse became dear to my heart when I was pastoring my seminary church in 1992. My wife, Tonya, and I went through the *Experiencing God* study along with our deacons and their wives. My journey of faith has been enhanced by the concept of trusting in the name of the Lord our God.

Trust is a fragile item in the life of a believer. Trust is like the petal of a rose. Trust can beautify a difficult path and create an aroma pleasing to Christ. Trust can also wilt when betrayed. Like a gem in the hand of a jeweler, trust in God can lead to an irresistible life in which God's glory radiates.

What do you trust in? In our society draped with affluence, it is so easy to trust in materialism. If we can only acquire one more object of our affection or jump into one more activity that produces an adrenaline rush, then we will be fulfilled...so we think. The things of this world just don't deliver what they promise. The chariots of our culture and the horses of our entertainment are not trustworthy. Only God can deliver on the magnitude of His promises. God always lives up to the level of His nature and character of perfection. There is no lack! There is no discrepancy! God is all sufficient and more than enough!

Fully rely upon God.

WHAT GOD WILL DO

Trust

"Commit your way to the LORD; trust in him and he will do this: He will make your righteousness shine like the dawn, the justice of your cause like the noonday sun." Psalm 37:5-6 (NIV)

A few months after I surrendered to preach, at age sixteen, God placed a true man of God in my life. His name was J.D. Scott. He had been preaching for over 55 years and was serving as an interim pastor. Pastor J.D. invited me to ride with him to his church and allowed me to preach in his pulpit. It was only my third time to ever preach. A few days later, I received a personal thank you letter in the mail from Pastor J.D., and next to his signature he wrote, "Psalm 37:5-6." As you can imagine, I immediately opened my Bible to read those verses to see what God wanted to say to me.

Your responsibility is to commit your way to the Lord and trust Him to do what He said He will do. God will take the imputed righteousness of Christ within your life and make it shine so that others may be drawn to Christ in you. Surrender your ambition, your desires, and your dreams to God, and trust Him to shine His penetrating light through you to touch the nations.

God will make the justice of your cause like the noonday sun. As you put feet to the purposes of God in your life, God will produce the momentum and establish the magnitude of your impact for His glory. Trust in God. Remember that God can do more through your life fully surrendered to His Lordship in a matter of minutes than you can do on your own. Let God have full reign in your life.

Will others see Jesus in you today? Will others be drawn to the Savior of the world because of your perpetual obedience and surrender to Him? You can trust Jesus with your life!

March 13
A Song Worth Singing
Trust

"He put a new song in my mouth, a hymn of praise to our God. Many will see and fear and put their trust in the LORD." Psalm 40:3 (NIV)

What is your life song? Has God put a new song in your mouth? As children of God, we have the life transforming message of Jesus. If you have been redeemed by the blood of Jesus, then you have a song to sing. It does not matter how musically inclined you are. What matters is that you have a song to sing! Your life in Christ is a song that others will observe.

Will others see Christ in your life song? Will they see and revere Jesus because of your life song? Will others place their trust in Jesus as a result of the song that your life sings? God has given us the wonderful and awesome privilege to be the tangible portrait of His grace on this planet. The conversations and interactions that you engage in on a daily basis are chords that vibrate the rhythm of God's love.

When you study the life of Jesus, you will notice that Jesus maximized the opportunities presented to Him each day. Jesus lived a life that radiated the love of God. People were drawn to Jesus because His life song declared the magnitude of God's abundant grace and mercy.

Maybe you are in a season currently that has inhibited the song in your mouth. Maybe you have not had a song to sing due to hurt, anger, or disappointment. Ask God to renew your mind and to renew your strength. Ask God to put a new song in your mouth to help you persevere and experience a breakthrough. God knows right where you are and exactly what you need. Trust God!

VICTORY IN JESUS
Trust, Victory, Enemies

"I do not trust in my bow, my sword does not bring me victory; but you give us victory over our enemies, you put our adversaries to shame."
Psalm 44:6-7 (NIV)

When you identify an area that you are gifted in or an activity that comes naturally to you, it is easy to place your confidence in that area or activity. Sometimes our competence becomes our confidence. We begin to trust the gifts and abilities that God has given us to the neglect of relying upon His strength. Sometimes we may even forget how we have become victorious. What do you trust in? Who are you relying upon to live the victorious Christian life?

- *"But blessed is the man who trusts in the LORD, whose confidence is in him. He will be like a tree planted by the water that sends out its roots by the stream. It does not fear when heat comes; its leaves are always green. It has no worries in a year of drought and never fails to bear fruit."* Jer 17:7-8 (NIV)
- *"What a wretched man I am! Who will rescue me from this body of death? Thanks be to God--through Jesus Christ our Lord!"* Romans 7:24-25 (NIV)

God gives us the victory. The credit does not belong to us for weathering the storms of life. God gives us the grace we need to both live and die. God provides us with His ample supply of Manna and quail. God multiplies the loaves and fish to nourish us.

Spend a few moments thanking God for coming to your rescue. Be mindful of how needy you are and how generous God is. Weigh the privilege of trusting God, and using the gifts and abilities He has given, in order to live for His glory.

March 15

GOD'S UNFAILING LOVE

Trust

"But I am like an olive tree flourishing in the house of God; I trust in God's unfailing love for ever and ever." Psalm 52:8 (NIV)

The supply of God's love never diminishes. God's love is unlimited and unwavering. You can trust in God's unfailing love. When you place your trust in the immutable character of God, you will be anchored to the Rock. The uncertainties of life in a fallen world cannot alter the unfailing love of God. You are never more secure than living under the canopy of God's love.

- *"Whoever does not love does not know God, because God is love." 1 John 4:8 (NIV)*
- *"This is love: not that we loved God, but that he loved us and sent his Son as an atoning sacrifice for our sins." 1 John 4:10 (NIV)*

You can flourish in this life regardless of your circumstances by trusting in God's unfailing love. You can move beyond relying on feelings that come and go by trusting in the consistent flow of God's love. Before you were born, God established you in His love. Before you took your first breath, God demonstrated His love for you by giving you His only Son to die so that you could live forever.

Finding Refuge
Trust, Refuge, Sufficiency

"I will say of the LORD, 'He is my refuge and my fortress, my God, in whom I trust.'" Psalm 91:2 (NIV)

When answers are beyond your reach, trust in God. When your circumstances produce an element of fear, trust in God. When you feel as though the road of life has become filled with pot holes, trust in God. God is your refuge. He is your covering and your protection. Your fortification is found in God.

Jesus endured the agony of being falsely accused and ultimately crucified. The people went from waving the palm braches shouting "Hosanna" to waving their fists in the air shouting "crucify!" Jesus endured such opposition so that we could learn from Him the importance and value of taking refuge in God. Jesus entrusted Himself to the protective hand of God.

   • *"For we do not have a high priest who is unable to sympathize with our weaknesses, but we have one who has been tempted in every way, just as we are--yet was without sin. Let us then approach the throne of grace with confidence, so that we may receive mercy and find grace to help us in our time of need." Heb 4:15-16 (NIV)*

What kind of obstacles are you currently facing? Is there anything that is bothering you or causing you to lose sleep at night? Close your eyes and simply articulate your fears and frustrations before the Lord. Release your anxiety to God and allow Him to fill your questions with His abiding Presence. Trust in God's timing. Trust in God's unlimited supply. God knew that you needed Jesus to become your personal Savior.

You may not know what tomorrow holds; but you know who holds tomorrow. God has the whole world in His hands; that includes you.

March 17
FINDING STABILITY
Trust

"Those who trust in the LORD are like Mount Zion, which cannot be shaken but endures forever." Psalm 125:1 (NIV)

Can God use a shepherd boy to slay a giant? We all face giants in this life. Sometimes the giants are related to health, sometimes related to family or friends, and sometimes related to finances. The giants before us are not obstacles to overcome, but rather opportunities for our trust in the Lord to be developed and displayed. God gets the glory when the victory is won. When David faced his giant, Goliath, God received the glory.

- *"David said to the Philistine, 'You come against me with sword and spear and javelin, but I come against you in the name of the LORD Almighty, the God of the armies of Israel, whom you have defied. This day the LORD will hand you over to me, and I'll strike you down and cut off your head. Today I will give the carcasses of the Philistine army to the birds of the air and the beasts of the earth, and the whole world will know that there is a God in Israel. All those gathered here will know that it is not by sword or spear that the LORD saves; for the battle is the LORD's, and he will give all of you into our hands.'" 1 Sam 17:45-47 (NIV)*

Repeat this phrase aloud, "The battle is the Lord's." Just speaking forth that phrase reminds us that the battle is not about us, but about God and what He wants to accomplish in us and through us. The opposition you face in this life provides you with multiple opportunities to trust in God and demonstrate His ability to enable you to endure difficult circumstances. As long as you anchor your trust in God, you will not be shaken. The evidence of stability will be realized as you place your trust in God.

Now consider your giants. Is there anything you are facing that God cannot handle? Remember, the battle is the Lord's.

EXTENDING FORGIVENESS
Forgiveness, Decisions, Extending Forgiveness

"Forgive us our debts, as we also have forgiven our debtors." Matt 6:12 (NIV)

Forgiveness is always the best decision.

The Bible teaches us multiple facets of forgiveness. We have the privilege of receiving God's forgiveness provided by the atoning work of Jesus on the cross. This vertical forgiveness initiated by God allows us to be in a right relationship with God. We also have to come to the place of forgiving ourselves. Once we have received God's forgiveness for our sins, we need to forgive ourselves so that we can walk in the freedom Christ provides. Another facet of forgiveness is that of extending forgiveness to others.

In teaching His disciples how to pray, Jesus included the discipline of extending forgiveness to others. Before asking God to forgive us of our sins, we are to have already forgiven those who have sinned against us. In order to have a proper vertical relationship with God, we must ensure a proper horizontal relationship with others.

When it comes to extending forgiveness to others, you never have to pray and ask God if you should forgive someone. God expects us to extend instant forgiveness to others. To harbor bitterness or resentment breaks the heart of God. To fail to forgive others is to disobey God.

Spend some time in prayer asking God to search your heart. As God reveals elements of unforgiveness in your life, deal with them before God in prayer. The more specific you are in prayer, the more dynamic your experience in prayer will be. Forgiveness is always the best decision.

March 19
THE PROCESS OF FORGIVENESS
Forgiveness, Compassion, Trust

"Bear with each other and forgive whatever grievances you may have against one another. Forgive as the Lord forgave you." Col 3:13 (NIV)

Forgiveness is an event, followed by a process.

Perhaps you have found yourself in situations where you have had a hard time forgiving those who have wounded you. Maybe you have been wounded by hurtful words directed to you. Maybe you have been wounded by someone who withheld affection or affirmation from you. Doing life with others involves risks. Relationships can be risky.

In his letter to the church at Colosse, Paul identified the prominent role of forgiveness in the realm of relationships. We are commanded to patiently endure each other and to graciously forgive whatever grievances we may have against one another. In order to have a right relationship with God, we must have a right relationship with others. Conversely, in order to have a right relationship with others, we must have a right relationship with God.

The next time you begin thinking that someone doesn't deserve your forgiveness, ask this question, "How much has the Lord forgiven me?" That question places a unique perspective on the concept of forgiveness. In the midst of our hurt, extending forgiveness may not be in line with our true feelings.

Jesus is not asking you to do anything He has not already done for you. Jesus is not asking you to do anything that He has not already empowered you to do. Follow His example and trust in His provision to enable you to extend forgiveness. Forgiveness is an event, followed by a process. Ask Jesus to give you the compassion and courage to extend forgiveness.

FORGIVENESS AND TRUST

Forgiveness, Mercy, Trust

"For if you forgive men when they sin against you, your heavenly Father will also forgive you. But if you do not forgive men their sins, your Father will not forgive your sins." Matt 6:14-15 (NIV)

Would it not be hypocritical to receive God's forgiveness personally and then refuse to extend God's forgiveness to others? We do not earn God's forgiveness by forgiving others, but we demonstrate God's forgiveness as we forgive others.

You don't have to ponder the decision to forgive those who have wounded you. Forgiving those who have hurt you does not validate their behavior or condone their actions, but rather honors God by mirroring His forgiveness towards you. The grace and mercy that God lavishes on you becomes a blessing that flows through you to those who have wounded you.

Forgiveness is immediate; trust takes time. Just because you forgive someone does not mean that it is safe to trust that person. God is not asking you to extend forgiveness and then embrace a posture of vulnerability and susceptibility. You are to walk wisely. It takes time and multiple opportunities for a person to demonstrate trustworthiness.

Extend forgiveness immediately, and then pray for the person you have forgiven. Ask God to transform the one you have forgiven and to help that person become worthy of your trust. Extending forgiveness is not optional in God's economy.

In my daily quiet time, I came across this question by Henry Blackaby that God is using in my life, "Would you want God to forgive you in the same way you are presently forgiving others?"

March 21
CHOOSING TO FORGIVE
Forgiveness, Memory, Extending Forgiveness

"For I will forgive their wickedness and will remember their sins no more."
Heb 8:12 (NIV)

God, in His omniscience, has the capacity to remember our sins no more. God is infinite and we are finite. We do not have the capacity to forgive and forget. Of course, it seems at times that we forget what we need to remember and remember what we need to forget. Even after we have extended forgiveness to someone who has wounded us, it can be difficult to forget the experience and the pain involved.

You can be driving down the road or watching television or surfing the internet, and an image will trigger the memory of being wounded by someone you have already forgiven. Forgiveness includes memory. Forgiveness is not the ability to remember no more, but rather being able to say, "Though I remember, I choose to forgive."

Forgiveness is a choice. Harboring bitterness and resentment is a choice as well. I remember when I chose to visit my dad in jail to personally extend forgiveness to him for the hurt he had inflicted throughout my life due to his alcohol abuse. For years, I had chosen to allow unforgiveness to poison my life and to infuse my life with toxic bitterness. The day I chose to forgive my dad was the day I realized that, even though my dad was the one in prison, I had been imprisoned by my unforgiveness.

Yes, I remember the hurt and the pain of my dad's alcohol abuse, but in the swirling current of memory, I choose to forgive. God uses my memory to remind me of His abundant grace in my life. God is not asking me to do anything He has not already done for me.

The Best Decision

Forgiveness, Compassion, Cross, Extending Forgiveness

"Be kind and compassionate to one another, forgiving each other, just as in Christ God forgave you." Eph 4:32 (NIV)

Extending forgiveness is intentional and perpetual.

The words "just as" are powerful. In our key verse above, they mean to imitate and to emulate God's forgiveness. We are to forgive each other just as in Christ God forgave us. Let's consider going on a personal journey together in order to extend forgiveness to those who have wounded us.

Ask God to bring to your mind someone you need to forgive. This may induce feelings of hurt, betrayal, or neglect. Now that you have someone in mind, take that person with you to the cross in prayer. In fact, you may even need to take them by the hand as you kneel with them at the foot of the cross. Remember that Jesus knows him or her better than you do. Jesus loves him or her more than you do. Also, Jesus paid the full price for his or her complete forgiveness.

In prayer, say to the Lord, "Jesus, as you have graciously forgiven me, I now choose to forgive (insert his or her name)." Release that person from the prison of your unforgiveness. Genuinely extend forgiveness as in Christ God forgave you. Now entrust that person and your future to God.

Forgiveness is always the best decision.

March 23
HE IS RISEN
Resurrection, Life, Easter

"The angel said to the women, 'Do not be afraid, for I know that you are looking for Jesus, who was crucified. He is not here; he has risen, just as he said. Come and see the place where he lay.'" Matt 28:5-6 (NIV)

Are you looking for Jesus? He has risen! Death has been conquered. Sin has been atoned for. Forgiveness has been made available. Reconciliation has been established. Satan has been defeated. Hell has been invaded. Heaven has been decorated: gates of pearl, streets of transparent gold, river of the water of life, the tree of life, light from the Glory of God, light from the Lamb of God, no more night, no longer any curse, absence of tears, absence of mourning, absence of crying, absence of pain, and the presence of jasper, sapphire, chalcedony, emerald, sardonyx, carnilian, chrysolite, beryl, topaz, chrysoprase, jacinth, and amethyst.

- *"Now if we died with Christ, we believe that we will also live with him. For we know that since Christ was raised from the dead, he cannot die again; death no longer has mastery over him. The death he died, he died to sin once for all; but the life he lives, he lives to God." Romans 6:8-10 (NIV)*
- *"We were therefore buried with him through baptism into death in order that, just as Christ was raised from the dead through the glory of the Father, we too may live a new life." Romans 6:4 (NIV)*

Are you living in light of the resurrection of Jesus? Are you walking in anticipation of heaven? The same power that raised Jesus from the dead is available to you. The tomb is empty so that you can be filled by the Person of the Holy Spirit.

LIVING THE LIFE
Life

"He who has the Son has life; he who does not have the Son of God does not have life." 1 John 5:12 (NIV)

Are you living the life God has for you now?

Jesus is alive and the tomb is empty. Shouldn't that reality make an eternal difference in your life now? For some reason, we put life off until another day. We believe that life is right around the corner. It seems as though that corner never comes. Life is delayed until the next opportunity or the next breakthrough. Maybe life will kick into gear when we get our driver's license, or graduate, or get married, or get a home, or have kids, or land that perfect job, or send our kids off to college, or become grandparents, or retire. What's the holdup? Why isn't life happening now?

The eternal life God has given us in His Son is now. If you have the Son, then you have life now. God has taken the initiative to provide you the opportunity to receive the gift of eternal life. Once you place your faith in the completed work of Jesus on the cross, you become a child of God. In that moment, God graces you with the gift of eternal life. Eternal life for you does not begin after you die and go to heaven. Even if Jesus comes before you die and you get to experience the rapture, eternal life does not begin at that point. Eternal life for you begins the moment you trust Jesus as your personal Lord and Savior. Eternal life is now!

What are you doing with the life God has given you? Are you living it for His glory? Are you wasting your life on careless living? Are you delaying life until another day, week, month, or year?

Choose to live the life now!

March 25
DEALING WITH DELAYS
Delays, Life, Omniscience, Sovereignty, Unmet Expectations

"Jesus loved Martha and her sister and Lazarus. Yet when he heard that Lazarus was sick, he stayed where he was two more days." John 11:5-6 (NIV)

Delays are painful. We understand that God is all-knowing and that God is love, but we just don't always fully understand God's timing. When God doesn't respond in the time frame that we have established, we wonder if God really cares. Delays intensify our fears and magnify the reality of our meager faith.

Have you ever been between a rock and hard place and wondered if God would come through for you? Have your circumstances ever taken you to a place you never thought you would go? God allows us to go through those seasons and experience those places in order to come to know the depth of His love. God is for us. God always has our best interest in mind. Nothing happens to a child of God without His permission. If God permits it, then God will use it for your good and for His glory.

Martha and Mary experienced the full impact of a delay. Their brother, Lazarus, was sick and died before Jesus got there. They knew firsthand the trauma of unmet expectations. They had seen Jesus speak life into the dead. They had seen Jesus restore sight to the blind, speech to the mute, mobility to the lame, and hearing to the deaf. Yet, Jesus did not operate according to their personal time preference. Jesus delayed.

Why doesn't God show up to resolve your dilemmas sooner? Why does God seem to delay His response to your need for divine intervention? God's timing is perfect. He is never late. God, in His sovereignty, takes the confetti of our lives and produces a portrait of His grace.

Do you trust God? Are you entrusting your life and your circumstances to His care? Are you willing to obey God in the midst of a perceived delay?

GOD'S PURPOSE IN PROBLEMS
Life, Death, Glory, Sin, Sickness, Consequences

"When he heard this, Jesus said, 'This sickness will not end in death. No, it is for God's glory so that God's Son may be glorified through it.'" John 11:4 (NIV)

God has a purpose behind every problem.

Living the life in a fallen world includes unfavorable circumstances. The sin factor affects both the cause and the solution to problems in this life. You can trace sin, sickness, and death back to the garden when man fell. The residual effect of sin permeates every generation. We live our lives in a world that straddles daily the consequences of sin. As Steve Farrar writes in his book, *Finishing Strong*, "Sin will take your farther than you want to go, keep you longer that you want to stay, and cost you more than you want to pay."

God does not originate our problems, but He orchestrates the solution to our problems. The origin of our sin is linked through our family tree back to Adam and Eve. The solution to our sin is linked to God's provision of forgiveness through the atoning work of Jesus on the cross.

Martha and Mary grieved the death of their brother, Lazarus. They also grieved the fact that Jesus did not come to their rescue according to their personal preference of time. Jesus identified a higher purpose behind their problem. Jesus declared that it was for God's glory.

Watch to see how God reveals Himself and His glory through your circumstances. God's glory can radiate in your present circumstances and in the midst of your perplexing problems. God has a purpose behind every problem. Allow God's glory to shine even when the solution to your problems is delayed from your standpoint. God purpose will always prevail. Nothing can derail God's glory.

March 27
PLACING VALUE ON LIFE
Resurrection, Faith, I am sayings

"Jesus said to her, 'I am the resurrection and the life. He who believes in me will live, even though he dies; and whoever lives and believes in me will never die. Do you believe this?'" John 11:25-26 (NIV)

The value of life seems to go up when you come face to face with death. If you have ever had someone close to you die, you know what I mean. We tend to take life for granted until we brush up against the reality of death. Maybe you have leaned on the door of death personally through tragedy or health issues.

When I almost died in a Jet Ski accident on February 23, 1986, at 2:20pm at Buhlow Lake in Alexandria, Louisiana, the value I placed on life elevated exponentially. When I held my daughter, Tori, for the first time, the value I had placed on life catapulted again. Five years later, when I held my son, Austin, for the first time, the value I had placed on life skyrocketed yet again.

Martha expressed her faith in Jesus and acknowledged that her brother, Lazarus, would not have died had Jesus been there. Jesus, the One who establishes the value of a life, declared, "I am the resurrection and the life." Martha understood that her brother would rise again on the last day. She was looking to the distant future. Jesus reminded her of the immediate reality.

Do you believe that Jesus is who He says He is? The value of your life has already been established by the saving work Jesus did for you on the cross. Jesus took your place. You can know Jesus, the resurrection and the life, personally and eternally.

GROWING THROUGH GRIEF

Life, Humility, Grief, Humanity of Christ, Incarnation, Sympathy

"Jesus wept." John 11:35 (NIV)

Jesus wept aloud when He stood over unrepentant Jerusalem in their failure to recognize Him as Savior. But when Jesus stood before the tomb of Lazarus, He shed a tear. Jesus' expression of grief was not a loud lament, but rather an intimate display of grief over the reality of the consequences of sin. We get a glimpse of the humanity of Christ as He empathized with Mary and Martha. Of course, Jesus knew that He was about to raise Lazarus from the dead.

- *"He was despised and rejected by men, a man of sorrows, and familiar with suffering. Like one from whom men hide their faces he was despised, and we esteemed him not." Isaiah 53:3 (NIV)*
- *"For we do not have a high priest who is unable to sympathize with our weaknesses, but we have one who has been tempted in every way, just as we are--yet was without sin." Heb 4:15 (NIV)*

Jesus knows grief by personal experience. Jesus knows what you are going through right now. You will never go where Jesus has not already been. Draw near to Him. Place your burdens upon Him. Trust Jesus with your life, your hurts, your disappointments, and your dreams.

March 29
ALIGNING WITH GOD'S WILL
Prayer, Faith, Life, Obstacles

"So they took away the stone. Then Jesus looked up and said, 'Father, I thank you that you have heard me. I knew that you always hear me, but I said this for the benefit of the people standing here, that they may believe that you sent me.'"
John 11:41-42 *(NIV)*

When you contemplate the relational fortitude Jesus modeled in prayer, you gain insight into your personal need to stay connected to the Father. Jesus, as the Son of God and the Savior of the world, nurtured His love relationship with the Father through consistent conversation.

- *"Very early in the morning, while it was still dark, Jesus got up, left the house and went off to a solitary place, where he prayed."*
  Mark 1:35 *(NIV)*
- *"But Jesus often withdrew to lonely places and prayed."*
  Luke 5:16 *(NIV)*

Standing before the tomb of Lazarus, Jesus asked them to remove the stone, and they did. Before Jesus commanded Lazarus to come forth, He prayed. In fact, Jesus looked up and prayed to His Father in Heaven. Jesus prayed a prayer of thanksgiving and a prayer of affirmation.

Never underestimate the power of prayer. Your love relationship with God determines the level of your participation in God's agenda. As the world-renowned missionary, E. Stanley Jones, explained: "If I throw out a boathook from the boat and catch hold of the shore and pull, do I pull the shore to me, or do I pull myself to the shore? Prayer is not pulling God to my will, but the aligning of my will to the will of God." Jesus prayed and lived in alignment with the will of God. Are you ready to pull yourself to the shore?

REMOVING THE GRAVE CLOTHES
Freedom, Resurrection, Life, Miracle, Liberty

"When he had said this, Jesus called in a loud voice, 'Lazarus, come out!' The dead man came out, his hands and feet wrapped with strips of linen, and a cloth around his face. Jesus said to them, 'Take off the grave clothes and let him go.'"
John 11:43-44 (NIV)

Are you living the life God has given?

Jesus left heaven and came to earth to dwell among us and ultimately give His life in death upon the cross so that we could know and experience true life. Jesus has removed the obstacles and provided the only way to salvation. Jesus is the way.

Death could not prevent Jesus from bringing forth life, even to Lazarus, who had been dead four days. As the stench of death permeated the graveyard, Jesus called Lazarus by name to come forth from the dead. As Lazarus came out of the tomb, Jesus commanded them to take the grave clothes off and to let him go.

What is keeping you from living the life God has given? What kind of grave clothes have kept you bound? Release those things which prevent you from walking in the fullness of God's provision. Let go of those thoughts and attitudes that inhibit the flow of the Holy Spirit in your life. Jesus has paid full price for your freedom. Jesus has called you forth from the dead.

- *"As for you, you were dead in your transgressions and sins, in which you used to live when you followed the ways of this world and of the ruler of the kingdom of the air, the spirit who is now at work in those who are disobedient." Eph 2:1-2 (NIV)*
- *"So if the Son sets you free, you will be free indeed." John 8:36 (NIV)*

Take the grave clothes off, and walk in the grace God provides.

March 31
Embracing the Way of Jesus
Allurements, Divine Appointment, Frustration, Fulfillment

"Jesus answered her, 'If you knew the gift of God and who it is that asks you for a drink, you would have asked him and he would have given you living water.'"
John 4:10 (NIV)

Have you been there, done that, and left frustrated?

Life is filled with unlimited options and unimaginable opportunities. We are bombarded with advertisements positioned to convince us that we need the product being promoted. Our landscape is littered with attractions and allurements competing for our attention. It seems that the more we acquire, the more we desire. The more we attain, the more we strain to attain even more. Yet, at the end of the day, after the varied pursuits, we are left empty.

We meet a woman in the Gospel of John who has been there, and done that. In fact, she has had five husbands, and the one she is with now is not her husband. She has been looking for love in all the wrong places. She has been trying to make sense out of life through relationships with men. Each relationship has not delivered what it promised. This Samaritan woman meets a man, unexpectedly, who will transform her life.

Jesus is always at the right place at the right time. Jesus is always seizing opportunities to build bridges to broken people. The Samaritan woman experienced a divine appointment when she met Jesus. Jesus initiated the relationship that would ultimately change the Samaritan woman's life.

Are you frustrated with your life? Have you sought to fill the void in your life with good things at the expense of the best God has for you? Maybe it is time for you to meet Jesus at the well. Maybe it is time to give up on your personal journey to fulfillment, and embrace the way of Jesus.

PRACTICING SOLITUDE

Solitude, Intimacy with God, Habits

"Very early in the morning, while it was still dark, Jesus got up, left the house and went off to a solitary place, where he prayed." Mark 1:35 NIV

Can you imagine having a daily appointment with the Creator of the universe? What would you say? How would you prepare for such an important meeting? The reality is that you have that wonderful privilege of connecting with the Creator. Through the completed work of Jesus on the cross, the divine connection has been established. Can you hear me now?

The challenge for us is not making the connection. God took the initiative to bring us into a vibrant love relationship with Himself. The challenge is for us to carve out unhurried time to be alone with Him. Jesus modeled the value of solitude throughout His earthly ministry.

We must consciously practice solitude. Solitude becomes the environment by which we bend our ear and our will toward the echo of God's whisper. What needs to change in your daily routine to make room for connecting with our Creator? What adjustments do you need to make in order to practice solitude?

April 2
INSTEAD OF YOU
Justice, Love

"But the chief priests stirred up the crowd to have Pilate release Barabbas instead." Mark 15:11 (NIV)

Have you ever encountered injustice? Have you ever been treated unfairly? I think we have all been there. It hurts! The scars serve as a constant reminder. In our verse today, we find a word that compels us to contemplate. It is the soothing word, "instead." Let me take this punishment instead of you. Allow me to receive this penalty instead of you. Jesus will be flogged and crucified instead of Barabbas. The innocent man dies in his place. The guilty man goes free. Jesus receives what He doesn't deserve while Barabbas receives what he doesn't deserve. Jesus receives death! Barabbas receives life! Is that justice? Should the guilty go free?

It depends who takes the initiative. "But God demonstrates his own love for us in this: While we were still sinners, Christ died for us" (Rm. 5:8 NIV). Christ died instead of us! Yes, while we were still sinners!

How can you demonstrate that kind of love? Who in your sphere of influence needs to know what "instead" looks like? Forgive instead of holding a grudge. Show acceptance instead of forging a gap. Offer help instead of ignoring the need. Appreciate Jesus instead of taking Him for granted. It's your move!

MERCY CAME RUNNING

Mercy, Righteousness

"God made him who had no sin to be sin for us, so that in him we might become the righteousness of God." II Cor. 5:21 (NIV)

Try to measure the depth of God's mercy. When you weigh the purity of Christ's life and the contamination of our sinfulness, the scale drastically shifts to our side. We are guilty. We stand condemned.

Fortunately, God came to our rescue. Mercy came running! God made Jesus to be sin for us so that we could become righteousness.

Have you received what He offers? Have you come to the place in your life of recognizing your sin and your separation from our Holy God? God initiated the process to bring you into harmony with His purpose and plan. God's initiative demands a response. He did not make us robotic. He made us relational so that we could choose Him or refuse Him.

You can be in right standing before God by placing your faith in the completed work of Jesus on the cross. You can know the peace that passes all understanding. You can have the ultimate relationship with the One who demonstrated the ultimate portrait of mercy.

God did not give us what we deserve. Would you be willing to simply praise Him right now for extending His mercy to you?

April 4
PEACE HE GIVES

Peace

"But he was pierced for our transgressions, he was crushed for our iniquities; the punishment that brought us peace was upon him, and by his wounds we are healed." Isaiah 53:5 (NIV)

God always goes the extra mile. Just when you thought you could go no farther and had nowhere to turn, God steps in. He robes Himself in flesh and becomes like us so that we can become like Him. For thirty-three and a half years, Jesus walked upon earth to reveal the Father.

At His baptism at age thirty, Jesus heard the affirming words from His Heavenly Father, "This is my son, whom I love; with whom I am well pleased" (Mt. 3:17 NIV). Jesus passionately sought to fulfill the Father's will. Think about the implications of His pursuit. It meant sacrificing His own life on the cross to bring ultimate peace into our lives. He gave His all so that we could experience all that God has to offer.

Jesus was pierced, crushed, and punished so that we might experience the peace of God. He was wounded for the sake of our healing. Jesus took our place. He stepped in so that you could step up and know the One True and Living God personally and eternally.

What are you doing with the peace He gives? What is keeping you from embracing His abiding peace? I am reminded of the bumper sticker that says, "No Christ, no peace! Know Christ, know peace!" Are you full of peace?

GETTING WHAT YOU DON'T DESERVE

Grace

"One of the criminals who hung there hurled insults at him: 'Aren't you the Christ? Save yourself and us!' But the other criminal rebuked him. 'Don't you fear God,' he said, 'since you are under the same sentence? We are punished justly, for we are getting what our deeds deserve. But this man has done nothing wrong.'" Luke 23:39-41 (NIV)

Death row awaits with anticipation as the guard passes by one cell after another until he comes to your cell. The consequences of your criminal behavior reach the pinnacle as you intake your final few breaths. But wait, the guard unlocks the cell door and announces that you are completely free to leave the prison grounds. You have been pardoned! You will not have to pay for your sin!

Now wait a minute. How would you categorize such a transaction? Maybe there's a word that comprehends such an act. Consider the word, grace. Perhaps mercy is not getting what we deserve, and grace is getting what we do not deserve. Think about it. We do not deserve forgiveness, peace, a second chance, or love. But God gives us what we do not deserve.

Jesus responded to the repentant criminal on the cross by saying, "I tell you the truth, today you will be with me in paradise." Now that's giving the criminal something he does not deserve. I think that when it comes to our sinful state, we are all on death row! But, God gives us what we do not deserve. "For it is by grace you have been saved, through faith--and this not from yourselves, it is the gift of God--not by works, so that no one can boast" (Eph. 2:8-9 NIV).

April 6
RECEIVING GOD'S FORGIVENESS
Forgiveness

"When they hurled their insults at him, he did not retaliate; when he suffered, he made no threats. Instead, he entrusted himself to him who judges justly. He himself bore our sins in his body on the tree, so that we might die to sins and live for righteousness; by his wounds you have been healed. For you were like sheep going astray, but now you have returned to the Shepherd and Overseer of your souls." 1 Peter 2:23-25 (NIV)

Your greatest need has been met. The greatest gift has been given. Eternity has been radically altered. Your destination is now secure! How can this be?

Jesus bore our sins in His body on the cross and uttered the life changing words, "It is finished!" That's right! Our sin debt has been paid in full. Forgiveness has been provided. We can add nothing to what Jesus accomplished on the cross. We cannot work our way into salvation, and we cannot do anything to earn what He purchased for us.

We have the privilege of entrusting ourselves to Jesus just as He entrusted Himself to God's plan. We have the glorious opportunity to receive the comprehensive forgiveness that He provides.

What is different about your life today as a result of what Jesus did for you 2,000 years ago? What is keeping you from fully surrendering your life to His control? What is keeping you from trusting Him with your life daily and eternally? Have you received His forgiveness? You can be free!

No Condemnation

Righteousness, Freedom, Condemnation

"Therefore, there is now no condemnation for those who are in Christ Jesus, because through Christ Jesus the law of the Spirit of life set me free from the law of sin and death." Romans 8:1-2 (NIV)

What are you doing with the new life you have been given? As a child of God, your sin debt has been deleted, your name has been written in the Lamb's Book of Life, and your adoption has been completed. Satan is defeated! Jesus reigns!

Are you allowing Jesus to reign in your life? Are you living in light of your new identity in Christ? You are now free to live and express your God given potential. You are now free to share His love and shine His light. The shackles have been removed! Praise God!

There is now no condemnation! The righteousness of Christ has been deposited into your account. When God sees you, He sees the righteousness of Christ. The operation of the Holy Spirit has set you free from the operation of sin and death.

Carve out some time today to think through all that God has delivered you from. Spend a few moments praising Him for His deliverance. Bask in the reality of your relationship with our Heavenly Father. He is worthy! You are free!

April 8
LIVING IN LIGHT OF THE RESURRECTION
Resurrection

"He is not here; he has risen, just as he said. Come and see the place where he lay." Matt 28:6 (NIV)

Are you living in the power of the resurrection? Jesus is alive! The redemptive act of God has ushered forth new life and a new beginning. God is who He says He is and does what He says He will do. The resurrection of Jesus from the dead changes everything. The darkness has turned to light. Sin and death no longer have mastery over us. Both have been defeated.

Have you allowed the empty tomb to become a reality in your daily living? Are you walking in perpetual consciousness of God's redemptive activity? There's more to Easter than just dressing up and going to church. The fact that Jesus rose from the dead establishes our eternal destiny and enables us to proclaim His redemption story throughout the earth.

Praise the Living God today, for He rules and He reigns! Allow Jesus to have full access to your hurts, your habits, and your hang ups. Allow Him to bring His resurrection power to every area of your life so that you can live in fullness everyday.

DISCERNING WHAT GOD VALUES

Priorities, Time Management

"I am going to send you what my Father has promised; but stay in the city until you have been clothed with power from on high." Luke 24:49 (NIV)

What will your schedule look like today? How will your time be allocated? Just as Dave Ramsey says, "Tell your money where to go!" You must also tell your time and energy where to go. You have 86,400 seconds to allocate within the next twenty four hours.

Your priorities will determine how you invest your time and energy. If you value what God values, then His priorities will be reflected in your schedule.

If the disciples value what God values, then they are going to Jerusalem to await the coming of the promised Holy Spirit. Their number one priority is obeying God. Their priorities will be validated by their obedience to the command of Jesus. The good news is that 120 believers gathered in the Upper Room in Jerusalem and experienced ten days of anticipation and obedience.

They were willing to value what God values. They were willing to allow God's priorities to be their priorities. As a result, they cleared their schedule and allocated their time and energy to obey Jesus. What was the result? God blessed their obedience on the day of Pentecost with the indwelling Holy Spirit and the salvation of 3,000 souls!

Now let's take a look at your life. What does your schedule say about your priorities? What do you value? Are you willing to make necessary adjustments to bring your life into alignment with what God values? Take the initiative!

April 10
INSTANT OBEDIENCE
Obedience

"We know that we have come to know him if we obey his commands." I Jn 2:3 (NIV)

So what does the resurrection life look like? Instant obedience! Your number one priority is to obey God. Obeying God begins with surrendering to the Lordship of Christ and giving Him complete control of your life.

Acknowledge your sin and separation from our Holy God, and receive His provision for the forgiveness of your sin. Place your faith in the completed work of Jesus on the cross. Make obeying God the number one priority of your life.

To know Him is to obey Him. Obedience to God is not only a mark of spiritual maturity; it is the birthmark of being born again. Obeying God is a non-negotiable.

Satan's goal is to lure you into succumbing to one of his schemes. The enemy seeks to entice you with a shortcut to obeying God's best for your life. "Be self-controlled and alert. Your enemy the devil prowls around like a roaring lion looking for someone to devour" (I Pt 5:8). Don't give the devil a foothold. In fact, don't even give him a toehold.

The resurrection life is allowing the Holy Spirit to control your thoughts, your words, and your actions in such a way that the enemy doesn't have room to sneak in to devour. Post a "no trespassing" sign, and remind the enemy that he is trespassing on your Father's territory!

Instant obedience is always the best option for living the resurrection life. Sing with me, "Have thine own way Lord, have thine own way."

RESTING IN JESUS

Reliance, Rest

"Come to me, all you who are weary and burdened, and I will give you rest. Take my yoke upon you and learn from me, for I am gentle and humble in heart, and you will find rest for your souls. For my yoke is easy and my burden is light."
Matt 11:28-30 (NIV)

Jesus is always on time. He knows just what we need, right when we need it. His invitation to join Him and to find rest in Him is the antidote to our fast paced lifestyle. As one person said, "If we don't learn to come apart, we will come apart!"

Why do we feel guilty when we slow down? Why do we gravitate toward the performance trap and end up equating productivity with spirituality? Sometimes the most spiritual move we can make is to slow down and experience the rest Jesus offers.

Be sure to notice in our verses for today that there is a prerequisite to encountering His rest. We must be willing to come to Him. We must be willing to take the initiative to respond to His invitation. That just doesn't fit our adrenaline addicted society. We tend to long for the next high or the next rush. Maybe we can just capture a few more sips of caffeinated coffee. Will that deliver what we need most?

Perhaps the invitation is to come to the place of total reliance upon God. If I yoke up with Him, then I will have to be willing to go where He goes and embrace the pace He sets. Remember, His yoke is easy and His burden is light. Sounds refreshing!

April 12
PACE YOURSELF
Praise

"I will praise you, O LORD, with all my heart; I will tell of all your wonders."
Psalm 9:1 (NIV)

How do you begin each day of your life? Do you jump right out of bed and hit the floor running, or do you slowly drag yourself from beneath the sheets and gradually wake up to the approaching day? Either way, let me share with you a wonderful way to PACE yourself for each day.

Let's consider using PACE as an acrostic to get our day moving in the right direction with the Lord. Dr. Adrian Rogers shared this daily discipline with me several years ago. The "P" stands for "Praise!" The psalmist models this attitude and action by saying, "I will praise you, O Lord, with all my heart." To praise God is to give Him honor for who He is. To praise God is to acknowledge His sovereignty, His power, and His holiness.

Step number one: When you awaken each morning, lift your hands toward heaven and say, "Lord, I praise You!" That's right; as soon as your feet hit the ground, lift your hands, and speak it with sincerity and with passion. You may even choose to look up toward heaven as you say those precious words to our Living Lord.

Each of the next three days, we will unlock each letter of the word PACE to explore a simple yet captivating daily exercise to start each day off right. Now, let's practice this first step. Lift your hands toward heaven. Now look up and say it with me, "Lord, I praise You!"

He is worthy. We are blessed.

ACCEPTING GOD'S ACCEPTANCE

Acceptance

"God, who knows the heart, showed that he accepted them by giving the Holy Spirit to them, just as he did to us." Acts 15:8 (NIV)

Have you accepted God's acceptance of you? That's step number two in order to PACE yourself for the day. Remember, you start your day off by lifting your hands toward heaven and saying, "Lord, I praise you." Then, as you keep your hands lifted, you turn the palm of your hands toward each other and say, "I accept Your acceptance of me."

How did God demonstrate His acceptance of the Gentiles in the book of Acts? He demonstrated His acceptance by allowing the Holy Spirit to take up residence in them. God indwelt them by His Holy Spirit. He took the initiative through the shed blood of Jesus to make them fit for His habitation. "Do you not know that your body is a temple of the Holy Spirit, who is in you, whom you have received from God? You are not your own; you were bought at a price. Therefore honor God with your body" (1 Cor 6:19-20 NIV).

Who made us acceptable? Jesus! What should our response be to His acceptance of us? Accepting others! "Accept one another, then, just as Christ accepted you, in order to bring praise to God" (Romans 15:7 NIV).

Let's practice! Lift up your hands and say, "Lord, I praise You." Now, turn your uplifted hands toward each other and say, "I accept Your acceptance of me."

Now live in fullness everyday by accepting His acceptance of you!

April 14
SURRENDERING TO THE LORD'S CONTROL

Control, Lordship

"Now that I, your Lord and Teacher, have washed your feet, you also should wash one another's feet. I have set you an example that you should do as I have done for you." John 13:14-15 (NIV)

Who's your boss? To whom are you yielding allegiance? I hope your answer is Jesus. His desire is not only to be the Savior of your life, but to also be Lord of your life. In the language of the New Testament, "Lord" means one who has control over. Thus, to make Jesus Lord of your life is to yield to His control. The Lordship of Christ denotes submitting to His authority and embracing His agenda.

Let's continue to unfold our PACE acrostic. The letter "C" is for control. Include this in your daily routine: Lift your hands toward heaven, and turn your palms upward and say, "I surrender to Your control."

Now it is time to practice! Lift your hands toward heaven and say, "Lord, I praise You. I accept Your acceptance of me. I surrender to Your control."

Just in case you have not turned your life over to Jesus and allowed Him to become your Savior and Lord, consider this wonderful promise from God: "That if you confess with your mouth, 'Jesus is Lord,' and believe in your heart that God raised him from the dead, you will be saved" (Romans 10:9 NIV).

Let's surrender to His control, and see what happens!

EXPECTING GREAT THINGS FROM GOD

Expectation, Hope

"'For I know the plans I have for you,' declares the LORD, 'plans to prosper you and not to harm you, plans to give you hope and a future.'" Jer 29:11 (NIV)

Have you ever been through a season of uncertainty? Anxious thoughts race through your mind, and uneasiness permeates your emotions. You fear the unknown. Indecision imprisons you. Questions linger.

That's exactly the kind of season the Israelites experienced when they were exiled to Babylon from their homeland of Jerusalem. They were displaced, discouraged, and confused. Yet, in just the right moment, God met them at their point of need.

We serve an "on time" God! He is never late, and He always knows exactly what you need. Therefore, you can trust Him to accomplish His perfect plan in you and through you. He knows you by name, and even the hairs upon your head are numbered. Wow! He's good!

Are you ready for the final letter in our PACE acrostic? The "E" is for expectation. At this point, you pray with your hands outstretched, parallel to the ground (as though you are trying to fly) with the palm of your hands facing upward. Then you say, "I expect great things to happen today!"

Recognize God's sufficiency, and PACE yourself each day by embracing this spiritual discipline. Lift your hands toward heaven and say, "Lord, I praise You. I accept Your acceptance of me. I surrender to Your control. I expect great things to happen today!"

Now we're on shouting ground. Live in fullness everyday!

April 16
FINDING GOD IN THE ORDINARY
Ordinary

"Be strong and courageous. Do not be afraid or terrified because of them, for the LORD your God goes with you; he will never leave you nor forsake you."
Deut 31:6 (NIV)

Most of life is ordinary. Waking up, going to school or work, and of course, eating three times a day, and then sleeping, characterize life. You may say it is simply doing the ordinary routines that comprise our earthly existence.

Fortunately, droplets of surprise sprinkle the mundane. It may be a phone call that makes your day. Or it may be an email that touches your heart. The envelope in the mail as you open it reveals a refund you did not expect. Someone very special to you expresses love with a visit. Maybe you receive refreshing revelation as you read the Bible, and it prompts you to trust in God's timing.

Jesus will come to you, wherever you are. He will never leave you. He will never forsake you. He will never let you down. Are you willing to give Him access to your life? Are you willing to give Him the mineral rights to your fears and frustrations?

Where are you? Jesus will come to you.

The Comfort God Provides

Comfort

"Praise be to the God and Father of our Lord Jesus Christ, the Father of compassion and the God of all comfort, who comforts us in all our troubles, so that we can comfort those in any trouble with the comfort we ourselves have received from God." 2 Cor 1:3-4 (NIV)

The deadliest shooting in modern United States history took place on April 16, 2007, on the campus of Virginia Tech. Thirty-two students were killed, and the gunman committed suicide. Our hearts are broken, and our nation grieves for the families of those affected by this tragedy. Similar feelings erupted on September 11, 2001. Confusion looms. Questions linger.

My pastor, Dr. David Fleming, shared four timely promises that we can embrace from God's Word to help us navigate seasons of uncertainty.

1. Jesus will come to you wherever you are.

2. Jesus will walk with you through whatever.

3. Jesus will help you make sense of it all.

4. Jesus will turn your life around.

Our greatest need in this moment is the comfort God provides. He is more than enough. Allow God to speak to your heart and to extend His comfort to you. Then, PACE yourself and share your heart with God. Let Him hear the authentic cries of your heart. Express your trust in Him. Be comforted and seek to comfort others.

April 18
ANCHORING TO THE ROCK
Refuge

"The LORD is my rock, my fortress and my deliverer; my God is my rock, in whom I take refuge." Psalm 18:2 (NIV)

Who are you relying upon? What is your faith anchored to? Where do you run when the storm comes? Where do you go when life doesn't make sense? Can you affirm these words?

The LORD is my rock. He provides my stability!

The LORD is my fortress. He provides my serenity!

The LORD is my deliverer. He provides my solidarity!

The LORD God is my rock, in whom I take refuge. He provides my safety!

We are in desperate need of God's moment by moment provision. He is still on His throne and has given us everything we need to live out His plan and fulfill His purpose. God is not limited by our limitations.

God is eternal, holy, immutable, omnipotent, omniscient, and omnipresent. He is sovereign. His love endures forever, and His mercies are new every morning. You can take refuge in Him.

THE REAL ENEMY

Opposition

"Now the serpent was more crafty than any of the wild animals the LORD God had made. He said to the woman, 'Did God really say, "You must not eat from any tree in the garden"?'" Gen 3:1 (NIV)

God created a perfect world that sin infected. We now live on a broken planet with broken people who are fallen and flawed. Without Divine intervention, our situation is hopeless.

We have three enemies: the world, the flesh, and the devil. The serpent, known as Lucifer or the devil, is a created being who was once in right relationship with God and had authority to serve God. However, Lucifer sought to "de-throne" God (Is 14:12-15).

The sin of pride adversely affected Lucifer's relationship to God. He sought to de-throne God, and God responded by casting Lucifer out of heaven. Since that moment, the enemy has been on a mission to disrupt and to contaminate all that God has made.

Spend time today contemplating the presence of evil in our society. See if you can identify the source of the sinful behavior that permeates our earthly existence.

Let me pray with you. "Father, we acknowledge Your authority and Your sovereignty. You are infinite and we are finite. You are perfect and we are imperfect. You are holy, pure, and undefiled. We are desperate for You. Display Your glory throughout the earth today. Make Your Name great among the nations. Help us to walk in the light You have given. We submit to You in Jesus' Name, Amen."

April 20
LIVING IN THE READINESS MODE
Readiness

"Be self-controlled and alert. Your enemy the devil prowls around like a roaring lion looking for someone to devour." 1 Peter 5:8 (NIV)

If you decide to live a life of instant obedience to Jesus Christ, you will face opposition. The enemy will not rest until you are discouraged, disillusioned, and defeated. The devil is on the hunt to devour Christ followers.

This is not the time to coast into neutral. The Bible teaches us to be alert. That means to stay in the ready mode. We must embrace readiness!

- *"So then, let us not be like others, who are asleep, but let us be alert and self-controlled." 1 Thess 5:6 (NIV)*
- *"And pray in the Spirit on all occasions with all kinds of prayers and requests. With this in mind, be alert and always keep on praying for all the saints." Eph 6:18 (NIV)*

Opposition is as normal in the life of a believer as water is in the life of a fish. Jesus was never surprised by the enemy. Jesus was never unprepared to combat the enemy. Why? Because Jesus embraced readiness! Jesus chose to be alert!

Are you ready for today? Have you embraced readiness?

Declaring Sufficiency in Christ
Sufficiency

"For we do not have a high priest who is unable to sympathize with our weaknesses, but we have one who has been tempted in every way, just as we are--yet was without sin." Heb 4:15 (NIV)

Are you struggling? Are you hurting? Do you ever go through seasons of loneliness? Have you encountered frustration or disappointment? Have your dreams been shattered?

Jesus is more than enough! He can identify with our heartache and pain. He knows what it feels like to be misunderstood. His life was marked by ridicule, unfair treatment, and betrayal. Jesus is well acquainted with the onslaught of temptation. Was He tempted? Yes! Did He commit sin? No! Can He relate to the gravitational pull of sin? Yes!

Because Jesus was without sin, our insufficiency is transformed by His sufficiency. When we are weak, He is strong! When we are most susceptible to sin, Jesus consistently stands as the model to follow.

Remember, Jesus became like us so that we could become like Him.

April 22
APPROACHING THE THRONE OF GRACE
Confidence

"Let us then approach the throne of grace with confidence, so that we may receive mercy and find grace to help us in our time of need." Heb 4:16 (NIV)

Approaching the throne of grace with confidence is not equated with arrogance. Confidence is acknowledging your enablement through God working in you and through you. Arrogance is rooted in self worship.

God grants accessibility. He makes Himself available to us and allows us to approach His throne of grace. Now grace is receiving what we do not deserve while mercy is not receiving what we deserve. We do not deserve God's acceptance. We do not deserve God's provision of forgiveness, redemption, and eternal life. Because of our sin nature, we deserve death, alienation, punishment, and eternal damnation.

Praise God for His initiative to bring you into a vibrant love relationship with Himself. Now that you can approach the throne of grace with confidence, the question is: Are you taking advantage of the opportunity that God has provided for you to approach the throne of grace with confidence?

Think through your daily intimacy with God. How often are you intentionally approaching the throne of grace? Are you consciously accessing God's presence through prayer?

ELEVATING SOUL CONSCIOUSNESS

Soul Consciousness

"The harvest is past, the summer has ended, and we are not saved."
Jer 8:20 (NIV)

How much time do you have left on earth? How many people will die without a saving relationship with Jesus Christ within the next twenty-four hours? What difference will your life make in light of eternity?

Jesus modeled a deep abiding passion for souls. The Bible says, "For the Son of Man came to seek and to save what was lost" (Luke 19:10 NIV). Jesus never lost His focus of redeeming the lost. He did not neglect His mission to save the lost at any cost.

How many lost people are in your sphere of influence? What kind of relational bridge are you building to them? What are you willing to do to introduce them to a saving relationship with Jesus?

Pray this prayer with me. "Father, forgive me for my passive neglect. Forgive me for being so self-absorbed that I have minimized the urgency of soul-winning. Elevate my soul consciousness. Give me eyes to see lost people in their desperation. Anoint me with the courage of Jesus. Empower me to be your witness and to be your laborer in the harvest field. In Jesus' Name, Amen."

April 24
BEING AVAILABLE FOR GOD'S USE
Availability

"Now an angel of the Lord said to Philip, 'Go south to the road--the desert road--that goes down from Jerusalem to Gaza.' So he started out, and on his way he met an Ethiopian eunuch, an important official in charge of all the treasury of Candace, queen of the Ethiopians. This man had gone to Jerusalem to worship, and on his way home was sitting in his chariot reading the book of Isaiah the prophet. The Spirit told Philip, 'Go to that chariot and stay near it.'"
Acts 8:26-29 (NIV)

God blesses our availability. He is not limited by our ability or inability. God does His best work through those who make themselves available for His use.

So, the question is: Are you available for God's use? If so, then anticipate God's invitation for your participation in His Kingdom activity. God is always at work. Are you available to join Him in His work?

Philip made himself available for God's use. God responded to Philip's availability by inviting him to join Him in what He was already doing in the life of the Ethiopian eunuch. Did you notice that as Philip was on his way, and the eunuch was also on his way, that God made a way for the two to connect?

This divine connection would have never taken place had Philip not made himself available for God's use. Will you pray right now and make yourself available for God's use?

SENSITIVITY TO GOD'S ACTIVITY
Sensitivity

"Then Philip ran up to the chariot and heard the man reading Isaiah the prophet. 'Do you understand what you are reading?' Philip asked. 'How can I,' he said, 'unless someone explains it to me?' So he invited Philip to come up and sit with him." Acts 8:30-31 (NIV)

Is availability enough? If you make yourself available for God's use, will that be enough? No! Your availability must be accompanied by your sensitivity to God's activity.

Philip would have missed the divine connection with the Ethiopian eunuch had he not both made himself available to God and been sensitive to God's activity. In obedience to God, Philip ran to the chariot. Then, he was sensitive enough to hear the man reading Isaiah the prophet and to ask a probing question. In others words, Philip was sensitive to the opportunity that God had orchestrated.

God is always at work. Make yourself available and be sensitive to God's activity. Your sensitivity to God's activity will determine the level of connectivity with people God brings into your path.

Are you available? Are you sensitive to God's activity? Let's see what happens in your life today!

April 26
BUILDING INTENTIONAL RELATIONSHIPS
Intentionality

"The eunuch asked Philip, 'Tell me, please, who is the prophet talking about, himself or someone else?' Then Philip began with that very passage of Scripture and told him the good news about Jesus." Acts 8:34-35 (NIV)

Be intentional! Make a bee-line to the cross! Maximize the opportunities that God brings to you each day. Don't minimize your participation in God's activity.

Can God accomplish His plan without you? Sure He can! However, God chooses to use human instrumentality in the redemptive process. God chose to use Philip in bringing salvation to the Ethiopian eunuch.

Philip was available, sensitive, and intentional. It is not enough to just make yourself available. It is not enough to be sensitive to opportunities God interjects into your path. You must be willing to intentionally point people to Jesus.

Every interaction and every interruption in life can be used of God to bring people into a vibrant love relationship with Jesus. Don't miss the opportunity! Seize the moment! Be intentional!

IDENTIFYING WITH CHRIST THROUGH BAPTISM

Identification

"As they traveled along the road, they came to some water and the eunuch said, 'Look, here is water. Why shouldn't I be baptized?' And he gave orders to stop the chariot. Then both Philip and the eunuch went down into the water and Philip baptized him. When they came up out of the water, the Spirit of the Lord suddenly took Philip away, and the eunuch did not see him again, but went on his way rejoicing." Acts 8:36-39 (NIV)

When I served as pastor of First Baptist Church of Folsom, Louisiana, during my seminary days, I had the wonderful experience of creek baptisms. Every July 4th, we would have a special worship service at Pittman's Creek. Even though we had a heated baptistry in our worship center, many believers chose to be baptized in the freezing cold water at the creek. Those were memorable baptisms.

Have you been properly baptized by immersion following your conversion? If not, why not? What is keeping you from identifying with Christ through baptism?

The Ethiopian eunuch was passionate about following in believer's baptism. His life had been radically transformed by the saving grace of Jesus Christ. Now, he wanted to identify with Christ through baptism. He chose a creek baptism!

If you have already followed the Lord in believer's baptism, spend some time reflecting on that spiritual marker in your life. Thank God for allowing you to identify with Jesus through baptism.

If you have not been baptized, would you be willing to schedule your baptism within the next few days. Make it right! Give God your best! Jesus went all the way for you. Would you be willing to go the next step with Him and identify with Him through believer's baptism?

April 28
BEING STILL
Renewal

"Be still, and know that I am God; I will be exalted among the nations, I will be exalted in the earth." Psalm 46:10 (NIV)

Hit the pause button! Wait! Stop! Hold on a second! Don't move! Freeze! Relax! Be still! Why are we in such a hurry? Why are we sprinting in this marathon called life? Why do we choose to run on fumes?

Your life is structured for the results you are getting. If you are overwhelmed and stretched to the limit, then your life is currently structured to produce that reality.

Can you continue living at your present pace? Can you continue to function at the immediate level you are embracing? You may be feeling that if something doesn't change, you are going to explode or burn out. So the question is: What needs to change? If you keep living the way you are living, you will keep getting the results you are getting.

Maybe there is value in being still. Maybe there are healthy consequences to being still. I wonder if God created us to know that He is God. What if our knowing Him as God is proportionate to our willingness to be still?

Are you willing to try an experiment? Find a quiet place each day to just sit and reflect. Hit the pause button at least one time per day in order to be still. There's no agenda! There's nothing to fulfill! There's no deadline! Just be still, and see what God does to bring refreshment, renewal, and revival into your life.

MAKING A LIFE-CHANGING DECISION

Restoration

"When he came to his senses, he said, 'How many of my father's hired men have food to spare, and here I am starving to death! I will set out and go back to my father and say to him: Father, I have sinned against heaven and against you. I am no longer worthy to be called your son; make me like one of your hired men.' So he got up and went to his father." Luke 15:17-20 (NIV)

You are not a robot. God created you with the capacity to accept His plan or to reject His plan. He made you to be relational. You can respond to God's offer of restoration, or you can choose to go your own way.

God grants the freedom to accept Him or reject Him. By the power of His Holy Spirit, He comforts and convicts. He guides and He provides. However, God will allow you the freedom to choose a selfish path or a selfless path. He will alert you when you are taking a path that is not His best for you. Yet, God will allow you to maneuver in the direction of your choice.

The prodigal son made a poor decision when he selfishly requested his share of the estate so that he could carelessly spend it. Yet, God allowed him to get to the pigpen level of living. It was there that the prodigal son came to his senses and made the life-giving decision to get up and go back to his father.

Restoration awaits! How will you respond to God's offer?

April 30
MAKING UP YOUR MIND
Distractions

"Not long after that, the younger son got together all he had, set off for a distant country and there squandered his wealth in wild living." Luke 15:13 (NIV)

How does a runner prepare for a marathon? He removes distractions that would impede his progress and focuses his energy and effort on intentional training.

One of Satan's primary tools is to keep us distracted from God's plan. We begin to major on the minors and minor on the majors. We drift from our core values and seek to embrace superfluous agendas.

The prodigal son allowed the allurements of the distant country to distract him from his father's plan. He sought to bypass his father's protection and provision in order to court a cheap but appealing substitute. Sin never delivers what it promises!

What's the antidote to distractions? How do you overcome the lure of leaving the straight life? Here it is: Make up your mind!

- *"Since, then, you have been raised with Christ, set your hearts on things above, where Christ is seated at the right hand of God. Set your minds on things above, not on earthly things. For you died, and your life is now hidden with Christ in God." Col 3:1-3 (NIV)*

Pray this prayer with me: "Lord, I have made up my mind. Since I have been raised with You, I will set my heart on things above where You are seated at the right hand of God. Lord, I have made up my mind. I will set my mind on things above and not on earthly things. I have made up my mind. Since you died on the cross for me, my life is now hidden with You in God. I have made up my mind in Jesus' Name, Amen."

INVERTING DESPERATION

Desperation

"He longed to fill his stomach with the pods that the pigs were eating, but no one gave him anything." Luke 15:16 (NIV)

Desperate situations demand desperate measures. For a human being to get low enough to crave the slop that pigs eat defies logic. However, as Steve Farrar says in his book, *Finishing Strong*:

> Sin will take you farther than you want to go.
> Sin will keep you longer than you want to stay.
> Sin will cost you more than you want to pay.

Our appetite for sin will eventually take us down a road that leads to living below our new identity in Christ. The prodigal son reached the low point of sin's dreaded sway. He encountered the backside of the glitz and glamour of sin.

What would happen if you inverted your desperation? What if you decided to live in desperation for God? What if your appetite was refashioned from craving of sin to craving of righteousness?

Have you been to the desperate place? Have you ever reached the bottom? Now look within! Recognize your current condition. You are not made for the pigpen. Now look up! Resolve to live in light of your new identity in Christ.

May 2
MAKING WISE DECISIONS
Decisions

"So he got up and went to his father." Luke 15:20 (NIV)

There are so many options out there. Think about it. You will decide what to wear today. You will decide how you are going to interact with people today. You will decide where you will go throughout the day. You will decide what kind of attitude you will exhibit today.

God has enabled you to make decisions. As you know, with that kind of privilege comes an awesome responsibility to decide responsibly.

The prodigal son decided to leave his father's presence, protection, and provision in order to embrace a lifestyle of instant gratification. His perpetual poor decisions led him down the muddy path into the pigpen.

In the midst of the painful and devastating consequences proportionate to his poor decisions, the prodigal son made a decision that radically changed his future. He decided to get up and go back to his father.

Joshua illuminates the power of making wise decisions when he says, "Now fear the LORD and serve him with all faithfulness. Throw away the gods your forefathers worshiped beyond the River and in Egypt, and serve the LORD. But if serving the LORD seems undesirable to you, then choose for yourselves this day whom you will serve, whether the gods your forefathers served beyond the River, or the gods of the Amorites, in whose land you are living. But as for me and my household, we will serve the LORD" (Josh 24:14-15 NIV).

I deeply affirm a statement that I heard Louie Giglio make: "Long before you decided what to do with God, God decided what to do with you."

Now, it's your turn! What will your decision be?

CLOSING THE DISTANCE

Distance

"But while he was still a long way off, his father saw him and was filled with compassion for him; he ran to his son, threw his arms around him and kissed him." Luke 15:20 (NIV)

Have you ever felt a distance between you and God? Have you experienced seasons where God seemed far away? Who moved?

God allows us to distance ourselves from Him. Did you know that you determine the level of intimacy that you have with God?

God draws us near in salvation and we respond by drawing near to Him through daily intimacy. We navigate the relational proximity. "As you draw near to God, He will draw near to you" (James 4:8 NIV).

Remember, the prodigal son made the life altering decision to get up and go back to his father. Notice how the prodigal son was still a long way off when his father saw him and was filled with compassion for him. Who ran? Well, the son ran away from his father and then decided to return. Then, the father ran to his son. That blesses my heart. The father ran to his son! It sounds like "mercy came running!"

RECOGNIZING YOUR DISPOSITION
Disposition

"The son said to him, 'Father, I have sinned against heaven and against you. I am no longer worthy to be called your son.'" Luke 15:21 (NIV)

There is power in the recognition of your true disposition. You can shroud your persona with a facade that exudes perfection while your inner life embodies disarray. Disguising the reality of your inner self has the potential to delay being found out. However, the manifestation of your true disposition will appear at some point. God has a way of exposing our current reality.

When God asked Adam and Eve, "Where are you?" He was not perplexed that He had misplaced the crown of His creation. His question was not one of confusion related to an inability to find the couple that He created. His question was to heighten their recognition of their true disposition. God wanted Adam and Eve to recognize their current reality.

After Isaiah encountered God's holiness, he came face to face with his true disposition. A new standard of measurement became his conscious defining moment. Isaiah responded by saying, "Woe is me!" (Isaiah 6:5 NIV).

The prodigal son identified his true disposition and responded with the confession, "Father, I have sinned against heaven and against you. I am no longer worthy to be called your son" (Luke 15:21 NIV).

Consider the holiness of God. Are you sensing a need for confession in light of His holiness and your true disposition? His purity exposes our sinfulness. He graciously offers forgiveness.

UNCONDITIONAL LOVE
Dignity

"But the father said to his servants, 'Quick! Bring the best robe and put it on him. Put a ring on his finger and sandals on his feet. Bring the fattened calf and kill it. Let's have a feast and celebrate. For this son of mine was dead and is alive again; he was lost and is found.' So they began to celebrate." Luke 15:22-24 (NIV)

After a few minutes of channel surfing on your television you will discover that the media ruthlessly demeans human beings. Cynicism, pessimism, and sarcasm permeate the air waves.

In order to bestow dignity, you must value the other person. How you view others will directly affect how you treat others.

The prodigal son obviously negated his right for a welcome home party. He had dishonored his family name and wasted his family fortune. His lifestyle of gratifying his sinful appetite would have seemingly burnt the bridges back home.

However, the prodigal son's absence of dignity did not circumvent the presence of dignity the father beheld. The prodigal son's negligent behavior did not evaporate the father's love. The father was willing to look beyond his son's sin and embrace his son's value. The father was willing to retrieve the diamond in the rough.

The prodigal son's reception was not based on his sin but on the father's endless source of love. Sound familiar? God doesn't give us what we deserve. Now that is mercy! God also gives us what we do not deserve. Now that is grace! His love shines through our failure and selfishness in order to bring the dignity of Christ into our lives. Our value is based on His unconditional love.

May 6
FAITHFUL FATHERING
Distinction

"'My son,' the father said, 'you are always with me, and everything I have is yours. But we had to celebrate and be glad, because this brother of yours was dead and is alive again; he was lost and is found.'" Luke 15:31-32 (NIV)

If you have ever lost anything that you valued, then you know what it feels like to celebrate when the recovery is made. Can you imagine someone you treasure being displaced? Do you sense the anticipation of their return? How would you respond?

The prodigal son was fortunate to have a father waiting, watching, and anticipating his return. However, the older brother was not in a celebrative frame of mind. He was bitter and resentful. The older brother could not understand why his father would throw such a massive party for his young wayward brother. It just did not make sense.

The father made a distinction between the two brothers. Did you see it in the passage? The father affirmed the older son's distinction by acknowledging that their special connection was not hindered by the younger son's rebellion. On the other hand, the father made a clear distinction by identifying that the younger son was dead and is alive again; he was lost and is found. The prodigal son was in desperate need of the father's mercy, grace, and love.

Have you been there? Spend some time thinking about how God has fathered you through difficult times. Aren't you grateful that He doesn't give you what you deserve?

DEMONSTRATING COMPASSION

Compassion

"The LORD is gracious and righteous; our God is full of compassion."
Psalm 116:5 (NIV)

God's resources are unlimited. Try to measure the depth of God's love. Seek to weigh the hand that keeps the planets in orbit. Ponder the expanse of God's consistent flow of gracious compassion.

The prodigal son's father exhibited God's nature and character as he embraced his repentant son. The father's compassion demonstrated that he valued his son's return more than he judged his son's rebellion. What does righteousness in action look like? Well, it looks like a father showing compassion to a wayward son.

David painted a portrait of the nature and character of God as that of being full of compassion. Aren't you eternally grateful that our Living God is the God of Compassion? His compassion is His righteousness in action.

What does compassion look like in your life? When have you experienced the compassion of God? Imagine your life without God's righteousness in action. What if God withdrew His compassion from your life today?

Pray with me: "Father, thank You for being a God of communication. We praise You for making Your compassion known to us even while we were living in rebellion and disobedience. We marvel at Your patience with us. Enable us to live in light of Your compassion today. Empower us to extend Your compassion to others in the measure that You have extended Your compassion to us. May others see Jesus in us through every interaction and interruption that You allow. In Jesus' Name, Amen."

May 8
PERSONALIZING PRAYER
Personalization, Transgression

"Have mercy on me, O God, according to your unfailing love; according to your great compassion blot out my transgressions." Psalm 51:1 (NIV)

David came to the point of desperation after committing the sins of adultery and murder. God used the prophet Nathan to confront David. Nathan used a parable to personalize David's sin and then injected the piercing accusatory statement, "You are the man!" (2 Samuel 12:7 NIV).

Have you heard these lyrics before? "It's me! It's me O Lord, standing in the need of prayer!" Both David and the prodigal son would have embraced this song. It is common throughout our earthly existence to go through seasons of personalization. In fact, if you want to become Christ-like and reach your God-given potential, then you must be willing to acknowledge your sin personally.

Personalization is looking into the mirror and confronting the reality of your own sin before you start judging others. The next step is to personalize God's mercy, unfailing love, and compassion.

Now let's get personal. What specific area of your life is in desperate need of God's touch? Identify the sin that entangles you and trace Satan's strategy. How does the enemy attack you? When are you most susceptible to sin? Where are you when you are most vulnerable to the enemy's flaming arrows? Is it when you travel? Is it when you are home alone? Is it when you are at work?

Personalize Psalm 51:1 and pray it to God right now. Go ahead and pray this Scripture, and see how God reveals His mercy, unfailing love, and compassion.

FACING LIFE'S TRANSITIONS
Transition

"God is our refuge and strength, an ever-present help in trouble. Therefore we will not fear, though the earth give way and the mountains fall into the heart of the sea, though its waters roar and foam and the mountains quake with their surging." Psalm 46:1-3 (NIV)

Are you currently facing any of life's transitions? Maybe you are preparing for graduation and anticipating the future. Perhaps you are considering retirement and wonder if this is the right time. As a primary caregiver, you may be seeking God concerning transitioning a loved one into an assisted living center. It could be that you have purchased a new home and are trying to get settled and find order amidst the chaos. Regardless of your particular season of transition, God is more than sufficient to see you through.

For the elder brother, his transition was related to the reentry of his younger brother we know as the prodigal son. Can you relate? Has anyone re-entered your life recently? That's a transition that you must face. How will you make room in your life for the person? How will their presence affect you and your schedule?

The elder brother did not transition well. He was embittered by his father's gracious response. He was resentful of the forgiveness his younger brother received. He will have to choose how he will navigate this transition.

God is our refuge! God is our strength! We can go to Him. In fact, our first response to life's transitions should be to go to Him. He already knows what we are facing and what challenges we will face. Remember, He is all knowing!

Rest in Him. Give Him your worry. Give Him your confusion. Wait for God to show you the next step. Simply obey what you already know!

May 10
USING MEMORY FOR GOD'S GLORY
Memory

"For I know my transgressions, and my sin is always before me."
Psalm 51:3 (NIV)

How's your memory? Can you remember your favorite vacation from your childhood? Can you remember learning how to swim or braving the high diving board for the first time? Do you remember the day you got your driver's license? There's power in memory.

Memory can paralyze us with fear or mobilize us to persevere. Memory can blockade us like a brick wall or project us forward like a smooth water slide. It depends on how you utilize your memory.

Satan uses memory to ridicule and demean us. He uses our memory to stifle our growth and to discredit our progress. Satan will bring to our minds the darkness of our past in order to cripple us.

Yet, where Satan seeks to bring death and destruction, God can bring life and victory! God uses memory to remind us where we would be without His abundant grace and abiding peace. God allows us to remember our sin so that we will know where He brought us from.

David acknowledged his sin. David affirmed the reality of sin always being before him in his memory. The question is not: Why do I remember my sin? The question is: What will I do in response to my ability to remember my sin?

God wants us to remember that He rescued us from our sin so that we can live the abundant life. So, when Satan reminds you of your past, just remind him of God's provision of cleansing through the shed blood of His Son and our Savior, the Lord Jesus! Yes! Now that's using memory in victory!

PURSUING PURITY
Participation

"Create in me a pure heart, O God, and renew a steadfast spirit within me."
Psalm 51:10 (NIV)

God places the righteousness of Christ in us at salvation. His impartation of purity makes us fit for the Kingdom of God. Our response should be that of participation in the perpetual process of purity. We work out what God has worked in!

We are to take the initiative to purify our hearts. The constant pursuit of purity should be evidenced in our lives. We are living out the imputed righteousness of Christ. We take on the nature of Christ to live in obedience to God.

- *"But the father said to his servants, 'Quick! Bring the best robe and put it on him. Put a ring on his finger and sandals on his feet. Bring the fattened calf and kill it. Let's have a feast and celebrate.'"*
  Luke 15:22-23 (NIV)

Why would the father demand that the servants put a ring on the prodigal son's finger? The ring symbolizes relationship and partnership. The broken and confessional son received affirmation of his sonship. The father signified the partnership through a ring.

Are you connected to Jesus? Is your life hidden in Christ? Can you say that Christ is your life? Who will you partner with today in order to pursue a life of purity?

May 12
DIFFUSING BITTERNESS
Resentment

"But he answered his father, 'Look! All these years I've been slaving for you and never disobeyed your orders. Yet you never gave me even a young goat so I could celebrate with my friends. But when this son of yours who has squandered your property with prostitutes comes home, you kill the fattened calf for him!'"
Luke 15:29-30 (NIV)

Resentment is like acid in a relationship. It causes strife, discord, and animosity. Resentment has the capacity to keep you from experiencing meaningful relationships. The fruit of resentment is a heart full of bitterness.

The prodigal son received a loving reception from his gracious father, yet his older brother did not exemplify the same kind of response. Instead, he exhibited a major case of resentment. The older brother was unwilling to see his brother through the eyes of his loving father. He was quick to judge and condemn. There was no room for an expression of mercy, only a toxic display of bitterness and resentment.

Are there any relationships in your life that have caused you to grow bitter? Can you name a few individuals who have affected your life in a demeaning way? Where do you go from here?

Spend some time praying for people you have grown bitter towards. Acknowledge your struggle in prayer, and ask God to release you from the bondage of bitterness and the rope of resentment. Surrender your hurt and disappointment to God, and seek to reflect the father's heart and not the older brother's resentment.

LEAVING A LEGACY

Influence

"I have been reminded of your sincere faith, which first lived in your grandmother Lois and in your mother Eunice and, I am persuaded, now lives in you also."
2 Tim 1:5 (NIV)

My dad became a severe alcoholic which led to my parents' divorce when I was seven years old. As a result, I grew up in a single parent family. My mother sought to fulfill both roles of being a father and a mother to me and my older brother.

The one constant in our upbringing was church. My mother played the piano, and my Mamaw played the organ. Every Sunday morning and evening and Wednesday night, we would be at church. During those years of growing up without a dad, God raised up some godly men in our church who took us fishing, hunting, and camping.

The Apostle Paul is writing a very personal note to his son in the ministry, Timothy. He recalls Timothy's sincere faith which first became evident in the lives of Timothy's mother and grandmother. They effectively handed down their faith to their son and grandson, Timothy.

I can relate. My mother and Mamaw have consistently lived out their faith. God used their influence to bring me to the point of recognizing my need for Jesus to become my personal Lord and Savior. On March 28, 1979, I turned my life over to Christ and He saved me. Ever since that moment, I have had the wonderful privilege of knowing the Friend who sticks closer than a brother and the Father who will never let me down.

Who has God used to influence you to develop an abiding relationship with Jesus? Spend some time in prayer thanking God for the godly influences He has brought into your life.

May 14
NAVIGATING CONSEQUENCES
Decisions

"...and Jesse the father of King David. David was the father of Solomon, whose mother had been Uriah's wife," Matt 1:6 (NIV)

In the first chapter of the Gospel according to Matthew, four women are named in the genealogy of Christ: Tamar, Rahab, Ruth, and Mary. Uniquely, there is a fifth woman listed in the genealogy of Christ, but she is unnamed. She is simply identified as Uriah's wife. We know her name because we were introduced to her by name in II Samuel chapter eleven.

> • *"One evening David got up from his bed and walked around on the roof of the palace. From the roof he saw a woman bathing. The woman was very beautiful, and David sent someone to find out about her. The man said, 'Isn't this Bathsheba, the daughter of Eliam and the wife of Uriah the Hittite?'" 2 Sam 11:2-3 (NIV).*

Bathsheba's name means "daughter of abundance." She is blessed with a wonderful name, yet her name is not mentioned in chapter one of Matthew. We will find that she is abundantly blessed with God's grace.

She is a warrior's wife, and her husband has gone off to war. One evening while she is bathing, King David notices her and wants to know more about her. He asks about her and then discovers that she is Uriah's wife. He proceeds to have her brought to his palace and then ends up taking the relationship too far, and she gets pregnant.

Has life ever taken you to a place you never thought you would face? Take a few moments to reflect over your life, and try to recall some of those experiences that caught you by surprise. We have all been there. The question is: What will God teach us about ourselves and about Himself during those times?

BROKEN VESSELS
Formation

"This is the word that came to Jeremiah from the LORD: 'Go down to the potter's house, and there I will give you my message.' So I went down to the potter's house, and I saw him working at the wheel. But the pot he was shaping from the clay was marred in his hands; so the potter formed it into another pot, shaping it as seemed best to him." Jer 18:1-4 (NIV)

God specializes in using broken vessels. Jeremiah noticed the potter shaping the pot as seemed best to him. Our life will be useful to God if we continually remember that God is the potter and we are the clay.

Maybe you have been on the Potter's wheel in your life and you have experienced a season of suffering. God can use suffering to mold us and shape us. I remember a few years ago, I was going through a difficult season of personal suffering, and I decided to call one of my mentors. I remember asking him if maybe God was preparing me for my next assignment. He immediately responded by saying that, "God is always preparing you for your next assignment, but your next assignment may be right where you are!"

Suffering is part of living on a broken planet. We live in a fallen world, yet God has the capacity of utilizing that suffering for our spiritual formation. Don't expend your energy trying to detect the source of your suffering. Instead, ask God to show you what He wants to accomplish through your life in the midst of the suffering.

Are you willing to allow God to place you on the Potter's wheel to mold you and shape you into the image of Christ? Are you willing to allow God to develop your spiritual formation so that you can reach your full redemptive potential?

May 16

REDEEMING THE PAIN

Flawed

"But the pot he was shaping from the clay was marred in his hands..." Jer 18:4 (NIV)

Whenever you purchase an item that has an "as is" tag on it, you accept the fact that it may be flawed. In other words, the item may not be perfect.

The beauty of salvation is that God accepted us "as is" and brought us into a vibrant love relationship with Himself to move us from "as is" to "what could be" in His hands. Yes! We were marred in His hands, but He lovingly and patiently removes the imperfections of our attitude, behavior, and speech.

Being on the Potter's wheel can be painful at times. As God allows us to go through suffering and sorrow in this life, the areas of our life that do not reflect Christ-likeness will be dealt with. God will grow us through the pain. He will mold us and shape us through adversity.

Bathsheba endured some difficult seasons in her life. She experienced loneliness, grief, delays, disappointment, and shattered dreams. Yet, God redeemed all of those seasons in her life to bring her into a deeper relationship with Himself. She would have never become a Proverbs 31 woman without the adversity that God allowed her to face. She was marred in His hands. As a result of the loving touch of the Potter's hands, she became a masterpiece!

Are you on the Potter's wheel? Be patient. Allow God to mold you. He took you "as is", and He is shaping you for eternal significance.

WALKING IN GOD'S FAVOR

Favor

"And we know that in all things God works for the good of those who love him, who have been called according to his purpose." Romans 8:28 (NIV)

While you were sleeping, God was working. He does not sleep. God is always at work. His work is continuous and consistent. Whatever you are facing today, God is working. Whatever you are dreading today, God is working. Whatever you are fearing today, God is working.

In all things, God works! He takes the initiative. Regardless of how confusing your current circumstance may seem to you, God is at work. He takes the initiative to work for your good and His glory. In all things, God works for the good of those who love Him.

Do you love Him? Have you been called according to His purpose? Then you can walk in assurance today knowing that in all the things you face, in all the things you are wrestling with, in all the things that seem impossible, God works for your good. He will do what is best for you. He formed you and fashioned you, and He will orchestrate all of the circumstances that surround you in order to work for your good.

Now that is the favor of God! You are favored by God. You are His treasure. Trust Him.

May 18
CONFORMING TO CHRIST
Conformity

"For those God foreknew he also predestined to be conformed to the likeness of his Son, that he might be the firstborn among many brothers." Romans 8:29 (NIV)

How did Bathsheba make it into the genealogy of Christ in Matthew 1:6? How did you make it into the family tree of Christ? Bathsheba and you are products of the grace of God. The only way in is through the doorway of God's grace (Eph. 2:8-9).

You are in the Royal Family through the grace of God as evidenced in your faith in the completed work of Jesus on the cross. Now that you have been adopted into His family, God wants you to become like Christ.

The process of sanctification follows salvation. Once you are saved, God places you on a path to be conformed to the likeness of Christ. You have the wonderful privilege of participating with God in the process of conformity. God seeks to remove anything in us that doesn't look like Jesus.

Sometimes God will use the chisel of adversity, and sometimes God will use the hammer of silence. God will allow us to go through seasons of uncertainty to conform us into the likeness of Christ.

Reflect for a few moments on the level of Christ-likeness that has been attained in your journey thus far. What behavior and attitudes do you exhibit currently that just don't line up with Christ-likeness? Will you participate with God in the process of conformity?

GOD TOOK THE INITIATIVE
Abundance

"He who did not spare his own Son, but gave him up for us all--how will he not also, along with him, graciously give us all things?" Romans 8:32 (NIV)

The gas light just came on. You keep driving as you wonder how far you can go before you run out. The farther you drive, the more adrenaline pumps into your bloodstream. As you visualize the possibility of stepping out of your car to push it one full block to the gas pump, you decide it might be time to stop risking the inevitable and just take the time to fill up.

God's gas light never comes on. His tank never empties. He never runs on fumes. God is the God of abundance! His resources are unlimited! The beauty of His love is seen by His willingness to give us His very best, His own Son. God gave up His Son, Jesus, for us all. What an incredible portrait of His grace.

God did not wait until you had it all together. God did not wait until you cleaned your life up and eliminated the rough edges. God demonstrated His own love for us before we made a move toward Him (Rom. 5:8). God went first! God initiated the love relationship that we enjoy! How do we know that? While we were still bankrupt in our sinful condition, Christ died for us!

Notice what we truly deserve...death! Notice what we get instead...eternal life! How can that be? God, who graciously gives us all things, gives us the gift of eternal life. It cost Him everything, yet it is free to us.

Have you received the gift of eternal life? Are you in Christ? Your union with Christ will determine your eternal destiny.

May 20
WEARING THE JESUS JERSEY
Advantage

"What, then, shall we say in response to this? If God is for us, who can be against us?" Romans 8:31 (NIV)

Your jersey will determine your opposition. What team are you playing for? If you have turned your life over to Jesus Christ then you are wearing the Jesus jersey. You have been adopted into God's family, your name has been written in the Lamb's Book of Life, and you have been indwelt by the Holy Spirit. Your agenda is no longer about you and your plans. Your agenda is now the Head Coach's agenda. Now you live your life according to His game plan. Now your passion is to please the One who's Name you bear.

Remember, in all things God works for the good of those who love Him and are called according to His purpose. He is for you. He designed you. He determined who your parents would be and where you would be born.

If God is for you, who can be against you? This verse does not mean that you will not face opposition in this life. If you wear the Jesus jersey, you will face intense opposition. God's promise is that your opposition is not your opposition. The opposition you face in this life is God's opposition.

Satan knew he could not defeat God, so he decided to attack that which is closest to God's heart, you! So the opposition you are facing is really not about you, but about Satan trying to hurt God by attacking God's children.

The wonderful victorious news is that God is for you! If God is for you, then Satan doesn't have a chance!

EXPERIENCING HARMONY WITH GOD

Peace

"Grace and peace to you from God our Father and the Lord Jesus Christ."
Eph 1:2 (NIV)

Paul begins his letter to the church at Ephesus by identifying man's two greatest needs: grace and peace. The peace that Paul speaks of is not connected to circumstances and is not a reflection of your level of happiness. Peace comes from God and by His grace.

Remember that grace is God's riches at Christ's expense. We come to know God's grace by placing our faith in the completed work of Jesus on the cross.

- *"Therefore, since we have been justified through faith, we have peace with God through our Lord Jesus Christ, through whom we have gained access by faith into this grace in which we now stand."*
  Romans 5:1-2 (NIV)

I am justified. It is just-if-I'd never sinned. God sees me through the shed blood of Jesus. Now I have peace with God because I am a recipient of His grace.

- *"You will go out in joy and be led forth in peace; the mountains and hills will burst into song before you, and all the trees of the field will clap their hands." Isaiah 55:12 (NIV)*

Be still for a few moments and just reflect on the presence of God's peace in your life right now. Are you at peace with God? Are you experiencing harmony with God? Confess any sin that the Holy Spirit reveals. Rest in God's provision. Remember, only God can give you peace. Receive His peace and walk in the peace that God provides.

May 22
THE SACRED UNION

Union

"To them God has chosen to make known among the Gentiles the glorious riches of this mystery, which is Christ in you, the hope of glory." Col 1:27 (NIV)

When you say, "I do" to Jesus, there is a union formed that cannot be broken. You become one with Christ. You are united with Him.

Once you are "in Christ" there are eternal benefits and immediate realities. Notice how Paul uses the union reality in the first chapter of Ephesians through being "in Christ."

"...the faithful in Christ Jesus (1:1), ...blessing in Christ (1:3), ...he chose us in Christ (1:4), ...given us in the One he loves (1:6), ...in him we have redemption (1:7), ...which he purposed in Christ (1:9), ...in him we were also chosen (1:11), ...you also were included in Christ (1:12), ...marked in him with a seal (1:13)."

Let me ask you a question that has eternal consequences: Are you in Christ? Think about your life, and travel back in your mind to the place where you recognized your lostness and became aware of your need for union with Jesus. Do you remember the eternal transaction? Can you recall the moment you became a Christ follower and gave evidence of your union with Him?

What about now? Is it obvious to others that you are in Christ?

BEING BORN FROM ABOVE

Regeneration

"Now there was a man of the Pharisees named Nicodemus, a member of the Jewish ruling council. He came to Jesus at night and said, 'Rabbi, we know you are a teacher who has come from God. For no one could perform the miraculous signs you are doing if God were not with him.'" "In reply Jesus declared, 'I tell you the truth, no one can see the kingdom of God unless he is born again.'"
John 3:1-3 (NIV)

Jesus encountered Nic at night. Nicodemus was a very religious man but did not have a relationship with Jesus. He was an outstanding law abiding citizen, as far as society was concerned, but missed the mark of God's perfection. He recognized Jesus as a unique teacher but failed to recognize Jesus as the Messiah.

The encounter shifted as Jesus announced that a person must be born again to see the kingdom of God. Nicodemus thought Jesus meant that a person must be born again physically. However, Jesus was speaking of a spiritual rebirth.

To be born again means to be born from above. It means to be born into. At conversion, you are born from above which means God regenerates, redeems, and reconciles you. When you place your faith in Jesus alone for salvation, you are born into His family.

When you are born again, your new identity is that of being "in Christ." Once you are "in Christ" you become the recipient of God's treasures as affirmed in Ephesians chapter one.

Read Paul's letter to the church at Ephesus, and underline or highlight the phrase "in Christ" each time you see it. Then, close your eyes, smile, and express your gratitude to God for your new identity.

May 24
Unleashing God's Promises
God's Promises, If/Then

"When Solomon had finished the temple of the LORD and the royal palace, and had succeeded in carrying out all he had in mind to do in the temple of the LORD and in his own palace, the LORD appeared to him at night and said: 'I have heard your prayer and have chosen this place for myself as a temple for sacrifices. When I shut up the heavens so that there is no rain, or command locusts to devour the land or send a plague among my people, if my people, who are called by my name, will humble themselves and pray and seek my face and turn from their wicked ways, then will I hear from heaven and will forgive their sin and will heal their land. Now my eyes will be open and my ears attentive to the prayers offered in this place.'" 2 Chron 7:11-15 (NIV)

God's love is unconditional. Some of God's promises are conditional. For example, see if you can locate God's conditional promise to Solomon.

Did you find it? God's conditional promise to Solomon had an if/then element. If my people will...then I will. Yes! We want God to hear from heaven, and we want God to forgive our sin, and we want God to heal our land. Yet, God's promise is conditioned by our willingness to humble ourselves, pray, seek His face and turn from our wicked ways.

In the first chapter of Ephesians, Paul gives us an if/then promise without using the words if and then. He unveils the realities of being "in Christ."

Now that you have underlined or highlighted Paul's use of "in Christ" in the book of Ephesians, see if you can detect the benefits or realities of being "in Christ." For example, if I am in Christ, then I am...! Write down each reality, and spend some time reflecting on one reality at a time. Over the next few days, we will explore each reality together.

BEING SET APART BY GOD

Identity, Saint

"Paul, an apostle of Christ Jesus by the will of God, To the saints in Ephesus, the faithful in Christ Jesus:" Eph 1:1 (NIV)

In her book, *Breaking Free*, Beth Moore reminds us of our position in Christ in the following affirmations:

> God is who He says He is.
> God can do what He says He can do.
> I am who God says I am.
> I can do all things through Christ.
> God's Word is alive and active in me.

Seek to memorize these five statements, and speak them aloud each morning to start your day off in the right frame of mind. It will affect your outlook and attitude in a life giving way.

Focus with me on the third affirmation: I am who God says I am. Repeat that phrase to yourself and allow it to sink in. Let's see how we can connect this truth with Paul's "in Christ" realities.

If you are in Christ, then you can affirm this reality:

Reality #1: I am a saint.

If you are in Christ, then God says that you are a saint. A saint is one who has been set apart by God. Your faith in the atoning work of Christ on the cross transfers your identity to that of a saint. It doesn't mean that you are perfect and immune to the presence of sin. It means that God positions you as a saint. You have a new standing before God and with God.

May 26
BLESSED WITH EVERY SPIRITUAL BLESSING
Blessed

"Praise be to the God and Father of our Lord Jesus Christ, who has blessed us in the heavenly realms with every spiritual blessing in Christ." Eph 1:3 (NIV)

You are God's treasure. Can you imagine the Creator of the universe being the reason for your existence? You are not an accident. God purposed for you to be born. You were planned by God.

Another reality of being in Christ is that you are blessed. If you are in Christ, then you can say, "I am blessed." Go ahead and say it aloud!

God has blessed you in the heavenly realms with every spiritual blessing in Christ. God's resources are unlimited. He never runs out! He never runs dry! His shelves are never empty! Our God of abundance has blessed you with every spiritual blessing in Christ.

When someone asks you today, "How are you doing?"...don't say, "Oh, I'm doing alright." Instead, say with conviction and confidence and assurance, "I am blessed!"

Doesn't that make you want to shout? Don't ever forget who you are and Whose you are! You are a child of the King! You are blessed and highly favored by the Lord. Walk in the new identity you have in Christ.

BEING RIGHTLY RELATED TO GOD
Relationship, Staying Vertical

"The most important one,' answered Jesus, 'is this: "Hear, O Israel, the Lord our God, the Lord is one. Love the Lord your God with all your heart and with all your soul and with all your mind and with all your strength." The second is this: "Love your neighbor as yourself." There is no commandment greater than these."' Mark 12:28-31 (NIV)

What really matters in this life? It depends on your point of reference. If you are living for what can be seen, then the answer may be very complex. However, if you are living for that which is unseen, then the answer is very simple.

Love God and love others. Jesus modeled this kind of focus in His earthly ministry. He stayed connected to the Father through daily intimacy. He guarded His priorities. He protected His love relationship with the Father. Jesus allocated His time to reflect His core values.

Are you loving God with all of your heart? Are you loving God with all of your soul, mind, and strength? This represents your vertical relationship. Your vertical relationship is your number one priority. Your effectiveness in the Kingdom of God will never rise above the level of your intimacy with God.

Think about the cross for a moment. Notice the vertical beam. This represents your relationship to God. Are you rightly related to God through faith in Jesus Christ? Are you daily nurturing your love relationship with Him?

Stay vertical!

May 28
EMPLOYING YOUR UNIQUENESS

God's Creation, Unique

"But you are a chosen people, a royal priesthood, a holy nation, a people belonging to God, that you may declare the praises of him who called you out of darkness into his wonderful light." 1 Peter 2:9 (NIV)

What do fingerprints, DNA, and snowflakes have in common? Each has been uniquely designed by God and there are no two alike. Out of 6.4 billion people alive on planet earth today, there is no one exactly like you. Even if you are an identical twin, there are unique differences between you and your look alike.

God made you uniquely to fulfill His purpose and to bring Him glory on the earth. As a child of the King, you have been identified as chosen. You were selected by God to be part of His family. You were chosen to be part of His royal priesthood, His holy nation, and His possession.

How does your uniqueness benefit God? You were uniquely chosen by God to declare His praises. You have a song to sing! He called you out of darkness. Do you remember where you were when God came to your rescue? He brought you into His wonderful light. From darkness into the light is the theme of our praise.

You are uniquely designed by God and for God. You are His. Are you willing to allow Him to shine through your uniqueness to impact the nations for His glory? Are you willing to uniquely know Him and uniquely show Him to your family, your friends, and your future relationships?

CHOSEN BY GOD

Chosen

"I have chosen the way of truth; I have set my heart on your laws." Psalm 119:30 *(NIV)*

Have you ever wondered what makes people do good things? Why would someone choose the way of truth? Why would someone set their heart on God's laws? Perhaps one's behavior is related to one's position in Christ.

We have been exploring the "in Christ" realities found in Paul's letter to the church at Ephesus.

> Reality number one: I am a saint!
> Reality number two: I am blessed!
> Reality number three: I am chosen!

- *"For he chose us in him before the creation of the world to be holy and blameless in his sight." Eph 1:4 (NIV)*

Did you choose God or did God choose you? That's right...you were chosen by God long before you were even born. The song says, "While He (Jesus) was on the cross, I was on His mind." Even before Jesus came to earth to live a sinless life, die a substitutionary death, and defeat sin and death, you were chosen by God. Before God splattered the stars in the universe, you were chosen. Before God spoke light into existence, you were chosen. Before God separated the day from the night, you were chosen.

Why were you chosen? You were chosen by God to be holy and blameless in His sight. Can you pull that off by yourself? No! Does God expect you to pull that off by yourself? No! Jesus came so that you could live the life of choseness.

May 30
ADOPTED INTO GOD'S FAMILY
God's Family, Adopted

"Yet to all who received him, to those who believed in his name, he gave the right to become children of God." John 1:12 (NIV)

Solidify the "in Christ" realities...

> Reality number one: I am a saint.
> Reality number two: I am blessed.
> Reality number three: I am chosen.
> Reality number four: I am adopted.

If you are in Christ, then you are adopted. God gave the right for you to become a child of God. In love, God predestined you to be adopted as his child through Jesus Christ.

> • *"For he chose us in him before the creation of the world to be holy and blameless in his sight. In love he predestined us to be adopted as his sons through Jesus Christ, in accordance with his pleasure and will--to the praise of his glorious grace, which he has freely given us in the One he loves." Eph 1:4-6 (NIV)*

God's grace is the gateway to our adoption into His family. Your adoption is formalized at conversion. God takes the initiative to draw you by convicting you of sin and convincing you of His righteousness. He gives you the freedom to choose Him or refuse Him. His salvation is available to all but only effective for those who place their trust in the completed work of Jesus on the cross.

Adoption is not an option. Adoption is a reality for those who are in Christ. Spend some time thanking God for His willingness to adopt you into His family.

LAVISHED BY GOD'S LOVE

Love, Position

"How great is the love the Father has lavished on us, that we should be called children of God! And that is what we are! The reason the world does not know us is that it did not know him. Dear friends, now we are children of God, and what we will be has not yet been made known. But we know that when he appears, we shall be like him, for we shall see him as he is." 1 John 3:1-2 (NIV)

Try to measure God's love. There isn't a scale large enough to calculate His love. You become a child after your physical birth. However, you do not become a child of God until you respond to His offer of salvation.

At salvation, you are not made righteous, you are declared righteous by God. He lavishes you with His love, and you become a child of God. Your new position in Christ enables you to enjoy peace with God and assurance of eternal life.

Rejoice that you are a child of God, and recognize that the best is yet to come. What you will be has not yet been made known. One day, you will be like Jesus and see Him as He is.

There's more to come! Enjoy each day walking with Jesus. Focus on knowing Him intimately and making Him known globally. Your position in Christ changes everything, including the here and now, as well as the hereafter.

June 1
THE REALITY OF REJECTION
Rejection

"He then began to teach them that the Son of Man must suffer many things and be rejected by the elders, chief priests and teachers of the law, and that he must be killed and after three days rise again." Mark 8:31 (NIV)

Rejection hurts. Have you been there? When you don't feel that you measure up to a standard that has been established or an expectation that has been articulated, rejection seeps in. You begin to experience pain, discontentment, and insecurity. During those times when you are misunderstood, rejection begins to shadow your vision and stifle your optimism.

Jesus lived in the midst of steep legalism in His day. The elders, chief priests, and teachers of the law sought to shackle others by their self-imposed rules and regulations. They promoted religion by works, which embodied excessive "do's and don'ts", that totally bypassed intimacy with our Heavenly Father.

The suffering of Jesus included rejection. He was not accepted by those who claimed to be religious. Rejection was perpetual during His three and a half year public ministry. His being rejected ultimately led to His being crucified.

What kind of rejection are you currently facing? How long has the rejection lingered? There is good news on the way that will give you a whole new perspective on how to respond to rejection. Spend some time sharing your hurt with Jesus in prayer. Let Him hear you express your pain as you call out His Name.

ACCEPTING GOD'S ACCEPTANCE

Accepted

"...to the praise of his glorious grace, which he has freely given us in the One he loves." Eph 1:6 (NIV)

How do you respond to rejection? Do you allow it to inject you with insecurity or do you challenge the rejection? It's time to verbalize your "in Christ" realities:

> I am a saint.
> I am blessed.
> I am chosen.
> I am adopted.
> I am accepted.

Have you accepted God's acceptance of you? He took the initiative to demonstrate His acceptance of you by freely giving you His grace in Jesus. Do you measure up to His standard of righteousness? No! However, God declared you righteous when you accepted the atoning work of Jesus on the cross.

When rejection surfaces, combat lies with the truth of God's acceptance of you. Your peace in this life will be proportionate to your acceptance of God's acceptance of you. Your acceptance of God's acceptance of you will give you lasting peace and eternal security. Some people may reject you. Some people may misunderstand you. However, you can respond to rejection by living in light of your acceptance of God's acceptance of you. "But God demonstrates his own love for us in this: While we were still sinners, Christ died for us" (Romans 5:8 NIV).

Your acceptance has permanence!

June 3
ACCEPTING OTHERS
Accepting Others

"Accept one another, then, just as Christ accepted you, in order to bring praise to God." Romans 15:7 (NIV)

Hurting people hurt people. Have you been wounded by someone recently? What is your natural reaction? You probably want to wound them for wounding you. But is it possible to look at the person behind the behavior? Maybe they are deeply hurting personally. Maybe they are searching for something to anesthetize their pain.

You cannot control how they treat you. However, you can control how you respond to their treatment of you. When you react, it is you reacting. When you respond, it is the Holy Spirit living in you expressing His nature and character through you.

Jesus is the ultimate pattern for us to model our lives after. He exemplified how to respond to difficult people. Rather than retaliating, Jesus entrusted Himself to the Judge who is all-knowing and all-seeing.

God doesn't miss even a fragment of an interaction that you have with others. Entrust yourself to His care. He knows what you are dealing with. By the way, He created the person who has wounded you. In fact, God even gave them His best by allowing Jesus to die on the cross for them, also.

Accepting others will not come naturally. Accepting others, especially difficult people, comes supernaturally as you surrender your life completely to the Lordship of Christ. Allow Him to be Lord of your life and your interactions with people who may potentially hurt you. Jesus specializes in pain management.

SHARPENING ONE ANOTHER

Nurturing

"As iron sharpens iron, so one man sharpens another." Proverbs 27:17 NIV)

God wants you to grow spiritually. What does that look like? Spiritual growth looks like a believer who is becoming a fully devoted follower of Christ. It is a process by which you participate with God in His activity. God does not expect you to fly solo. Being a Christ follower is a commitment to walk in fellowship with God and other believers.

So how do you grow? You grow by feeding on God's Word. You grow by reading and applying the Bible. My mentoring group decided to read the book of Ephesians everyday as part of our spiritual devotion and development.

My pastor, Dr. David Fleming, preached expositionally (verse by verse) through the book of Ephesians. As I read through all six chapters of Ephesians each day, my walk with God was enriched. Meditate on this powerful verse from Ephesians:

"I keep asking that the God of our Lord Jesus Christ, the glorious Father, may give you the Spirit of wisdom and revelation, so that you may know him better." Eph 1:17 (NIV)

Commit to read Ephesians each day for several days as you nurture the life of Christ in you? Let's walk together through God's Word so that we may know Him better. Write down verses that God uses to speak into your life directly. You may want to memorize a few verses to recite from time to time. Allow God's Word to come alive in you.

Invite someone to go on this journey with you. As iron sharpens iron, you will sharpen each other. Your life will be enriched by the relationship and encouraged by the the consistent intake of God's Word.

June 5
REJOICING IN YOUR NEW IDENTITY
Redemption

"In him we have redemption through his blood, the forgiveness of sins, in accordance with the riches of God's grace that he lavished on us with all wisdom and understanding." Eph 1:7-8 (NIV)

Our position of being "in Christ" unlocks the treasure chest of His resources. It is imperative that you make certain that you are in Christ. Your union with Him will determine your "in Christ" realities.

> I am a saint.
> I am blessed.
> I am chosen.
> I am adopted.
> I am accepted.
> I am redeemed.

Redemption in the language of the New Testament carries the idea of purchasing (or redeeming) a slave in order to set him free. Jesus purchased you with His blood in order to set you free. He ransomed you through His death.

Do you realize how valuable you are in God's sight? Do you understand that Jesus paid your sin debt in full? You have been redeemed!

I am reminded of the song, "He paid a debt He did not owe. I owed a debt I could not pay. I needed someone to wash my sins away." Thank God for His redeeming love! Rejoice in your new identity that Christ purchased!

Choosing the Best Option

Options, Lordship

"Now fear the LORD and serve him with all faithfulness. Throw away the gods your forefathers worshiped beyond the River and in Egypt, and serve the LORD. But if serving the LORD seems undesirable to you, then choose for yourselves this day whom you will serve, whether the gods your forefathers served beyond the River, or the gods of the Amorites, in whose land you are living. But as for me and my household, we will serve the LORD." Josh 24:14-15 (NIV)

Before the foundation of the world, God chose you. However, God gives you options. You can choose Him or refuse Him. You can accept His offer of forgiveness through the shed blood of Jesus or reject His offer of forgiveness. You can receive the gift of eternal life by placing your faith in the completed work of Jesus on the cross, or you can deny the gift of eternal life.

You have options. That's the power of God's love. We are not robots. We are not plastic. We are real human beings with real feelings and real thoughts. We have the capacity to activate our will to choose a certain direction in life. There are many paths available to us, but they do not lead to life. There's only one path that leads to life.

Jesus is the only way (John 14:6). Are you willing to choose Him? Joshua did not vacillate. He resolved to serve God. He took ownership for leading his family spiritually. He included his family in the commitment to serve the Lord. He lived out what he expected of his family.

Yes, you have options. In fact, the enemy will place many attractive options before you. Don't give in. Choose to surrender fully to Jesus and serve him wholeheartedly.

June 7
ALIGNMENT THROUGH PRAYER

Alignment, Prayer

"Therefore, since we have a great high priest who has gone through the heavens, Jesus the Son of God, let us hold firmly to the faith we profess. For we do not have a high priest who is unable to sympathize with our weaknesses, but we have one who has been tempted in every way, just as we are yet was without sin. Let us then approach the throne of grace with confidence, so that we may receive mercy and find grace to help us in our time of need." Heb 4:14-16 (NIV)

Prayer is aligning your life with God's agenda. God has a plan for your life. He has a purpose for you to fulfill. How do you get connected to that purpose and plan? Through alignment!

Prayer is the avenue through which we connect with God. He has already broken down the barriers that separated us. God grants us access to Him through prayer based on the atonement of Christ. Because Jesus paid the penalty for our sin, we have the privilege of communing with God through prayer.

As a Christ follower, you have direct access to God through Jesus. Seize the opportunity to live in the presence of God. Don't miss the moment. God has granted you access. You can have unbroken communion with the Creator of the universe. The One who designed you, pursued you, and reconciled you invites you to walk intimately with Him. The language of your relationship is prayer.

What does your prayer life look like? Do you practice the presence of God? Do you rush your time alone with God? Align with God's agenda through an ongoing vibrant prayer life. Commune with God perpetually and persistently. Jesus, as the High Priest, has provided the way!

Receiving God's Forgiveness

Forgiveness, Redemption

"In him we have redemption through his blood, the forgiveness of sins, in accordance with the riches of God's grace that he lavished on us with all wisdom and understanding." Eph 1:7-8 (NIV)

Are you ready for the next "in Christ" reality? You can say it now: I am forgiven. If you are in Christ, then you are forgiven. Because of Christ's atonement, you have been declared righteous. Your sins have been forgiven. Notice the key in the above verse is, "through his blood."

"In fact, the law requires that nearly everything be cleansed with blood, and without the shedding of blood there is no forgiveness" (Heb 9:22 NIV).

Jesus shed His blood to pay the debt of your sin in full. Have you received God's forgiveness? Confess your sins and God will forgive you of your sins (1 Jn 1:9). Jesus atoned for your sin by dying on the cross as the perfect and sinless sacrifice. His payment for you sin was sufficient to provide for your cleansing.

Claim your "in Christ" realities today:

> I am a saint.
> I am blessed.
> I am chosen.
> I am adopted.
> I am accepted.
> I am redeemed.
> I am forgiven.

Now walk in the reality of being in Christ. You are forgiven.

June 9
FINDING YOUR SABBATH
Sabbath

"They brought to the Pharisees the man who had been blind. Now the day on which Jesus had made the mud and opened the man's eyes was a Sabbath. Therefore the Pharisees also asked him how he had received his sight. 'He put mud on my eyes,' the man replied, 'and I washed, and now I see.'"

"Some of the Pharisees said, 'This man is not from God, for he does not keep the Sabbath.'" John 9:13-16 (NIV)

Jesus placed the needs of others above the legalistic views of the Pharisees. He was willing to do something helpful and holy on the Sabbath. Yet, Jesus was criticized for His actions.

What are you willing to do on the Sabbath? What kind of Saturday will you experience? Sometimes the most spiritual activity you can embrace on a Saturday is to disconnect from the rush and routine of your everyday life. Maybe a day of rest could be the healing that Jesus desires to give you.

For you, it may mean turning your cell phone off. It may mean carving out time to simply not be available or accessible for anyone for a period of time.

Jesus embraced the discipline of getting away from the crowds and the tugs of life. He frequently went up on a mountainside to commune with our Heavenly Father. Yet, Jesus was willing to seize the opportunity to extend personal touch ministry. Because of His willingness to embrace a Sabbath rest, He had something to give those in need.

What does your day look like? Are you overextended or overcommitted? Have you said "yes" too often and not said "no" enough? May God give you Sabbath rest!

SECURING YOUR ETERNITY

Guarantee, Security of the Believer, Holy Spirit

"Now it is God who makes both us and you stand firm in Christ. He anointed us, set his seal of ownership on us, and put his Spirit in our hearts as a deposit, guaranteeing what is to come." 2 Cor 1:21-22 (NIV)

Perhaps you have heard the expression, "Life has no guarantees!" Well, that's just not true. If you are "in Christ", then you have a guarantee that no one can disrupt. God guarantees your safe and secure eternal destiny. How does God indicate the security of our future? "Now it is God who has made us for this very purpose and has given us the Spirit as a deposit, guaranteeing what is to come" (2 Cor 5:5 NIV).

God gives His Holy Spirit to us at conversion. The moment we confess Jesus as Lord and embrace the reality that God raised Him from the dead, we are saved and filled with His Holy Spirit. The Holy Spirit indwells us permanently. He does not move in and then move out. His indwelling Presence becomes our guarantee.

You are made fit by God for the Holy Spirit's habitation. At the moment of your conversion, the Holy Spirit comes to live inside of you. You become the walking Tabernacle of His Presence. The Holy Spirit guarantees what is to come. Your eternal security is enveloped by the indwelling Presence of the Holy Spirit.

Have you received God's deposit? Read Ephesians 1:13-14 and reflect on your current reality.

June 11
UNVEILING THE MYSTERY
Mystery, God's Will

"And he made known to us the mystery of his will according to his good pleasure, which he purposed in Christ, to be put into effect when the times will have reached their fulfillment--to bring all things in heaven and on earth together under one head, even Christ." Eph 1:9-10 (NIV)

The mystery Paul is speaking of is not mysterious. He is speaking about something once hidden now made known. God is a God of revelation. As Henry Blackaby says, "God reveals Himself, His purposes, and His ways." God wants you to know His will. God invites you into a relationship through which you come to learn how to walk with Him.

Read these two verses again and notice how many times God's activity is revealed.

> He made known...
> The mystery of His will...
> According to His good pleasure...
> Which He purposed...
> Under one Head...
> Even Christ.

Have you noticed the activity of God in your life? There's no mystery here! God is at work! It brings God pleasure to reveal His will to you. God is moved by the relational interaction between Himself and the one He pursues. You are that one! God pursues you with His everlasting love in order to bring you into harmony with His purpose and plans. You are treasured by God.

Spend some time tracing the activity of God in your life. You may want to write down some spiritual markers in your life that have identified God's activity in and through your circumstances.

WISDOM FOR GOD'S WORK

Wisdom, God's Will

"In him we have redemption through his blood, the forgiveness of sins, in accordance with the riches of God's grace that he lavished on us with all wisdom and understanding." Eph 1:7-8 (NIV)

God gives you wisdom to know and comprehend the redemption you have received. God's wisdom enables you to embrace your new identity in Christ. His wisdom gives you the ability to walk in His ways. Yet, without the Holy Spirit living in an individual, the things of God will not make sense. A person without the indwelling Holy Spirit will not be able to detect the activity of God (1 Cor. 2:14). It will not make sense to them.

Spiritual realities are detected by spiritual sight. The wisdom God grants enables us to see His realities. The things that come from the Spirit of God can only be discerned by spiritual vision. Your ability to see God's activity is proportionate to the wisdom God gives you. Illuminating the path God wants you to take, the Holy Spirit works in you to enable you to recognize and respond to God's will.

If you are lacking God's wisdom, then just ask Him for wisdom without doubting (James 1:5-6). When God lavised you with His grace at salvation, you also became the recipient of His enablement. God equips you to fulfill His agenda. You need God's wisdom to do God's work.

June 13
UNDERSTANDING AND DOING GOD'S WILL
Understanding, Application, Obedience

"Get wisdom, get understanding; do not forget my words or swerve from them."
Prov 4:5 (NIV)

We know more than we obey. Wisdom is to know and comprehend. Understanding is to apply what we know and comprehend. Application of God's Word indicates fullness in Christ.

Just as a treadmill will not benefit your health unless you get on it and use it, God's Word will not bring understanding until you apply it. Application leads to clarification, maturation, and transformation. Wisdom and understanding become evidence through application. Put God's Word and God's wisdom into practice.

Where do you start? You start by reading God's Word. Next, you meditate on God's Word. Then, you apply God's Word. Instead of leaning on your own understanding, trust in the Lord and acknowledge His ways (Prv. 3:5-6). Instead of swerving from God's Word, get His wisdom and His understanding (Prv. 4:5). Instead of coasting through life, diligently get understanding (Prv. 4:7).

Obey what you know! Apply what God has spoken into your life with understanding! Walk in the light God gives you! The adventure continues as you walk with God and entrust your life to His care. God has special plans for you that will bring you into a closer relationship with Him. You will need God's wisdom and understanding to participate with Him in His agenda.

June 14

GOD'S ORCHESTRATION

Orchestration, Sovereignty of God

"In him we were also chosen, having been predestined according to the plan of him who works out everything in conformity with the purpose of his will, in order that we, who were the first to hope in Christ, might be for the praise of his glory."
Eph 1:11-12 (NIV)

Has your life ever become complicated and messy? Have you traveled down a road you never thought you would navigate? Living in a fallen world tends to cause us to experience unexpected turns in life. Sometimes we make poor choices, and sometimes the decisions of others negatively affect us. It could be that a relationship has diverted into unhealthy patterns, or personal behaviors have drifted away from God's best.

The good news is that God is sovereign. He rules and He reigns. He always has the final say in any and every situation. Even when you make a disastrous move, God can orchestrate your path for your good and His glory. Notice how our Bible verse says that God works out everything in conformity with the purpose of His will. He is God! There is nothing that is impossible with Him. He can handle your situation. He can handle your relationships.

God orchestrates everything we encounter to bring about His will. Right now your current challenge may seem like an uphill climb dragging two dead elephants. God can take any difficult situation and orchestrate the details to conform to His plan.

Are you willing to surrender your hurts, your frustrations, your disappointments, and your fears to God? Release them and entrust them to God's sovereign care. He is the master conductor in the orchestra called life.

June 15
INCLUDED IN CHRIST
Included, Salvation

"And you also were included in Christ when you heard the word of truth, the gospel of your salvation. Having believed, you were marked in him with a seal, the promised Holy Spirit, who is a deposit guaranteeing our inheritance until the redemption of those who are God's possession--to the praise of his glory." Eph 1:13-14 (NIV)

Our in Christ realities continue to grow. Now you can say, "I am included." Let's take a look at the in Christ realities so far in our journey through Ephesians.

> I am a saint.
> I am blessed.
> I am chosen.
> I am adopted.
> I am accepted.
> I am redeemed.
> I am forgiven.
> I am blessed with wisdom and understanding.
> I am included.

Remember, it's not about your story that God plays a part in. It's about God's story that you play a part in. The wonderful news is that you are included! I am reminded of the lyrics from a powerful hymn by Johnson Oatman, Jr., "Jesus included me, Yes, He included me, When the Lord said, 'Whosoever,' He included me."

Do you realize how much God treasures you? Before you chose Him, He chose to include you in His redemptive plan. Let that concept settle in for a few moments. Now, how will this "in Christ" reality impact your attitude and behavior today? What will be different about your outlook on life?

SEALED BY THE HOLY SPIRIT

Sealed, Holy Spirit, Security

"And you also were included in Christ when you heard the word of truth, the gospel of your salvation. Having believed, you were marked in him with a seal, the promised Holy Spirit, who is a deposit guaranteeing our inheritance until the redemption of those who are God's possession--to the praise of his glory."
Eph 1:13-14 (NIV)

If you believe, you will recieve. At the moment of conversion, you receive the baptism of the Holy Spirit. It is an instantaneous experience, not a subsequent event. The indwelling presence of Christ, the Holy Spirit, comes to live inside of you. Having believed on the gospel of Jesus Christ, you were marked in Christ with the seal of the Holy Spirit.

The seal speaks of authenticity. The seal speaks of identification. You belong to God. You are His creation. You became His child and were adopted into His family when you placed your faith in Jesus alone for salvation. You were marked with a seal. That seal is the Person of the Holy Spirit.

Did you notice the Trinity in these two verses? God the Father, God the Son, and God the Holy Spirit are expressed in verses thirteen and fourteen. Look closely and you will see "Christ", and then "Holy Spirit", and then "God" which form the Trinity, which means three in one.

God created you. Jesus redeemed you. The Holy Spirit inhabits you. Your conversion is the real deal which has been sealed. Now it is time for you to claim your "in Christ" reality: I am sealed!

June 17
SEALED AND SECURE
Security of the Believer

"And you also were included in Christ when you heard the word of truth, the gospel of your salvation. Having believed, you were marked in him with a seal, the promised Holy Spirit, who is a deposit guaranteeing our inheritance until the redemption of those who are God's possession--to the praise of his glory."
Eph 1:13-14 (NIV)

If you are in Christ, then you are sealed. If you are in Christ, then you are filled. If you are in Christ, then you are secure. Your security in Christ is not dependent on you. Your security is dependent on God who has sealed your security by filling you with His Holy Spirit.

Celebrate your security in Christ. Express your gratitude to God for your secure position in Christ. He gave you what you did not deserve. He placed you in the firm reality of being a child of the King. You are royalty. You are God's possession. God made it possible for you to be sealed and secure.

How will your position in Christ affect your relationships? How will your security in Christ impact your decisions and level of courage? What fears have been alleviated by God's seal of security in your life?

FATHERHOOD OF GOD

Fatherhood of God

"For you did not receive a spirit that makes you a slave again to fear, but you received the Spirit of sonship. And by him we cry, 'Abba, Father.' The Spirit himself testifies with our spirit that we are God's children." Romans 8:15-16 (NIV)

How does Father's Day impact you personally? Is it a day of warmth and wonderful memories, or is it a day of hurtful reminders of neglect? Your earthly father may be all that you have dreamed he would be, or he may be lacking in your concept of what an earthly dad should be.

My dad became an alcoholic when I was a child. Before my seventh birthday, my parents divorced. The devastation of divorce caused me to search for a father who would never let me down. On March 28, 1979, I found that Father when I turned my life over to Jesus Christ. He gave me a new identity, a new righteousness, and a new reason to live. Through my relationship with Jesus, I have come to know what unconditional love looks like and feels like. "Because you are sons, God sent the Spirit of his Son into our hearts, the Spirit who calls out, 'Abba, Father'" (Gal 4:6 NIV).

Are you embracing the Fatherhood of God? He is the ultimate Father! He will never leave you. He will never let you down. He will keep you in His care both in this life and the life to come. He will place your feet on higher ground. God will show you a love that is unmatched and unlimited.

June 19
TRUSTING GOD
On Mission, Trust

"The LORD had said to Abram, 'Leave your country, your people and your father's household and go to the land I will show you. I will make you into a great nation and I will bless you; I will make your name great, and you will be a blessing. I will bless those who bless you, and whoever curses you I will curse; and all peoples on earth will be blessed through you.'" Gen 12:1-3 (NIV)

Has God ever asked you to do something that was uncomfortable? Have you ever sensed that God wanted you to make a decision that would alter your current reality?

Abram was confronted with a word from God that would drastically change his path. God's instructions were not specific. In fact, God just told Abram to leave and go to a land He would show him. Abram was not on a mission, but on mission with God.

Being on mission with God is relational. If you want to obey God and trust Him to reveal His plan for your life, then you must be willing to walk with Him and get to know His voice. God does not need you to be on a mission. God wants you to make a choice to be on mission with Him. He is in charge. He has an agenda for you to fulfill.

Abram had to trust God to show Him the way. As Abram obeyed, God would reveal his next step. Does that connect with you? Are you coming to the place where you realize that God wants you to simply choose to be on mission with Him and trust Him with the details? As you obey, God will reveal the way.

TAKING THE NEXT STEP
Obedience, Faith

"So Abram left, as the LORD had told him; and Lot went with him. Abram was seventy-five years old when he set out from Haran." Gen 12:4 (NIV)

What is keeping you from obeying God? Do you fear the unknown? Are you uncomfortable making a move without having more information? Maybe God has chosen to limit His revelation to match your obedience. Once you obey what He has already said, then He will show you the next step.

Abram took God at His word! He simply obeyed God. God told Abram to leave and go to a land that He would show him. Guess what? Abram left, as the Lord told him. He obeyed.

You can never go wrong obeying God. His way is always the best way. Even when it doesn't make sense or seem remotely logical, God's way is the right way. If you are confused about your next step, just obey what He has already said. Start there!

Identify what you are wrestling with right now. What is keeping you from taking the next step? Place that fear or frustration before the Lord in prayer, and see how He helps you take the next step.

God is patient with you and understands your fears and limitations. Entrust your future to God. His plan is your best option. Stay close to the Lord and lean into His heart for you. Be still and listen for His voice. Choose to respond in obedience to what God shows you. As you obey, He will illunimate the way!

June 21
WAIT FOR GOD'S TIMING
Delays, Waiting

"God also said to Abraham, 'As for Sarai your wife, you are no longer to call her Sarai; her name will be Sarah. I will bless her and will surely give you a son by her. I will bless her so that she will be the mother of nations; kings of peoples will come from her.' Abraham fell facedown; he laughed and said to himself, 'Will a son be born to a man a hundred years old? Will Sarah bear a child at the age of ninety?'" Gen 17:15-17 (NIV)

Can you imagine becoming a parent at age ninety or a hundred? That's difficult to fathom. However, the greater challenge would be to desire parenthood and having to wait until you were almost a century old to realize the dream.

Abraham and Sarah had to learn to live with delays. God had promised to bless them and to make them into a great nation. However, they had to walk in obedience to God and wait for His timing.

Have you noticed how our personal timetable doesn't always line up with God's timetable? We tend to want our blessing now. We don't usually "wait" very well.

God has a divine purpose in our delays. Sometimes, delays are a result of poor choices we have made, and sometimes, a consequence of poor choices others around us have made. Either way, God can use delays to portray His grace. God has the final say, doesn't He? Nothing happens without God's permission. If God allows a delay in your life, He will utilize the delay. Now rest in God's timing. Entrust your life to Him.

Preparing for Worship

"Early the next morning Abraham got up and saddled his donkey. He took with him two of his servants and his son Isaac. When he had cut enough wood for the burnt offering, he set out for the place God had told him about. On the third day Abraham looked up and saw the place in the distance. He said to his servants, 'Stay here with the donkey while I and the boy go over there. We will worship and then we will come back to you.'" Gen 22:3-5 (NIV)

Abraham prepared for worship. Worship is our response to God. Our worship reveals our level of obedience to God. Abram demonstrated absolute passion and submission to God through his worship of God.

I once heard someone say, "We don't come to church to worship, we come to church worshipping." That's sounds like the lifestyle that Abraham embraced. His preparation for worship was in fact an outflow of his lifestyle of worship.

Everybody worships something or someone. Who is the focus of your worship? How do you prepare for that expression of worship? God deserves your best. God deserves your affection, appreciation, and adoration.

Worship is expressing your love to God. Abraham expressed his love to God both in preparation for worship and in the presentation of worship. So, how's your worship? Do you prepare to bring God your best?

June 23
GUARDING YOUR TOP PRIORITY
Sacrifice, Priorities

"When they reached the place God had told him about, Abraham built an altar there and arranged the wood on it. He bound his son Isaac and laid him on the altar, on top of the wood. Then he reached out his hand and took the knife to slay his son." Gen 22:9-10 (NIV)

Is there anything in your life that takes priority over your relationship with Jesus? Are there any allurements sifting your affection away from your devotion to Christ? Do you have an Isaac in your life that you are unwilling to sacrifice?

Abraham demonstrated absolute loyalty and devotion to God by his willingness to sacrifice his promised son. Abraham and Sarah were beyond child bearing years. Yet, God provided the miracle of Isaac's conception. Now God is asking Abraham to sacrifice that which was promised to him.

What is standing in the way of your realization of unbroken fellowship with God? What is taking the number one place of prominence in your life which is reserved for God? Whatever that item, ambition, or person is, may be your Isaac.

Could it be that God wants you to sacrifice that Isaac in your life to enable God to have top priority in your life? God wants first place in your daily walk. God wants to be the supreme object of your energy and affection. He not only deserves it, but He demands it.

Spend a few moments taking inventory of your current priorities, and identify what is preventing God from being your top priority.

GOD'S PROVISION

Provision, Trust

"Abraham looked up and there in a thicket he saw a ram caught by its horns. He went over and took the ram and sacrificed it as a burnt offering instead of his son. So Abraham called that place The LORD Will Provide. And to this day it is said, 'On the mountain of the LORD it will be provided.'" Gen 22:13-14 (NIV)

God's provision always exceeds our sacrifice. Just when you think you have given God your all, He surpasses your sacrifice with His provision. God will never ask you to do anything that exceeds His provision. God's timing is not limited by our schedule. His provision always comes through at the perfect moment. God is never late.

We serve an on-time God. Sometimes it may seem as though God waits until you are in the fourth quarter with only a few seconds left on the clock. Yet, God's provision appears right on time.

Abraham obeyed God and demonstrated his reverence for God. In response, God provided a substitute for Isaac at the exact moment of greatest need.

What did Abraham learn about God through his willingness to trust and obey God in every situation? He learned that God was dependable and trustworthy. In response to the encounter of God's provision, Abraham acknowledged God as Jehovah Jireh, the Lord Will Provide.

What is keeping you from obeying God and trusting Him to provide?

June 25
LUMINARIES FOR THE LORD
Visible, Influence

"You are the light of the world. A city on a hill cannot be hidden. Neither do people light a lamp and put it under a bowl. Instead they put it on its stand, and it gives light to everyone in the house. In the same way, let your light shine before men, that they may see your good deeds and praise your Father in heaven." Matt 5:14-16 (NIV)

Are you making Jesus visible to others?

Jesus is the light of the world. When you become a Christ follower, you become His light in the world. As you let your light shine for Jesus, your good deeds will be visible to others, and they will praise God.

Writing from prison, Paul acknowledges the Ephesians for their strong faith in the Lord and their vibrant love for the other believers. Their Christian walk became evident to others in their part of the world. "For this reason, ever since I heard about your faith in the Lord Jesus and your love for all the saints, I have not stopped giving thanks for you, remembering you in my prayers" (Eph 1:15-16 NIV).

How did Paul hear about their faith and their love? Could it be that their lives visibly demonstrated their growing relationship with Jesus?

Be a luminary for the Lord. Let the light of Jesus shine brightly through your life and through your circumstances to illuminate the dark world you live in. Let others see Jesus in you. Go light your world for the Lord.

June 26
STAYING VERTICAL
Jesus, Love, Witness

"For this reason, ever since I heard about your faith in the Lord Jesus and your love for all the saints, I have not stopped giving thanks for you, remembering you in my prayers." Eph 1:15-16 (NIV)

The most incredible relationship you can ever have is vertical. Having a right relationship with God through Jesus Christ is the ultimate relationship. Think about the vertical beam of the cross. Allow it to represent your relationship with God. What does that relationship look like currently in your life?

Paul identified the evidence of one's right relationship with God as faith expressing itself through love. When you are living in harmony with God, your faith will be apparent. The Ephesians embraced their vertical relationship with God to the extent that Paul heard about their faith from his prison cell.

What is your faith relationship with God saying to those in your sphere of influence? In what environment is your faith in God most tested? How is your vertical relationship with God expressed in your home, at work, at church, and in your neighborhood?

Spend some time assessing your vertical relationship. Let God have His way in your life so that your faith will be evident to all.

177

BLESSED TO BE A BLESSING

Love, Generosity

"If anyone has material possessions and sees his brother in need but has no pity on him, how can the love of God be in him?" 1 John 3:17 (NIV)

When you pull up to a traffic signal and notice a man holding a cardboard sign saying, "Need food! Please help!", what kind of thoughts race through your mind? Do you wrestle with the notion to roll down your window and extend a dollar bill, or maybe even a five dollar bill? Then again, you may start pondering what that person might spend the money on. In your mind, you are thinking that he may take the money and go buy alcohol, cigarettes, or a lottery ticket. You question whether he will really use the money to buy food as his sign advertised.

Does God expect us to use good judgment? Yes! But, God also expects us to help meet needs. Remember this concept: God does not bless you based on how that person spends the money you give. God blesses you based on your heart in giving to meet needs.

John takes the concept of meeting needs into the arena of the family of God. We are to help fellow believers. In fact, if we are unwilling to use the resources God has blessed us with to help a brother in need, then how can the love of God be in us. In other words, God's love is evidenced as we meet needs.

God's love compels us to be generous. Generosity will not flow naturally. It is a supernatural experience. God has blessed us to be a blessing. Ask God to show you some needs this week that He wants you to meet for His glory!

STRATEGIC PRAYING

Strategic Praying

"I have not stopped giving thanks for you, remembering you in my prayers."
Eph 1:16 (NIV)

Is somebody praying for you? I want you to begin to calculate where you would be had it not been for the people who have prayed for you. Your name, your circumstances, and your future have been placed before the throne of God by those people who have prayed for you.

God has a unique way of prompting people to pray for you. He will nudge them with a gentle reminder of your life. They may respond by praying for you to realize God's will. Maybe they pray for you to have a heightened awareness of God's Presence and activity.

Paul exhibited a deep love for the saints in Ephesus. He constantly thanked God for them, and for their obvious faith in the Lord, and their love for their fellow believers. Paul consistently remembered them in his prayers. They were as natural to his prayer life as water to a fish.

Carve out a few moments right now to thank God for the people who have prayed for you. This could get emotional! It's okay. You matter to God, and He deeply loves you and cares for you. God has brought you to the minds of specific people in order for them to intercede on your behalf. You are being strategically prayed for.

Are you willing to be used of God to intercede for others? Are you willing to pray for others as God brings them to your mind? Be strategic in your praying. Seek to get in their skin as you pray for them.

June 29
RECEIVING GOD'S WISDOM
Wisdom, Impartation

"I keep asking that the God of our Lord Jesus Christ, the glorious Father, may give you the Spirit of wisdom and revelation, so that you may know him better." Eph 1:17 (NIV)

God's passion is for you to know Him intimately and accurately. However, you cannot know Him without the illuminating work of the Holy Spirit.

The Holy Spirit imparts wisdom to the child of God so that the believer can know God on an intimate level. Wisdom is the God-given ability to discern truth. Truth is not a cafeteria of facts, but rather the second Person of the Trinity, Jesus. "The man without the Spirit does not accept the things that come from the Spirit of God, for they are foolishness to him, and he cannot understand them, because they are spiritually discerned" (1 Cor 2:14 NIV).

The third Person of the Trinity, the Holy Spirit, imparts wisdom to the believer which awakens spiritual sight. This illumination enables the believer to detect the activity of God.

Are you allowing the Holy Spirit to impart God's wisdom in your life? Have you sought Him today and asked for the Spirit of wisdom? He freely gives to His children. God wants you to walk in His wisdom and to draw near to Him.

THE TEACHING COUNSELOR

Revelation, Holy Spirit

"But the Counselor, the Holy Spirit, whom the Father will send in my name, will teach you all things and will remind you of everything I have said to you."
John 14:26 (NIV)

Our God is a God who speaks. He desires to communicate His love to His creation. In his study, *Experiencing God*, Henry Blackaby taught that God speaks by the Holy Spirit through the Bible, prayer, circumstances, and the church to reveal Himself, His purposes, and His ways.

God is a God of revelation. He unveils that which was once hidden. God passionately reveals His truth so that we can know Him, and serve Him, and fulfill His plan.

Paul, in his prison prayer, is praying for the saints in Ephesus. His focus is asking God to give them the spirit of revelation. The Holy Spirit enables the believer to understand and apply God's Word.

Meditate on this verse for a few moments. Notice how the Holy Spirit is identified as a Teacher and a Reminder. God, through the Holy Spirit gives us wisdom to appropriate His Word in our daily living. The Holy Spirit teaches us God's Word and reminds us of what God has spoken.

As you read God's Word, pray and ask God to give you the Spirit of wisdom so that you may know Him better. Are you growing in your knowing?

July 1
KNOWING GOD

Knowing God

"I keep asking that the God of our Lord Jesus Christ, the glorious Father, may give you the Spirit of wisdom and revelation, so that you may know him better."
Eph 1:17 (NIV)

God wants you to know Him intimately. God invites you into the process. You must participate with God in developing and maintaining intimacy with Him. He makes the relationship possible through the atoning work of Jesus on the cross. You get the privilege of knowing God and growing in your knowledge of God.

Paul had a loving desire to see the saints at Ephesus grow in their relationship with God. From prison, he prayed for their sanctification. Meditate on his prayer.

Why would Paul pray that God would give the saints at Ephesus the Spirit of wisdom and revelation? He prayed that specifically so that they would know God better. In other words, there is room to grow. Yes, there's more to explore.

We are finite. God is infinite. There's so much more to know about God and more to explore in knowing God. The beauty of a love relationship with God is that it is progressive. You can continually grow to know God more. What a privilege! What an honor! What a responsibility!

SPIRITUAL HEART SURGERY

Heart, Love, Passion

Jesus said, "Love the Lord your God with all your heart and with all your soul and with all your mind and with all your strength." Mark 12:30 (NIV)

Your heart matters to God. God wants you to put your heart into loving Him. Your heart represents your thinking, knowing, and understanding. God desires for you to activate your will to demonstrate your love for Him.

In Paul's prison prayer for the saints at Ephesus, he prayed specifically for their hearts. He had such a profound love for them and exhibited compassion for them as he prayed for their spiritual perception. "I pray also that the eyes of your heart may be enlightened in order that you may know the hope to which he has called you, the riches of his glorious inheritance in the saints" (Eph 1:18 NIV).

In the language of the New Testament, the Greek word for heart does not refer to emotions. It refers to your capacity to know and comprehend. Your heart represents your understanding informed by·God. God does not deposit His deepest treasures in the shallow waters of your emotions. God entrusts His treasures to your heart.

Take heart! Let's get to the heart of the matter! Has your heart been deeply touched by God's amazing love? What are you doing with the heart God has given you? Are you growing in your knowing? Have you given God full access to your heart?

July 3
ENLIGHTENED TO KNOW HIS HOPE
Enlightenment, Heart

"I pray also that the eyes of your heart may be enlightened in order that you may know the hope to which he has called you, the riches of his glorious inheritance in the saints." Eph 1:18 (NIV)

Do you remember the Polaroid cameras that produced the photo within a minute of you taking the picture? Now we have digital cameras that provide a picture instantly. The old Polaroid cameras were considered innovative back then. You would take a picture and then watch it develop right before your eyes.

That process of development is similar to the Greek word, photizo, which Paul uses in his letter to the saints in Ephesus. This particular Greek word is translated as "enlightened."

Your heart, which represents your capacity to understand and comprehend God's truth, has room to grow. Your ability to know, grasp, and understand has the potential to develop. You can grow in your knowing.

God wants you to be enlightened. God desires for you to develop in your knowledge of Him. Personalize Ephesians 1:18 and pray through it by asking God to open the eyes of your heart. God will unveil His Word to you in a personal and powerful way.

THE HOPE GOD OFFERS

Hope, Calling

"And the God of all grace, who called you to his eternal glory in Christ, after you have suffered a little while, will himself restore you and make you strong, firm and steadfast." 1 Peter 5:10 (NIV)

Have you ever faced a seemingly hopeless situation? How did it make you feel? Hopelessness erodes passion for living. However, for the follower of Jesus Christ, hope awaits. Hope is made available to every believer by God.

Remember, life is not about our story that God plays a part in. Life is about God's story that we get to play a part in. God has an agenda for us to fulfill. We get to join Him in His activity.

As a child of God, you have the confident expectation of the hope to which He has called you. God called you to Himself in salvation, and God calls you to Himself in sanctification. Your calling involves life, in time, on planet earth, and in eternity, in heaven.

Can you echo Paul's words to his son in the ministry, Timothy? "Fight the good fight of the faith. Take hold of the eternal life to which you were called when you made your good confession in the presence of many witnesses" (1 Tim 6:12 NIV). It's not how you start. It's how you finish!

Do you know the hope to which God has called you? Are you secure in His calling? God has paved the way for you to live a life of hope.

July 5
ROYAL TREASURE

Riches, Holy Spirit, Lordship

"You, however, are controlled not by the sinful nature but by the Spirit, if the Spirit of God lives in you. And if anyone does not have the Spirit of Christ, he does not belong to Christ." Romans 8:9 (NIV)

At conversion, you get Jesus and He gets you. You become a saint, blessed, chosen, adopted, redeemed, forgiven, included, sealed, and secure. When you become a follower of Jesus Christ, you get all of Him. He permanently indwells you by His Spirit.

As a believer, you have the royal treasure of the Holy Spirit living in you. You become the walking Tabernacle of the Presence of God. He lives in you and expresses Himself through you.

Those who have been adopted into God's family are the riches of Jesus' glorious inheritance. We get Jesus and He gets those of us who have placed our faith in Him alone for salvation. Jesus sees us as His treasured possession. We are His glorious inheritance. The beauty of this reality is seen in the persistence of Christ to form us into His image. This process of sanctification is ongoing. We are still in process. We are perpetually on the Potter's wheel to be molded and shaped by the Master's hand.

Think of where you are now in your relationship to God in Christ. Imagine where you will be in your relationship with God as you continue to walk with Him daily and consistently yield to His Lordship and leadership in your life.

POWERED BY GOD

Power, Holy Spirit

"I keep asking that the God of our Lord Jesus Christ, the glorious Father, may give you the Spirit of wisdom and revelation, so that you may know him better. I pray also that the eyes of your heart may be enlightened in order that you may know the hope to which he has called you, the riches of his glorious inheritance in the saints, and his incomparably great power for us who believe. That power is like the working of his mighty strength, which he exerted in Christ when he raised him from the dead and seated him at his right hand in the heavenly realms, far above all rule and authority, power and dominion, and every title that can be given, not only in the present age but also in the one to come." Eph 1:17-21 (NIV)

Do you fully know the power made available to you as a Christ follower? When you made the divine transaction by trusting Jesus as the Lord and Savior of your life, you were indwelt by the Holy Spirit. His power became part of your spiritual DNA.

Paul prayed for the saints at Ephesus to come to fully know the resurrection power made available to them. His prayer should be your prayer as well.

The power that God exerted to raise Jesus from the dead is made available to you. The same power that ascended Jesus to heaven and exalted Him to the right hand of our Heavenly Father is the same power that empowers you to live out the Christian life. God does not expect you to be Christ on earth in your own strength. His power is more than enough to empower you and equip you to be the salt of the earth and the light of the world.

July 7
DAILY DOMINION
Dominion, Supremacy of Christ

"And God placed all things under his feet and appointed him to be head over everything for the church, which is his body, the fullness of him who fills everything in every way." Eph 1:22-23 (NIV)

The supremacy of Christ is affirmed in Paul's letter to the saints in Ephesus. God, the Creator and Sustainer of the entire universe, positioned Jesus as head of the church. Jesus is in charge. All things are under His feet. Remember, anything over your head is beneath His feet. "And he is the head of the body, the church; he is the beginning and the firstborn from among the dead, so that in everything he might have the supremacy" (Col 1:18 NIV).

Our function in the body is to manifest the Head. As His body, the church is to express the love of the Head. We are His dominion. We are made by Him and for His glory. As His dominion, we are under the control of His Lordship. Our desire is to please Him and to fulfill His agenda. He empowers us to live for His glory on the earth. May our obedience to Christ impact every continent.

You are living under His dominion. Since you are a part of the body of Christ, you express the fullness of God to a lost and dying world. As Jesus reigns in your life, you will reign in this life. Jesus is supreme. Give Him first place in your life. Live in such a way as to demonstrate your love and your loyalty to Christ.

FULLNESS IN CHRIST

Fullness, Salvation

"For God was pleased to have all his fullness dwell in him, and through him to reconcile to himself all things, whether things on earth or things in heaven, by making peace through his blood, shed on the cross." Col 1:19-20 (NIV)

How much of Christ did you receive on your day of salvation? Did you only get a part of Him and then, at a later date, receive a little bit more of Him? Or, did you receive all of Him?

When you placed your faith in the completed work of Jesus on the cross, you received all of Jesus. Instantly, upon your profession of faith in Jesus, you received the fullness of Christ.

- "For in Christ all the fullness of the Deity lives in bodily form, and you have been given fullness in Christ, who is the head over every power and authority." Col 2:9-10 (NIV).

The question is not, "Did you get all of Him?" The question is, "Did He get all of you?" At salvation, you get all of Christ. In sanctification, He gets more and more of you. You must daily surrender your life to His Lordship in order to give Him all of you. You have all of Him. You are full of Christ. That's right! You have been given the fullness of Christ!

How will you express the fullness of Christ today? Will it be evident to others that you are full of Him?

July 9
DEAD IN TRANGRESSIONS

Dead, Sin

"As for you, you were dead in your transgressions and sins." Eph 2:1 (NIV).

What were you before you came to Christ? Go there for a moment and ponder your condition. I remember as though it were yesterday. My parents were divorced and I was a few weeks shy of my tenth birthday when I came to the place of decision. The Holy Spirit had convicted me of my lostness and convinced me of my need for a Father who would never let me down. On March 28, 1979, I turned my life over to Jesus Christ and He saved me. Before that moment of decision, I was dead.

Paul reminded the saints at Ephesus about their condition before they came to know Christ in a life-altering way.

Before Christ came into your life, you had no spiritual sensitivity. You were dead! It may have appeared that you were alive since you demonstrated some level of life physically. However, you were spiritually dead.

Do you remember the story Jesus told about a father who had two sons? The younger son took his share of the father's estate and wasted it in riotous living and then hit rock bottom in the pig's pen. He came to his senses and decided to go back home to his father. Notice how the father responded to the son's return home. "For this son of mine was dead and is alive again; he was lost and is found.' So they began to celebrate" (Luke 15:24 NIV).

What were you before you turned your life over to Jesus? What are you now in Christ? Jesus came to resuscitate you spiritually and eternally. You will never be the same!

Moving Beyond What You Were

Transgressions, Sin, New Beginning

"As for you, you were dead in your transgressions and sins." Eph 2:1 (NIV)

What do an eraser, white-out, and a delete button have in common? Each item provides compensation for our mistakes. If you make a mistake on a document, then all you have to do is erase it, white-it-out, or delete it.

Don't you wish that the mistakes we make in life could be handled that succinctly? The reality is that we are flawed and live in a fallen world. Life gets messy and we make mistakes. We deliberately choose our own way, and sometimes we may deviate from God's best. Sometimes we make poor choices and break the heart of God. A name for that willful disobedience is called transgressions. We select a path that does not honor God, and therefore, we commit a transgression.

Before Christ, we were spiritually dead which was evidenced by our willful disobedience. Our transgressions flowed from our state of decay. We were dead! Thus, in our deadness, rebellion came naturally. We acted according to our spiritual reality.

Let the word "were", in verse one, capture your heart for a few moments. Meditate on what you were when you were dead in your transgressions. Weigh the reality of "were" and see if your level of appreciation for God's intervention escalates.

You don't have to continue to be what you were. It's a new day! God has provided the way, in Jesus, for you to experience a new beginning.

July 11
THE REALITY OF SIN
Sins, Consequences

"For all have sinned and fall short of the glory of God." Romans 3:23 (NIV)

Imagine our world without sin. Prisons would be empty. Crime would be absent. Poverty would be eliminated. Corruption would be nonexistent.

The reality is that sin is rampant throughout society and the world. To sin is to miss the mark. Failing to obey God is sin. When you sin, you break the heart of God. As Steve Farrar identified in his book, *Finishing Strong:*

> Sin will take you farther than you want to go.
> Sin will keep you longer than you want to stay.
> Sin will cost you more than you want to pay.

Sin never delivers what it promises. God promises that sin will produce spiritual death. So why do people sin? Why is there a natural bent toward sin? It all goes back to the fall of man when Adam sinned against God. We inherited the sin nature.

Our only hope is the transforming grace of Jesus Christ. He is our only hope. Spend some time confessing to God the specific times that you missed the mark of His holiness and righteousness. Acknowledge your dependency upon God and walk in His way.

DISCERNING THE REAL ENEMY

Evil, Devil, Enemy

"For our struggle is not against flesh and blood, but against the rulers, against the authorities, against the powers of this dark world and against the spiritual forces of evil in the heavenly realms." Eph 6:12 (NIV)

People are not the enemy!

Your spouse, your children, your brother, your sister, your mom, your dad, your boss, your neighbor, or your in-laws are not the enemy. Your enemy is the Devil and his demons. Your enemy is his spirit at work in this world. Your enemy is the Devil's evil spirit trying to coerce your flesh to follow its natural fallen cravings.

Spend some time thanking God that you are no longer what you "used to" be. Praise Him for what you are now "in Christ" and what you are becoming as you work out what God has worked in. "Therefore, my dear friends, as you have always obeyed--not only in my presence, but now much more in my absence--continue to work out your salvation with fear and trembling, for it is God who works in you to will and to act according to his good purpose" (Phil 2:12-13 NIV).

God has equipped you to combat the real enemy. Pray for those in your life that have become difficult, and remember that they are not the enemy. In fact, God gave them His best when He gave His only Son, Jesus, to die for them. Oh, and He gave His best for you! You were worth dying for.

July 13
Choosing the Appetite
Cravings, Sin Nature

"All of us also lived among them at one time, gratifying the cravings of our sinful nature and following its desires and thoughts. Like the rest, we were by nature objects of wrath." Eph 2:3 (NIV)

If you have ever had surgery, you know that it takes time for you to regain your appetite. You have been blessed with a God-given appetite for food. That appetite can be a blessing and help you grow and develop. However, that appetite can be abused and cause your body harm.

Your sinful nature has an appetite for sin. It craves sinful indulgence. Whatever you feed grows, and whatever you starve dies. When you feed your sinful nature, it grows. When you starve your sinful nature, it dies.

As a believer, your appetite for sin is transformed into an appetite for righteousness. Your new nature in Christ craves purity and holiness. "So I say, live by the Spirit, and you will not gratify the desires of the sinful nature. For the sinful nature desires what is contrary to the Spirit, and the Spirit what is contrary to the sinful nature. They are in conflict with each other, so that you do not do what you want" (Gal 5:16-17 NIV).

What will you choose to feed today? Will you choose to feed the cravings of your sinful nature or the cravings of the Spirit? What will you choose to starve today? Will you choose to starve the cravings of your sinful nature or the cravings of the Spirit?

Objects of Wrath
Wrath, God's Love

"All of us also lived among them at one time, gratifying the cravings of our sinful nature and following its desires and thoughts. Like the rest, we were by nature objects of wrath." Eph 2:3 (NIV)

An honest look at what we were before Christ keeps us humble and teachable. We live in light of our "in Christ" realities, but we keep an eye on our "before Christ" reality to remind us of what we have been delivered from.

In Paul's letter to the saints in Ephesus, he identified the believer's condition before submitting to the Lordship of Christ. Notice what we were before Jesus became Lord of our lives.

Why would we be objects of God's wrath? God is holy! The Psalmist affirms, "God is a righteous judge, a God who expresses his wrath every day" (Psalm 7:11 NIV).

The wonderful news is that, in Christ, we are no longer objects of God's wrath, but rather objects of God's love. Sin must be punished. Sin must be atoned for. God's grace has changed our desperate situation.

You are treasured by the Creator of the universe. God took the initiative to make a way for you to be in right standing before Him. His way is the only way. Through faith in the atoning work of Jesus on the cross, you are delivered from being the object of God's wrath. Now we are on shouting ground! Walk in light of your new identity in Christ. You are victorious!

July 15
ALIVE WITH CHRIST

Alive with Christ, Mercy

"But because of his great love for us, God, who is rich in mercy, made us alive with Christ even when we were dead in transgressions--it is by grace you have been saved." Eph 2:4-5 (NIV)

Why would God go to such lengths to rescue us and redeem us? God's great love and rich mercy are two reasons God comes to our rescue. His love is limitless. His mercy is proportionate to His love.

Even when we were dead in our sinful indulgence, God made us alive with Christ. We were hopeless and destitute, but God resurrected us from our deadness. God did for us that which we could not do for ourselves. "In the same way, count yourselves dead to sin but alive to God in Christ Jesus. Therefore do not let sin reign in your mortal body so that you obey its evil desires" (Romans 6:11-12 NIV).

What is your response to God's initiative? Have you turned your life over to Christ and fully submitted to His Lordship? Have you measured His love and received His mercy? Then, you have been made alive with Christ. You are dead to sin but alive in Christ.

Will you allow Christ to live His life through you today? The best is yet to come!

RAISED WITH CHRIST

Bible, Inspiration, Perspective

"Since, then, you have been raised with Christ, set your hearts on things above, where Christ is seated at the right hand of God. Set your minds on things above, not on earthly things." Col 3:1-2 (NIV)

The Bible is divided into two sections: Old Testament and New Testament. There are sixty-six books in the Bible: thirty-nine in the Old Testament and twenty-seven in the New Testament. God inspired forty human authors over a period of sixteen hundred years to record His Word to humanity. The Bible's overall theme is that of God revealing Himself and His persistence in redeeming fallen man. We are the recipients of the transforming grace of God through Jesus Christ as revealed in the Bible. Identify your position in Christ as a result of God's initiative.

You cannot raise yourself up. You cannot live the new life in Christ outside of God's provision. It's not about what you can do. It's all about what God has done in Christ to raise you up so that you may live a new life. Stop trying to live for God, and start allowing His resurrection power to flow through you as He lives His life through you.

What is your response to being raised with Christ? Set your heart on things above. In other words, allow your passion to be fueled by God's agenda. Set your mind on things above. Nurture a heavenly perspective to orient your life in alignment with what God values. Employ an eternal perspective so that your decisions will reflect the mind of Christ.

July 17
SEATED IN THE HEAVENLY REALMS

Spiritual Blessing, Heaven

"And God raised us up with Christ and seated us with him in the heavenly realms in Christ Jesus." Eph 2:6 (NIV)

Jesus prayed that God's Will be done on earth as it is in heaven. His desire is to see heaven's reality realized on earth. What is keeping that from happening? Sin!

Yet, in Christ, we have the reality of heaven authenticated in our love relationship with God. We are living in the Spirit realm whereby our identity in Christ is secure.

Our current reality in the Spirit realm is that of being seated with Christ. It speaks of our position in Christ. It speaks of our being adopted into His family. It also speaks of our future glorification and exaltation. Notice the intimate communion between Jesus and our Heavenly Father during one of Jesus' prayer times while on the earth. "Father, I want those you have given me to be with me where I am, and to see my glory, the glory you have given me because you loved me before the creation of the world" (John 17:24 NIV).

In His promise to the church at Laodicea, which includes those of us who are followers of Jesus Christ, Jesus affirmed our future reality when we get to heaven. "To him who overcomes, I will give the right to sit with me on my throne, just as I overcame and sat down with my Father on his throne" (Rev 3:21 NIV). So, where are you seated?

DISPLAYING GOD'S GRACE

Display, Grace, Witness

"Here is a trustworthy saying that deserves full acceptance: Christ Jesus came into the world to save sinners--of whom I am the worst. But for that very reason I was shown mercy so that in me, the worst of sinners, Christ Jesus might display his unlimited patience as an example for those who would believe on him and receive eternal life." 1 Tim 1:15-16 (NIV)

During my sophomore year in high school, I worked in a large grocery store. After spending a week outside fetching grocery carts, I was promoted to mopping floors on the inside. A few weeks later, I catapulted to the next level, that of being a display clerk. My job was to build captivating displays at the end of each aisle. Customers who came in just for milk and bread would often be drawn to one of the displays and end up purchasing one of the featured items.

God specializes in displaying His grace by featuring His children. One of God's featured converts was Saul, who became Paul. God intersected Saul's path on the road to Damascus and transformed his life (Acts 9). Saul became Paul and was transformed from being a persecutor of the church to a preacher of the Gospel. He was transformed from a murderer to a minister. Later in Paul's life, he writes to one of his young sons in the ministry, Timothy, to describe how God specializes in placing His children on the display of His transforming grace (1 Tim. 1:15-16).

God will display what He transforms. God will show off those who have experienced His grace, expressed in His kindness to them in Christ. Will you allow His grace and kindness expressed to you be put on display this week? Are you willing to start viewing others through the lens of God's tenderness and patience that He extends to you?

July 19
TRANSFORMING GRACE
Grace, Salvation, Heaven, Soulwinning

"For it is by grace you have been saved, through faith--and this not from yourselves, it is the gift of God-- not by works, so that no one can boast." *Eph 2:8-9 (NIV)*

How refreshing to receive something special that you did not deserve! That's grace in action. God saved us by His transforming grace. In mercy, He did not give us what we deserved. In grace, He gave us what we did not deserve.

Grace is unique compared to mercy. Grace is the blessing that places us in Christ. Once we are in Christ, we live the rest of our lives in light of our new identity in Christ. We are blessed with a new position, a new power, and a new purpose. "Therefore, if anyone is in Christ, he is a new creation; the old has gone, the new has come" (2 Cor 5:17 NIV).

How many portraits of grace have you known? Whenever you are tempted to judge others who may not be in Christ, consider what they could be if they had an abiding relationship with Christ. What if they became a portrait of God's grace?

What kind of portrait of grace have others seen in you? Does your life bear witness to the grace of God? You have a new position in Christ that enables you to launch into shining His light and sharing His love. You have a new power that enables you to testify of His marvelous grace with boldness and clarity. You have a new purpose that keeps you focused on eternity and that elevates your soul-consciousness.

You are saved by God's grace through faith. Now, invest the rest of your life leading others to the wonderful grace that you have experienced so they can spend eternity in heaven, too.

Faith, Salvation

"For it is by grace you have been saved, through faith--and this not from yourselves, it is the gift of God--not by works, so that no one can boast."
Eph 2:8-9 (NIV)

Religion is like a vaccination. It will give you just enough to keep you from getting the real thing. Religion is our attempt to reach up to God.

God desires relationship. Relationship is demonstrated by God coming down to us. The Creator chose to come down to His created ones. Though we are fallen, flawed, and fall short, God, in His love and through His grace, comes down to us.

Our love relationship with God is made possible by His grace. Yet, this eternal relationship is transacted through our faith response. Our faith, plus works, does not bring forth justification. Our faith response to God's offer of salvation opens the door to justification, which in turn, produces an outflow of good works.

Faith includes accurate knowledge, belief, and commitment. It is not enough to know that Jesus lived and died and rose again. You must believe that Jesus is the sinless, spotless, and sacrificial Lamb of God who paid the penalty for your sins. Faith involves belief that results in commitment and full surrender of your life to the Lordship of Christ.

Got faith?

July 21
GOD TOOK THE INITIATIVE
Gift, Initiative, Salvation

"But we ought always to thank God for you, brothers loved by the Lord, because from the beginning God chose you to be saved through the sanctifying work of the Spirit and through belief in the truth." 2 Thess 2:13 (NIV)

How much of your salvation depends on God and how much depends on you? If you say that it all depends on God, then what role do you play in the salvific process? If you say that it all depends on you, then what role does God fulfill?

The danger is to think that you did all you could do and then God did the rest. See if you can detect the clarity of what you bring to the salvation package in the following verse. "For it is by grace you have been saved, through faith--and this not from yourselves, it is the gift of God--not by works, so that no one can boast" (Eph 2:8-9 NIV).

Let's focus on the phrase, "and this not from yourselves." We have been saved by grace through faith. Where did that come from? Who made that possible? God! Salvation was not our idea. It was and is God's idea. God's redemptive activity is His loving response to fallen humanity.

God initiates and we respond. Salvation originates with God. God thought it, Jesus bought it, and the Holy Spirit wrought it. God graciously provides us with the opportunity to receive or reject His offer of salvation. God created us to be relational, not robotic. Choose life! Choose to receive God's gift of eternal life. If you have already done so, then be an irresitible influence for Christ so that others may choose to receive God's eternal gift.

RESCUING OTHERS

Pride

"Where were you when I laid the earth's foundation? Tell me, if you understand."
Job 38:4 (NIV)

Sometimes we forget how big God is and how small we are. That is one factor that makes salvation so amazing. God as the Creator of the entire universe has taken the initiative to rescue, redeem, and restore fallen humanity. God became like us so that we could become like Him. Wow!

So what do we bring to the table? Out of over 6.7 billion people on planet earth, what does one individual add to the equation of God's redemptive activity?

Remember, we are saved by His grace through faith (Eph. 2:8-9). Salvation is a gift, not a reward. We do not earn salvation by our works or deeds. Thus, there is no room for pride. Pride says, "Look at what I have done! Look at what I have accomplished!" The reality is that we cannot add to the completed work of Jesus on the cross. "May I never boast except in the cross of our Lord Jesus Christ, through which the world has been crucified to me, and I to the world" (Gal 6.14 NIV).

How will you respond to God's transforming grace? How will you interact with people this week in light of God's redemptive activity in your life? Join God in His redemptive activity. Begin viewing others through the lens of God's redeeming love. God rescued you so that you could participate with Him in rescuing others. Be a life-saver for the Lord!

July 23
SALVATION WORKS
Workmanship, Salvation

"For we are God's workmanship, created in Christ Jesus to do good works, which God prepared in advance for us to do." Eph 2:10 (NIV)

Salvation is a gift, not a reward. You cannot perform enough good works to earn salvation. You receive the gift of eternal life by the grace of God, through faith, in the completed work of Jesus on the cross. If salvation is a gift, how do good works add value?

God graciously gave His best, Jesus, to pay the sin debt you owed. It is a gift. If you try to pay for the gift one has given, then you cheapen the gift. What can you add to the finished work of Jesus on the cross? His atoning work is complete.

You were uniquely designed by God and for God. You are His masterpiece, His treasure, and the apple of His eye. You are His workmanship. He formed you and fashioned you for His glory. You are not an accident! You are here on purpose!

You cannot add to the salvation that God provided to you by His grace through faith. However, as His workmanship, you are created to do good works. You don't work for salvation; you work as a result of the salvation gift you have received. Good works are a result of a grateful heart. Show gratitude for what God has initiated and what faith has activated.

You are His workmanship created in Christ Jesus to do good works! Who will benefit from your life today?

Inside the Ark

Noah, Workmanship, Waiting

"This is the account of Noah. Noah was a righteous man, blameless among the people of his time, and he walked with God." Gen 6:9 (NIV)

God's workmanship included Noah. When we meet him in Scripture, we are drawn to Noah because he is the kind of daddy every child desires. He is in right standing with God and other people. Noah lives in harmony with God. Noah walks with God.

It sounds like Noah is a finished product. When we read about him in this verse, it appears that Noah has arrived. Where can he go from here? Yet, God takes Noah on an aquatic journey that is preceded by a perpetual dry season.

As God's workmanship, Noah has to learn how to trust God when circumstances do not make sense and delays are as frequent as the waves of the sea. Noah's life becomes a consistent pattern of waiting.

Can you relate? Are you agonizing over something in your life that seems to linger? Waiting does not come naturally to us. We live in a high-tech world that delivers information faster than the blink of an eye. We expect instant responses and instant results. Yet, God does not seem to be on our timetable.

Could it be that part of being God's workmanship includes more than just us employing good works? Maybe God wants us to see His value in the process more than the finished product. Maybe it's not so much about the ark. Maybe it's more about what is on the inside of the ark. God is really passionate about the interior of our lives.

While you are waiting, God is working!

July 25
WALKING WITH A LIMP
Jacob, Workmanship, Suffering

"So Jacob was left alone, and a man wrestled with him till daybreak. When the man saw that he could not overpower him, he touched the socket of Jacob's hip so that his hip was wrenched as he wrestled with the man." Gen 32:24-25 (NIV)

Have you ever wrestled with God? Who won? Wrestling is part of being God's workmanship. Jacob, as God's workmanship, came to know God in a new way after a night of wrestling. Just like in weight training, without resistance there is no growth.

God allows us to go through seasons of uncertainty. God allows us to experience seasons of silence and yes, even seasons of suffering. We wrestle with God in those seasons. Our faith is challenged and often our prayer life is stretched. We come to know God by experience. Sometimes that experience involves pain.

As God's workmanship, Jacob came away from the night of wrestling with a limp and a new name. You don't come into close proximity with the living God and leave the same. "Then the man said, 'Your name will no longer be Jacob, but Israel, because you have struggled with God and with men and have overcome'" (Gen 32:28 NIV).

God is for you. God is willingly to go to any length to bring you into a vibrant, intimate, and growing relationship with Him that is eternal. Walking with a limp is a constant reminder of our dependency upon God and His patience with us.

FROM THE PIT TO PROMINENCE

Joseph, Workmanship, Omnipotence

"Now Israel loved Joseph more than any of his other sons, because he had been born to him in his old age; and he made a richly ornamented robe for him. When his brothers saw that their father loved him more than any of them, they hated him and could not speak a kind word to him." Gen 37:3-4 (NIV)

Favored does not always equate to invincible. Joseph was favored by his father and hated by his brothers. Jealousy is like acid that erodes relationships and dissolves family unity. The seed of jealousy would germinate into a vine of hurtful branches in Joseph's life.

Joseph journeyed from the pit to the palace and then from the prison to the place of prominence. His life was like a vine climbing the rubble of a collapsed brick fence. Yet, through it all, the Lord was with Joseph.

God never abandons His workmanship. You are created by the Master architect. Your unique design comes from Almighty God. Nothing happens to you without the permission of your Creator. Whatever God orchestrates, He navigates. You are safe in His Hands. He knows what you are going through. He knows your past, your hurts, and your hang-ups. He knows every wound you have incurred. The Lord is with you and for you.

Here are a few lessons from Joseph's Life: God never abandons His children, God navigates what He orchestrates, and God nestles a mess into a masterpiece. You are safe in His care.

July 27
MOSES & THE PALACE
Moses, God's Provision

"When the child grew older, she took him to Pharaoh's daughter and he became her son. She named him Moses, saying, 'I drew him out of the water.'"
Ex 2:10 (NIV)

Amram and Jochebed were the parents of the baby that we come to know later as Moses. In response to Pharaoh's order to throw every boy that is born into the Nile, they sought to preserve his life by placing him into a floating basket and into the Nile River. He floated down the crocodile-infested Nile safely into the view of Pharaoh's daughter. When he grew older, he was brought to her, and she named him Moses.

God was clearly at work. God provided for Moses to go from being a helpless baby targeted by the death sentence of Pharaoh to being reared in the palace. Only God can maneuver someone from the awful plight of persecution to the panacea of the palace.

God thrives in hopeless situations. When your circumstances are desperate and impossible, God performs His greatest work. There is nothing beyond His grasp. He can surprise you with the exact provision at the exact time of need.

As God's workmanship, Moses encountered an unusual beginning. He was born in an environment that was not in his favor. Everything seemed to be against him. Yet, God was for him and made a way when there seemed to be no way.

Have you ever felt like you were in the turbulence of the Nile? Have circumstances ever weighed you down and depleted your emotional reserves? God is fully in tune. He invites you to come to Him as you are and rest in His care. You are His workmanship and He knows what you need. God knows. God cares. Rest in Him.

REDEEMING THE DRY SEASONS
Moses, God's Provision, Dry Seasons

"But Moses said to God, 'Who am I, that I should go to Pharaoh and bring the Israelites out of Egypt?'" Ex 3:11 (NIV)

What benefits were available to Moses in the desert that were unavailable to him in the palace? What could God teach Moses in the dusty desert that he could not learn in the palatial palace?

I remember going through a difficult season in ministry and felt led to call one of my mentors. I shared with him that perhaps God was preparing me for my next assignment. I'll never forget his response. He said, "Stephen, God is always preparing you for your next assignment. However, your next assignment may be right where you are."

Moses probably felt that way. He likely wondered what God could possibly be up to by allowing him to remain in the desert for forty years. God allowed Moses to experience forty years in the palace, to prepare him for the forty years in the desert, to prepare him for the forty years of leading the children of Israel to the Promised Land.

God does not waste our desert experiences. God uses those dry times in our lives to reveal Himself in a way that we would not comprehend otherwise. He is always preparing us for our next interaction, our next appointment, our next interruption, and our next assignment.

God will redeem the season you are in. Are you willing to trust God with your life? Are you willing to submit to His prompting?

July 29
MOVING WITH GOD
Moses, God's Movement

"In all the travels of the Israelites, whenever the cloud lifted from above the tabernacle, they would set out; but if the cloud did not lift, they did not set out-- until the day it lifted. So the cloud of the LORD was over the tabernacle by day, and fire was in the cloud by night, in the sight of all the house of Israel during all their travels." Ex 40:36-38 (NIV)

God makes His Presence known. For the children of Israel, God revealed His Presence through the glory cloud. God guided the Israelites by the visible manifestation of the cloud during the day, and fire, by night. When the cloud lifted and shifted, the Israelites moved. The Tabernacle was constructed in a way that emphasized ease of mobility. This enabled the Israelites to move when God moved.

As God's workmanship, where did Moses learn that kind of sensitivity to God's movement? Did he learn it in the palace during his first forty years on the earth, or perhaps, during the second forty years of his life as a shepherd in the desert? The burning bush experience obviously made an abiding difference in his sensitivity to God's Presence.

God is always at work. Are you sensitive to His activity? You can experience God's Presence moment-by-moment as you commune with Him through prayer and feed on His Word. You can experience God's Presence as you maintain a posture of expectation and anticipation. You always find what you are looking for. If you are looking for the activity of God, you will find it. Now, move with God.

EXCLUDED MEMORY

Excluded, Included, Salvation

"Therefore, remember that formerly you who are Gentiles by birth and called 'uncircumcised' by those who call themselves 'the circumcision' (that done in the body by the hands of men)-- remember that at that time you were separate from Christ, excluded from citizenship in Israel and foreigners to the covenants of the promise, without hope and without God in the world." Eph 2:11-12 (NIV)

You are either a Jew or a Gentile. In the New Testament period, Jews did not associate with Gentiles. In fact, the Jews viewed the Gentiles as unclean. Jesus made a way for the two to become one in the family of God.

Paul is reminding the saints at Ephesus of their former condition. He was placing a mirror in front of them and giving them a look into their life before conversion. They had to face the painful reality that they were actually separate from Christ and excluded from citizenship in Israel. Their former status was that of desperation.

Being excluded from citizenship meant overt rejection. Exclusion means that one does not measure up. It means that one does not meet the standards for inclusion. Paul is reminding the believers in Ephesus of their former reality.

Calculate for a moment what it would mean for you to be excluded from God's family. Think about the separation anxiety related to not being included in God's family tree. Do you remember what it felt like to not be in Christ? Do you remember being lost, hopeless, and separated from Christ?

Let the panic subside. Now, spend some time thanking God for including you in His redemptive plan. Let our Heavenly Father know how much you appreciate Him for including you in the salvation package.

July 31
BROUGHT NEAR
In Christ, Blood of Christ, Intimacy

"But now in Christ Jesus you who once were far away have been brought near through the blood of Christ." Eph 2:13 (NIV)

If you have ever traveled internationally, you know how it feels to be on the other side of the world. You know the impact of being twelve time zones away from home. There is a touch of insecurity which echoes the reality of being far away.

You can experience being far away in relationships. You can feel very close to someone at one time, and then feel far away from that person even when the physical proximity has not changed.

It is possible to be far away from God even though God is omnipresent. There is nowhere God is not. Yet, relationally you can be far away from God. You can walk closely with God and then, in a subtle way over time, drift until you are far away.

The refreshing news is that you don't have to stay far away. God's desire is for you to walk in daily intimacy with Him. He initiates the relationship and gives you the capacity to respond.

Don't waste your life. Don't live your life far away from God. There are no benefits to living far away from God. You will experience isolation and alienation. The only way to eliminate the gap is in Christ. Draw near!

Brought Near

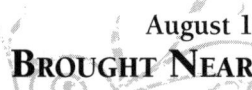

Spiritual Blessing, Separation

"But now in Christ Jesus you who once were far away have been brought near through the blood of Christ." Eph 2:13 (NIV)

I remember one of my childhood family vacations in Florida when my dad decided that we needed to experience the freedom that sailing brings. He had never been on a sailboat before. However, the longer my brother and I played on the beach, the more time my dad had to stare at the sailboats nearby. He convinced my mom that this would be a memorable exploration for our family to enjoy.

After a few minutes of instruction from the sailboat renter, we were charting new waters. My dad was the captain and my mom, brother, and I were the captive audience. The first hour was fun in the sun. Then, darkness came upon the sea rapidly. We were abruptly entangled in a massive storm that made the waters turbulent. The most frightening part of the adventure was the reality that the beach became smaller and smaller. Before long, my whole family was in panic mode, including the captain! I thought we were fashioning our final memory as a family unit. Fortunately, the sailboat renter came to our rescue. If he hadn't, I don't know that I would be here today.

It is a frightening reality to be far from God. There is not a darker or more isolated experience than that of being far from God. The truth is that every Christ follower was once far from God. The wonderful and liberating news is that we have been brought near. God took the initiative to mobilize His rescue package. He provided the atoning work of Jesus on the cross to bring us near.

Contemplate the desperation of being far from God. Look into the mirror first to get an honest glimpse of your proximity to God. Then, make yourself available today to be an agent to bring others near to God.

August 2
THE BLOOD SHED FOR YOU
Blood, Sacrifice, Forgiveness

"In fact, the law requires that nearly everything be cleansed with blood, and without the shedding of blood there is no forgiveness." Heb 9:22 (NIV)

Why blood? Have you ever wondered if God could have brought salvation to fallen man through another means? Jesus even prayed in the Garden of Gethsemane asking if it were possible for the cup of wrath to be passed. Yet, Jesus submitted to the Father's will. Why would blood be necessary to produce redemption?

God is holy, righteous, and pure. There is not a fraction of sin in God's nature or character. He is perfect. God's character demands perfection from His creation. As you know, we live on a broken planet and we inherited the sin nature from Adam. In and of ourselves, we are without hope. There is not a chance that we could ever erase the curse that keeps us from knowing God and coming into His Kingdom.

God took the initiative by demonstrating the necessity of the blood sacrifice in response to providing covering for Adam and Eve after they fell. God killed an animal in order to atone for their sin and to cover their nakedness (Gen. 3:21). Later, God instituted the blood sacrifice through the tabernacle and then the temple. The blood sacrifice is the non-negotiable for the removal of sin.

Jesus is the sinless sacrificial Lamb of God. Jesus became the substitute for our sin. He shed His own blood so that we could be made right with God and experience His abiding peace and live in the assurance of His eternal security. Have you made that transaction? Have you confessed your sin and received God's gift of eternal life? If so, say so! Let somebody know about your spiritual story this week. Testify of God's redeeming love!

GETTING CONNECTED
Church, Connected, Spiritual Maturity

"Now you are the body of Christ, and each one of you is a part of it."
1 Cor 12:27 (NIV)

Did you know that God's plan for your life begins with two invitations? God invites you to believe in the completed work of Jesus on the cross, and God invites you to belong to the local expression of His body, the church.

Do you believe? Have you settled that fact of God's salvation by grace through faith in Jesus alone? If so, then you have been adopted into God's family. You are now a child of the King. Your eternity is secure and your identity is firmly rooted in Christ.

Do you belong? If you believe, then you belong to the family of God. You are a citizen of heaven. However, God invites you to belong to the local visible expression of His body, the church. Notice that I did not ask you if you go to church. I want to know if you belong. Are you connected? Have you become a member of the local church and connected to a small group Bible study where you can know God and grow spiritually with those your age and life stage?

As Bruce Wilkinson says, "What you believe determines where you will spend eternity." Where you belong determines how you will fulfill God's purpose through His local body, the church. Invest your life in a vibrant, healthy, and growing Christ-honoring church that passionately seeks to fulfill the Great Commission. Get connected to one of the small group Bible studies where you can do life with fellow believers. We do better together!

August 4
REMOVING THE BARRIER
Serving, Believing, Church

"For he himself is our peace, who has made the two one and has destroyed the barrier, the dividing wall of hostility, by abolishing in his flesh the law with its commandments and regulations. His purpose was to create in himself one new man out of the two, thus making peace, and in this one body to reconcile both of them to God through the cross, by which he put to death their hostility." Eph 2:14-16 (NIV)

The former complexity of believing and belonging in the Old Covenant has been replaced by the simplicity and sufficiency of the New Covenant that Jesus completed. The paradigm shift involves moving from the ritual of religion to nurturing a vibrant love relationship with God through Jesus Christ.

How will you respond to the removal of the barrier? Jesus has made it possible for you to believe and to belong. Jesus has taken the full wrath of God for your sin. The ultimate price has been paid so that you can have the ultimate relationship that moves through this life and into the life to come.

Your eternal destination has been radically relocated as a result of your faith response in Jesus. Now it is your turn to live in response to His sacrificial gift. Do you believe? Do you belong? Express your faith by serving through the local church. Demonstrate your belief through your behavior. Allocate time to serve Christ through His church. Choose to contribute to the life of your local church. Jesus has removed the barrier to your salvation. Choose to remove the barriers that are keeping you from serving.

PRIVILEGED ACCESS
Access, Jesus, Intimacy with God

"For through him we both have access to the Father by one Spirit."
Eph 2:18 (NIV)

We would be stunned to receive a personal invitation for a private meeting with the president of the United States. Our mind would immediately be bombarded with thoughts of excitement, anticipation, and wonder. We would call, email, and text our friends and family members. Word would get out quickly. Then our focus would be on deciding what to wear for the special occasion and what to say to the Commander-in-Chief.

Now compare that to the reality of the personal invitation from the Creator of the entire universe to daily and perpetually come into His presence. Ponder the treasure of having unrestricted access to our Heavenly Father.

Through Jesus we have been granted access! What a wonderful reality of our relationship with Christ. You don't have to wait in line. You don't have to rigorously step through ritualistic hoops to enter God's presence. You have the unlimited back stage pass. How can this be?

Jesus removed the barrier. Jesus eliminated the wall of hostility. Jesus provided the way. Jesus granted the access. Jesus made us acceptable. Jesus built the bridge.

Does your level of intimacy with God represent the level of access to God made possible by Jesus? Don't waste the privilege!

August 6
THE OLD TESTAMENT TABERNACLE
Tabernacle, Holy Spirit

"Then have them make a sanctuary for me, and I will dwell among them. Make this tabernacle and all its furnishings exactly like the pattern I will show you." Ex 25:8-9 (NIV)

Three chapters of the Bible are given to the details of God's creation activity. Yet, fifty chapters of our Bible are focused on the details of the construction and utilization of the Tabernacle in the Old Testament. The Tabernacle was God's instrument to come to us and for us to come to Him. Remember, the purpose of the Tabernacle was connected to the Old Covenant prior to the New Covenant that Jesus ushered in. Let's take a journey back into the Old Covenant to capture God's redemptive activity.

God revealed to Moses the architectural dimensions, interior design, and precise function of the Tabernacle. Picture over two million Jews encamped in an area that would cover about twelve square miles. If you lived on the outskirts of the encampment, then you would have to walk nearly six miles to bring your sacrifice to the Tabernacle. From the distance, you would be able to view God's glory cloud descending from the sky down into the Most Holy Place.

God demonstrated in the Old Testament through the Tabernacle that His desire is to dwell with His people. As His Tabernacle, God has chosen to dwell in you permanently. God indwells you by the Holy Spirit. Did you know that you are the walking Tabernacle of God's presence (1 Cor 6:19-20)? What kind of Tabernacle are you being for His presence to dwell? Have you given Him full control of your life, your desires, your ambitions, and your fears?

ALTAR OF BURNT OFFERING

Tabernacle, Intimacy, Altar of Burnt Offering

"Build an altar of acacia wood, three cubits high; it is to be square, five cubits long and five cubits wide. Make a horn at each of the four corners, so that the horns and the altar are of one piece, and overlay the altar with bronze."
Ex 27:1-2 (NIV)

When you think about relationships, there are different levels of intimacy. Some relationships are emotionally distant and surfaced whereas some relationships have the capacity to be more consistent and feature an element of closeness. Then there are those relationships where the interaction is meaningful, transparent, and magnetic.

The Encarta Dictionary defines the word intimacy as a close personal relationship; a detailed knowledge resulting from a close or long association. One of my favorite definitions of intimacy is: "in to me you see."

God desires intimacy with you. In the Old Testament, the portrait of intimacy was the formation and utilization of the Tabernacle. God made a way for His people to experience intimacy with Him through a religious relationship.

As you enter the Tabernacle, the first item you encounter is the altar of burnt offering. The New Testament equivalent is the cross of Jesus Christ. Jesus became the ultimate sacrifice for your sin. As you pray through the Tabernacle, spend some time at the "altar of burnt offering" to praise God for His ultimate love gift and for Jesus being willing to pay the penalty for your sin.

August 8

THE BASIN OF WATER

Tabernacle, Intimacy, Basin of Water

"Then the LORD said to Moses, 'Make a bronze basin, with its bronze stand, for washing. Place it between the Tent of Meeting and the altar, and put water in it.'" Ex 30:17-18 (NIV)

The second step to intimacy with God involves "the basin of water" found in the Old Testament Tabernacle. We are touring the furnishings within the Tabernacle. After acknowledging God's gift of salvation through the atoning work of Jesus on the cross as symbolized by the altar of burnt offering, we now move to the basin of water.

The basin of water represents our cleansing provided by the shed blood of Jesus. In our prayer time, we move from praising God for His salvation gift to our confession of sin and receiving His forgiveness.

How can a Christ follower stay clean while living in a dirty world? You stay clean by consecrating your life before the Lord daily. That is not only to be conscious of your sin, but also to specifically confess your sin. "If we claim to be without sin, we deceive ourselves and the truth is not in us. If we confess our sins, he is faithful and just and will forgive us our sins and purify us from all unrighteousness" (1 John 1:8-9 NIV).

Are you obeying instantly and confessing sin immediately? Don't allow sin to linger.

THE TABLE

Intimacy, Tabernacle, Table of the Bread of the Presence

"Make a table of acacia wood--two cubits long, a cubit wide and a cubit and a half high. Overlay it with pure gold and make a gold molding around it. Put the bread of the Presence on this table to be before me at all times." Ex 25:23-24, 30 (NIV)

Where do you go for nourishment? How do you refuel your soul after you have depleted your emotional love tank? Is there a place to receive nourishment?

As we tour the Old Testament Tabernacle, we find the place for nourishment is the Table of the Bread of the Presence. It speaks of communion, fellowship, and nourishment.

As clarified in the New Testament, we don't go to a place for nourishment. Instead, we go to a person. Jesus! He is our Manna from Heaven! He is our daily bread! "Then Jesus declared, 'I am the bread of life. He who comes to me will never go hungry, and he who believes in me will never be thirsty'" (John 6:35 NIV).

In a moment, close your eyes and begin visualizing Jesus as the bread of life. Begin acknowledging His daily provision in your life. Think about seasons when you did not know how you would make it another day and Jesus showed up with abundant resources. Reflect on the transitions in your life where Jesus provided a way for you when there seemed to be no way.

Jesus is the ultimate way-maker! He is all you need! Surrender to His tender care. He will see you through. He has already been where you are going.

August 10
THE GOLDEN LAMPSTAND
Intimacy, Golden Lampstand, Tabernacle

"Make a lampstand of pure gold and hammer it out, base and shaft; its flowerlike cups, buds and blossoms shall be of one piece with it. Then make its seven lamps and set them up on it so that they light the space in front of it. Its wick trimmers and trays are to be of pure gold. A talent of pure gold is to be used for the lampstand and all these accessories. See that you make them according to the pattern shown you on the mountain." Ex 25:31, 37-40 (NIV)

Have you ever driven through a neighborhood in December to behold the captivating path of luminaries? It is so moving to capture the sight of the streets outlined with paper bags illuminated with candles flickering in the night.

The Golden Lampstand illuminated the Holy Place of the Tabernacle. It provided light to the table of the Bread of the Presence and the Altar of Burning Incense. The lampstand had seven oil lamps that provided light for the priest to serve.

A candle consumes itself whereas an oil lamp consumes the oil. Jesus has positioned us to be His light in this dark world. The Holy Spirit is the oil that fuels our gracious illumination. Is your neighborhood a brighter place because of your influence? Is your school or workplace different as a result of allowing the light of Christ to shine through you? "When Jesus spoke again to the people, he said, 'I am the light of the world. Whoever follows me will never walk in darkness, but will have the light of life'" (John 8:12 NIV).

Jesus has made you the light of the world. Don't hide His light. Allow His light to shine through you today in the interactions you embrace as well as the interruptions you face. Is the light of Jesus shining through you? You are a luminary for the Lord.

THE ALTAR OF BURNING INCENSE

Intimacy, Tabernacle, The Altar of Burning Incense, Prayer

"Make an altar of acacia wood for burning incense. It is to be square, a cubit long and a cubit wide, and two cubits high--its horns of one piece with it. Overlay the top and all the sides and the horns with pure gold, and make a gold molding around it. Put the altar in front of the curtain that is before the ark of the Testimony--before the atonement cover that is over the Testimony--where I will meet with you." Ex 30:1-3, 6 (NIV)

In the Holy Place of the Tabernacle, we have identified the Table of the Bread of the Presence and the Golden Lampstand. The next item is the Altar of Burning Incense. God instructed Moses on the details for the Altar.

Take inventory of your life right now. What are you offering up to God? How are you allocating your time and your energy? Are you living to bring glory to God in all things?

As you pray, your prayers rise like burning incense. As you live out your faith in Christ, your life becomes an aroma pleasing to God. As you offer your body to God for His glory, you are expressing worship to God. The Altar of Burning Incense represents your life made by God and for God.

Intercessory prayer and obedience to God demonstrate your passion to please Him and to honor Him with your life and your lips. Does your conversation honor God? Does your conduct move God's heart? May God's smile be your goal today!

August 12
THE CURTAIN

Intimacy, Tabernacle, The Curtain

"Make a curtain of blue, purple and scarlet yarn and finely twisted linen, with cherubim worked into it by a skilled craftsman. Hang it with gold hooks on four posts of acacia wood overlaid with gold and standing on four silver bases. Hang the curtain from the clasps and place the ark of the Testimony behind the curtain. The curtain will separate the Holy Place from the Most Holy Place." Ex 26:31-33 (NIV)

In the Old Testament Tabernacle, only the High Priest could enter the Most Holy Place. He would have to enter through the curtain which separated the Holy Place from the Most Holy Place. The wonderful news is that God has given every believer access into His Presence. How did He provide the way? "And when Jesus had cried out again in a loud voice, he gave up his spirit. At that moment the curtain of the temple was torn in two from top to bottom. The earth shook and the rocks split" (Matt 27:50-51 NIV). The sacrificial death of Christ granted access for every child of God.

God initiated the process to bring us into position to be reconciled to Himself. God gave us His best! God gave His only Son to die in our place and to pay our sin debt. We now have confidence to enter the Most Holy Place through the curtain that Jesus provided (Heb. 10:19-22).

How will you respond to God's redemptive activity? What will be different about your outlook on life? Are you sensing the need to draw near to God? He has done all the work!

The Ark of the Covenant
Intimacy, Tabernacle, The Ark of the Covenant

"Behind the second curtain was a room called the Most Holy Place, which had the golden altar of incense and the gold-covered ark of the covenant. This ark contained the gold jar of manna, Aaron's staff that had budded, and the stone tablets of the covenant." Heb 9:3-4 (NIV)

Being in Christ changes everything. Your position in Christ gives you direct access to God. In the Old Testament Tabernacle, only the High Priest was granted access into the Most Holy Place which contained the Ark of the Covenant (Ex. 25:10-11,22).

Now, every child of God has the privilege of approaching God with freedom and confidence. What makes that possible? Our position in Christ which is a result of our faith in Christ gives us direct access to our Heavenly Father.

When I pray through the Tabernacle each morning I choose to stop speaking to God and simply wait before Him as I enter the Most Holy Place. I often quote Samuel by saying, "Speak, LORD, your servant is listening" (1 Samuel 3:10). It is at this time that God begins to place people on my heart that He wants me to intercede for. Also, this is the specific time that God will bring truths from His Word to my attention that He wants me to focus on for the day.

Carve out some time to spend unhurried time alone with God. Sometimes the most spiritual thing you can do is to simply be still before God and wait for Him to speak. How long should you wait before the Lord? Wait long enough for Him to reveal His thoughts to you.

August 14
APPREHENDED BY THE GOSPEL

Prisoner, Gospel, Soulwinning, Lordship

"For this reason I, Paul, the prisoner of Christ Jesus for the sake of you Gentiles--"
Eph 3:1 (NIV)

My dad was given a ten year prison sentence for committing five consecutive DUI's during my childhood. As you can imagine, anytime I hear the word "prisoner", my heart rate escalates. I remember going to see my dad in prison for the first time and seeing him hand-cuffed and shackled in his prison orange jump suit. That memory is fixed in my mind.

When Paul, who is writing from prison to the saints in Ephesus, continues his epistle by identifying himself as a prisoner, my attention is arrested.

Paul was captured by the Gospel of Jesus Christ. He viewed himself as one bound to Christ for the sake of others. His life was fully surrendered to the Lordship of Christ. Therefore, Paul willingly gave his life to the vision of seeing Gentiles come to faith in Jesus Christ. His loyalty was to Christ. His devotion was to Christ. He lived to please the One who sacrificed His life for others.

Have you been captured by the Gospel of Jesus? Has the Good News apprehended you? Whose life will be influenced for Christ as a result of your loyalty to Him? Don't be imprisoned by fear. You have been armed with the greatest news that has eternal implications. God wants you to participate with Him in setting prisoners free.

THE MIRACULOUS MYSTERY

Mystery, Salvation, Soulwinning

"This mystery is that through the gospel the Gentiles are heirs together with Israel, members together of one body, and sharers together in the promise in Christ Jesus." Eph 3:6 (NIV)

When we hear the word mystery, we usually think of something that doesn't make sense or add up. We use the word to denote something strange or unfathomable. However, in the language of the New Testament, mystery refers to something hidden in God, but not hidden from God. God is all-knowing, all-seeing, and all-powerful. There is nothing hidden from His sight.

God determines our level of comprehension of His revelation. He chooses what to reveal and what to conceal. God unveils the mystery to Paul by revelation. That is, God unveiled the truth of the gospel to Paul. That which was once hidden from Paul became visible to Paul by God's revelation.

Under the inspiration of the Holy Spirit, Paul conveys to the saints at Ephesus the reality found within the mystery. Paul is saying that the mystery is that through the gospel both Gentiles and Jews come together in the Body of Christ and share in the promise. The wall of separation has been demolished by Christ. The separation wall collapsed and the unifying bridge was built.

Are you embracing the mystery of the gospel? Have you decided to live in light of God's revelation? God's revelation is realized in our participation in the divine nature (2 Peter 1:4).

August 16
SERVANT OF THE GOSPEL
Servant, Serve, Jesus

"I became a servant of this gospel by the gift of God's grace given me through the working of his power." Eph 3:7 (NIV)

The resounding phrase that reverberates throughout the line at Luby's is, "Serve you? Serve you?" As you sift through the many options available to you, you continually hear these soothing words from those serving the food.

Jesus is the ultimate example of servitude. "For even the Son of Man did not come to be served, but to serve, and to give his life as a ransom for many" (Mark 10:45 NIV). Jesus was willing to wash feet and to feed the hungry. Jesus served humanity. Jesus is the epitome of servitude. As followers of Christ, we are to do what Jesus did.

Paul identified himself as a servant of the gospel. His disposition was that of placing the needs of others before his own. He lived his life to benefit others. His motivation was to populate Heaven by getting the gospel to as many people as possible in his lifetime. Paul was passionately focused on spreading the Good News.

Where's your towel? Are you wearing it under your chin as though it were a bib declaring your desire to be served? Or can you honestly say that the towel is lapped over your forearm in the position to identify you as a servant? Seize opportunities today to serve others. Serve you? Serve you?

BRINGING CLARITY TO A CONFUSED WORLD

Clarity, Gospel, Jesus

"Although I am less than the least of all God's people, this grace was given me: to preach to the Gentiles the unsearchable riches of Christ, and to make plain to everyone the administration of this mystery, which for ages past was kept hidden in God, who created all things." Eph 3:8-9 (NIV)

Have you ever met someone who was great and they didn't know it? In other words, they were simply being who God made them to be and didn't build a tower of recognition for themselves.

Paul was great and didn't know it. He understood that his usability was proportionate to God's dispensing of immeasurable grace. His validation came through recognition of his desperation for God's mercy and grace.

Only through Paul's humility and dependency upon God was he enabled to hyper-focus on the mission of bringing clarity to the mystery of the gospel for the people in need of salvation. Paul stayed connected to the reality of God's grace. His past was a constant reminder of God's amazing grace.

Does your behavior bring clarity to the gospel for those watching your life? Are you drawing people to Christ or repelling them from Christ? May the fog lift and the gospel clearly go forth through opportunities God gives you this week to make Jesus known. Is there any greater vision to give your life to than that of bringing the gospel to the nations? Begin right where you are. Make plain the mystery of the gospel.

August 18

CONNECTING TO THE CHURCH

Church, Body of Christ, Serve

"His intent was that now, through the church, the manifold wisdom of God should be made known to the rulers and authorities in the heavenly realms, according to his eternal purpose which he accomplished in Christ Jesus our Lord."
Eph 3:10-11 (NIV)

Who makes up the church? According to Paul, the church is made up of those who are in Christ. Their reality is that of being saints, blessed, chosen, adopted, redeemed, forgiven, included, sealed, and secure. As believers in the completed work of Jesus on the cross, we are His body, the church.

The church is both local and global. The church has local expressions such as Champion Forest Baptist Church in Houston, Texas. The church also has a global expansion inclusive of all believers on the planet regardless of ethnicity. Jesus is the Head of the church and the One who creates unity in the midst of diversity.

Peter confessed that Jesus was the Christ (Mt. 16:18). Jesus acknowledged that He would build His church, not on Peter, but on the God-revealed confession. Jesus is the Christ!

God's desire is to manifest His manifold wisdom through the church. God's glory will be revealed through the Body of Christ, the church. In other words, God's church is the world redemption center.

Are you connected to the local church? Are you serving through the ministry of the local church? Make yourself available for God's use. Become a conduit of blessing for the One who bestows the blessings.

SUFFERING ON PURPOSE
Suffering, Salvation, Jesus

"I ask you, therefore, not to be discouraged because of my sufferings for you, which are your glory." Eph 3:13 (NIV)

The thought of someone suffering for you is a bit unsettling. What would motivate someone to suffer for you? The Bible calls it love. "To this you were called, because Christ suffered for you, leaving you an example, that you should follow in his steps" (1 Peter 2:21 NIV). Jesus was willing to die so that we could spend eternity with Him in heaven. Jesus suffered to benefit our forever.

Paul follows in Jesus' steps by giving his life for others. Paul's love for the saints in Ephesus is demonstrated by his perpetual concern for their spiritual maturity and unity. He is willing to suffer imprisonment, and at the same time, secure a measurable influence in their spiritual development. His suffering is for their glory. His suffering will be redeemed as they express their God-given potential.

Have you ever tried to measure the depth of Jesus' love for you? He really died for you. He gave His life so that you could live a life now that embodies His peace and a life forever that expresses His eternal nature. His suffering purchased your salvation. His resurrection secured your eternal life.

August 20

Staying Connected to the Source

Source, Prayer, Kneeling

"For this reason I kneel before the Father," Eph 3:14 (NIV)

Kneeling keeps you standing. Why would Paul assume the posture of kneeling in prayer on behalf of the saints in Ephesus? Paul had already surrendered his life and agenda to God. Kneeling was simply an outward expression of his inward position in Christ.

The Father is worthy of your humility and dependence. He alone is worthy of your passionate adoration and worship. Your heavenly Father is the source of life. He rescued you from the hell-bound path you were on. The Father willingly gave His best, Jesus, to take your place upon the cross. Your sin debt has been paid in full. Your salvation has been purchased by God's sinless and spotless Son, Jesus.

Now, what are you in need of? What do you need that your Heavenly Father has not provided? God is more than enough. His resources are unlimited. His generosity is immeasurable.

Has anything driven you to your knees lately? Have you been kneeling before the Father on behalf of someone in your sphere of influence? When you come to the place of desperation, you will find that your Heavenly Father has already been working. He is not surprised by your surprises. Nothing ever occurs to God. He already knows.

BEING IN GOD'S FAMILY

Family, Body of Christ, Church

"...from whom his whole family in heaven and on earth derives its name."
Eph 3:15 (NIV)

Family is God's idea. God is pro-family. Regardless of your upbringing, whether you grew up in a stable Christian environment or a broken home, you can be adopted into God's spiritual family.

God's family is known as the Body of Christ, the church. God's desire is for you to believe in His Son, Jesus. Once you place your faith in the completed work of Jesus on the cross, you become part of God's family. As you examine God's global family, you will detect instantly that God loves variety. He specializes in using all kinds of people to reach all kinds of people.

What kind of family member are you being within God's family? Are you adding value to what God is doing? Have you discovered your God-given gift mix? Are you serving through the ministry of God's local family, the church?

There is so much more that God wants to do through you than you can imagine. Begin asking God to reveal to you the next step that He wants you to take. Once God reveals the next step, be willing to obey instantly. It just may be something that will cause you to totally and completely depend upon His provision. God always provides for those He guides.

August 22
INNER STRENGTH
Strength, Power, Holy Spirit

"I pray that out of his glorious riches he may strengthen you with power through his Spirit in your inner being." Eph 3:16 (NIV)

God never intended for you to live the Christian life outside of His power. In fact, it is impossible to live the Christian life without God's power. For the believer, it is not a matter of being without God's power, but a matter of not appropriating the power God gives you at salvation.

Activation of God's power comes by trusting that God has the power to do what He has promised. Here is an example of a promise that every believer can claim. "But you will receive power when the Holy Spirit comes on you; and you will be my witnesses in Jerusalem, and in all Judea and Samaria, and to the ends of the earth" (Acts 1:8 NIV).

You do not ask God to give you something you already have in Christ. God promises that you will receive power when the Holy Spirit comes on you simultaneously at conversion and that you will be His witness locally, regionally, nationally, and globally.

At salvation, you received the Person of the Holy Spirit. He moved in as a permanent resident into His temple, your body. God gives you an inner strength so that you can fulfill the Great Commission in your generation. His strength is made perfect in your weakness. Be strengthened in His power to fulfill His mission.

ABIDING RELATIONSHIP

Abiding Relationship, Affirmation

"...so that Christ may dwell in your hearts through faith." Eph 3:17 (NIV)

We are by nature acceptance magnets and approval addicts. We want others to admire us and to affirm us. I heard about a basketball coach who instructed his players to always acknowledge their teammate who passed the ball to them which enabled them to make the shot. One of the players responding by asking the coach, "What if they aren't looking?"

The coach responded, "They'll look!"

Why would a basketball player who passed the ball off for a teamate to make a shot want to be acknowledged for his selflessness? He longs for acceptance, approval, admiration, and affirmation.

The ultimate demonstration of acceptance and approval is Jesus dying on the cross for our sins and being raised to life for our justification. The ultimate actualization of His acceptance and approval is the fact that He permanently dwells in our heart.

Jesus moves in so that we can have an abiding relationship with Him. "I am the vine; you are the branches. If a man remains in me and I in him, he will bear much fruit; apart from me you can do nothing" (John 15:5 NIV). To abide means to dwell and to take up residence and to feel at home. Is Jesus at home in your life? Have you given Him access to every area of your life?

August 24
Indescribable Love
Love, Jesus

"And I pray that you, being rooted and established in love, may have power, together with all the saints, to grasp how wide and long and high and deep is the love of Christ, and to know this love that surpasses knowledge--"
Eph 3:17-19 (NIV)

Is it possible to comprehend the love of Christ? Think about the person in your life who you feel currently loves you more than anyone else on the planet. Now that's a barge overflowing with love! However, that amount does not even come close to the love Christ has for you.

Interestingly, Paul clarifies that for a believer to grasp the love of Christ requires God's power. You must have the power of God to live the Christian life. You must also employ God's power to be able to grasp the width, length, height, and depth of Christ's love.

- *"But God demonstrates his own love for us in this: While we were still sinners, Christ died for us." Romans 5:8 (NIV)*
- *"How great is the love the Father has lavished on us, that we should be called children of God! And that is what we are! The reason the world does not know us is that it did not know him."*
  1 John 3:1 (NIV)

Have you come to know the love of Christ by experience? Are you allowing His love for you to impact how you treat others?

ABOUNDING FULLNESS

Fullness in Christ, Desire

"...that you may be filled to the measure of all the fullness of God."
Eph 3:19 (NIV)

Commercials, billboards, and newspaper advertisements remind us how food-driven our society has become. We are always asking about and searching for our next meal. Then we eat as though it is our last meal and then announce, "I'm full!"

Have you been there? Have you ever been so full that it hurt? God has given us an appetite for food. Of course, we are to use wisdom in making the right decisions regarding the food we intake.

There's another appetite that God has given us that cannot be satisfied by food. At salvation, God gives us a new nature that passionately desires His agenda, His desires, and His mission. His fullness becomes our reality.

When you receive God's gift of eternal life by placing your faith in Jesus alone for salvation, you receive the fullness of God in Christ. You are complete in Christ. Salvation is an event where you receive the fullness of Christ. Sanctification is a process where Christ expresses His fullness through you.

Have you fully surrendered your life to Jesus? Are you allowing Him to be Lord over every area of your life? Will the fullness of Christ be evident in your life today?

August 26
MORE THAN ENOUGH
Sufficiency of Christ, God's Character

"Now to him who is able to do immeasurably more than all we ask or imagine, according to his power that is at work within us, to him be glory in the church and in Christ Jesus throughout all generations, for ever and ever! Amen." Eph 3:20-21 (NIV)

There's more to explore! You are finite and God is infinite. You are limited. God is unlimited. You are vulnerable. God is invincible. You were born. God is eternal. He has always been and He will always be. You are flawed. God is perfect. You are weak. God is strong. You become. God is.

In Christ, you receive all that He is. The challenge is to discover what you have in Christ. The greater your awareness of His Presence in your life, the greater the results. It's not that you need more of Christ. He wants more of you. You have all of Christ. Does He have all of you?

God can do more than you ask or imagine. God can do more than you can fathom. He is able. He is able to bring victory and deliverance into any area of your life. God is able to help you overcome any harmful habit, hurt, or hang-up. He is able to bring relief to a broken heart. He is able to lift you up when you are feeling down. God is able to take an impossible situation and produce a miracle.

Spend a few moments in prayer asking God to heighten your awareness of His Presence in your life. Look to see where He is at work today so that you can join Him. There's more to explore! There's more to God than what you currently know.

Are you facing anything right now that is bigger than you? God is able!

THE FIRST NOT GOOD

Alone, Relationship

"The LORD God said, 'It is not good for the man to be alone. I will make a helper suitable for him.'" Gen 2:18 (NIV)

Is it possible to be in a crowd of thousands and still feel alone? We overload our lives with the confetti of activities and saturate our schedule with deadlines and diversions. We tend to overcommit and anesthetize our pain through the avenue of busyness. Constantly and persistently we are running from the lurking shadow of aloneness.

Have you identified the first "not good" in the Bible? After all that God had made and affirmed that it was good, He created man and then acknowledged that it was not good for man to be alone.

What's wrong with man being alone? Why would God have created man with a gap? There must be something to this aloneness that is counterproductive. Man being alone must not be a good thing in God's economy. Man alone may be prone to fill the void with something unacceptable or unhealthy.

God made man for relationship. God's antidote to Adam's aloneness was the creation of Eve. Adam experienced the "not good" of being alone until he met Eve. God designed Adam with a gap that only Eve could fill.

Marriage is a beautiful portrait of two becoming one flesh. Did you know that in temptation, Satan seeks to make the two, who have become one, two again? His goal is to create division, dysfunction, and distraction.

Jesus alone brings us into harmony with God. God has built us for relationship and companionship. How are your relationships?

August 28

Christian Conduct

Conduct, Integrity, Character

"As a prisoner for the Lord, then, I urge you to live a life worthy of the calling you have received. Be completely humble and gentle; be patient, bearing with one another in love." Eph 4:1-2 (NIV)

What does a life worthy of the calling you have received look like? It looks like humility, gentleness, patience, and forbearance in action. It is not enough to know to do right. You must place into action what you know. Application is the activation of faith. Jesus described that kind of life as a life of obedience to God's Word (Mt. 7:24-27).

Jesus authenticates that hearing God's Word is not enough. You must put feet to your faith by putting God's Word into practice. Application determines whether you are building on sand or on the rock. James affirms the teaching of Christ: "In the same way, faith by itself, if it is not accompanied by action, is dead" (James 2:17 NIV). Give your faith traction by putting your faith into action.

Is your faith dead or alive? Take a close look at your conduct both in private and in public. What does your conduct declare about your faith? Are you obeying what you know? Is your conduct consistent with the character of Christ? Live a life worthy of the calling you have received in Christ. Allow humility, gentleness, patience, and forbearance to become obvious realities in your life.

EXHIBITING THE CHARACTER OF CHRIST

Character, Unity

"Make every effort to keep the unity of the Spirit through the bond of peace."
Eph 4:3 (NIV)

Reputation is based on how others perceive you. Character is what you are in private. Character is revealed in crisis. Or another way to say it is that crisis reveals character.

Unity flows out of the character of Christ being developed in the life of a believer. God uses every circumstance and situation to build Christ's character in us. Christlikeness is a process.

- *"For those God foreknew he also predestined to be conformed to the likeness of his Son, that he might be the firstborn among many brothers." Romans 8:29 (NIV)*
- *"Not only so, but we also rejoice in our sufferings, because we know that suffering produces perseverance; perseverance, character; and character, hope." Romans 5:3-4 (NIV)*

God works to conform us into the likeness of Christ. God allows us to experience suffering which is vital in forming the character of Christ in us. God sprinkles godly people into our lives to model Christlikeness as well. Then there are times when we make poor decisions concerning the people we allow to influence our lives. The Bible identifies them as bad company (1 Cor. 15:33).

Are you allowing God to have His way in your life? Do you view suffering from God's perspective? What kind of people are you being influenced by? Is the character of Christ being formed in you?

August 30
THE UNITY OF COMMUNITY
Community, Unity, Diversity

"There is one body and one Spirit-- just as you were called to one hope when you were called--one Lord, one faith, one baptism; one God and Father of all, who is over all and through all and in all." Eph 4:4-6 (NIV)

What do you have in common with those in your sphere of influence? If you look closely, you will be able to discover some common ground even with those different from you.

God loves variety. Take a snapshot of creation. View the landscape, wildlife, and aquatic life, and you will quickly ascertain the variety God values.

God specializes in diversity. There are no two people alike. There are more than 12,000 people groups on our planet of 6.7 billion people. The wonder of God is displayed when He brings unity in the midst of diversity.

For example, there are over 400,000 churches in the United States. Each church is unique and diverse. Yet, God produces unity in the midst of diversity. That unity is the common unity that forms community within the local fellowship of believers.

Spend some time today looking for God's evidence of unity in the midst of diversity. Try to detect the common unity that God creates among those who have been adopted into His family.

CONNECTED TO THE BODY OF CHRIST
Connected, Body of Christ

"From him the whole body, joined and held together by every supporting ligament, grows and builds itself up in love, as each part does its work." Eph 4:16 (NIV)

Is anyone tracking you spiritually? Are you in a weekly environment where you can know and be known, love and be loved, care and be cared for? In other words, are you connected to a small group in weekly Bible study?

In this verse, God is describing the Body of Christ, the church, connected to each other in close relationship. The connectivity is realized by every person supporting each other, growing together, and serving together.

We do better together. God wants His family walking together in close proximity. There is a danger in being loosely affiliated with a church. God wants you to be deeply rooted and connected to His local body through a small group Bible study. In the church that I serve in, we call our small group Bible study environments Life Groups. These weekly small group environments allow people to study God's Word, share burdens, celebrate victories, and encourage spiritual maturity.

Are you connected? Are you supporting, growing, and serving together with other believers your age and in your life stage? Get connected!

September 1
ORDERING YOUR WORLD
Organization, Order

"Moses' father-in-law replied, 'What you are doing is not good. You and these people who come to you will only wear yourselves out. The work is too heavy for you; you cannot handle it alone.'" Ex 18:17-18 (NIV)

Where there is order, there is fruitfulness.

God is a God of order, not chaos. After leading the children of Israel out of Egypt, Moses faced an administrative nightmare. He was spending all of his time trying to solve all the problems among the people. All day long, he would sit and listen to each side of the story as people lined up for miles awaiting his hearing.

Fortunately, God sent Jethro to the rescue. Jethro was willing to speak truth into Moses' life and confront his leadership paralysis. Jethro challenged Moses to delegate to entrusted men. "Have them serve as judges for the people at all times, but have them bring every difficult case to you; the simple cases they can decide themselves. That will make your load lighter, because they will share it with you" (Ex 18:22 NIV).

Does that sound advice minister to you? "That will make your load lighter, because they will share it with you." Who is sharing your load? Are you connected to a church organized to mobilize you in ministry? Are you doing life with a small group committed to sharing your load and allowing you to share your life?

Order your life. Make needed adjustments to simplify your life so that you can focus on what really matters in this life.

FOCUS YOUR LIFE
Focus, Spiritual Maturity

"Instead, speaking the truth in love, we will in all things grow up into him who is the Head, that is, Christ." Eph 4:15 (NIV)

You become what you focus on.

Diffused light is weak. Focused light can cut steel. God blesses a life that is focused on His mission. His mission involves knowing, growing, and going. God wants you to know Him personally and intimately through an abiding relationship with Jesus. God wants you to grow in Him through prayer, Bible study, and connecting with other believers in a small group. God wants you to go into the world shining His light and sharing His love.

Is your life focused? Joshua focused his life and his family on serving the Lord (Josh. 24:15). Jesus focused His life on doing the will of God and finishing His work (John 4:34). Paul focused his life on forgetting what was behind and straining toward what was ahead (Phil. 3:13-14).

Is your life fragmented? Are you trying to keep too many plates spinning? Maybe God wants you to downsize from thirty spinning plates to three. Fix your eyes on Jesus. Jesus is the author and finisher of your faith (Heb. 12:2). Focus your life on knowing Jesus, growing in your love relationship with Him, and going for Him to make Him known throughout the earth. Eternity is at stake! Every moment matters!

What do you need to stop doing? What do you need to start doing? What do you need to continue doing? Live for God!

September 3
THE MOTION OF SPIRITUAL MATURITY
Spiritual Maturity, Christlikeness

"It was he who gave some to be apostles, some to be prophets, some to be evangelists, and some to be pastors and teachers, to prepare God's people for works of service, so that the body of Christ may be built up until we all reach unity in the faith and in the knowledge of the Son of God and become mature, attaining to the whole measure of the fullness of Christ." Eph 4:11-13 (NIV)

The goal of your spiritual maturity is Christlikeness.

Until you become just like Christ, you are not through. You are in the process of becoming who you are in Christ. Are you on a path of spiritual growth and development? Are you being intentional about becoming more and more like Christ?

If you are not in motion to become more like Jesus, then you are creating a commotion within the Body of Christ. Each person in the Body of Christ must grow personally. Each person must be in motion being equipped for service and being encouraged towards spiritual maturity.

Where are you heading? What are you aiming for? How are you going to achieve spiritual maturity? Do you have an action plan? "Like newborn babies, crave pure spiritual milk, so that by it you may grow up in your salvation, now that you have tasted that the Lord is good" (1 Peter 2:2-3 NIV). Unity and spiritual maturity are indicators of your Christlikeness.

CHARACTERIZED BY STABILITY

Stability, Spiritual Maturity

"Then we will no longer be infants, tossed back and forth by the waves, and blown here and there by every wind of teaching and by the cunning and craftiness of men in their deceitful scheming." Eph 4:14 (NIV)

Spiritual maturity will ensure stability.

God blesses the pursuit of spiritual maturity. His strength and stability become evident in the devoted life of the child of God. What are you striving to become? How are you allocating your time and energy? What eternal benefits are you producing by your daily decisions?

We combat three enemies: the world, the devil, and the flesh. These three are anti-God. They are opposed to God's agenda. God's purposes do not align with this world's system. Thus, to become a fully devoted follower of Christ will require a life of resistance. Just like in physical fitness, without resistance there is no growth.

God desires for every believer to grow deeper. Stability comes when you are grounded in God's Word and anchored to the Rock, Jesus. Instability is the result of spiritual immaturity and lethargy. God wants you to know Him more. Paul affirmed his pursuit of knowing Christ intimately. "I want to know Christ and the power of his resurrection and the fellowship of sharing in his sufferings, becoming like him in his death" (Phil 3:10 NIV).

Is your current walk with God characterized by stability? Are you building your life on the deep truths of God's Word?

September 5
SPIRITUAL HEALTH AND GROWTH
Spiritual Maturity, Health

"I planted the seed, Apollos watered it, but God made it grow." 1 Cor 3:6 (NIV)

Where there is health, there is growth.

A healthy body will grow. A healthy believer will grow spiritually. A healthy church will grow both numerically and spiritually.

You determine the level of participation in the process of maturation. God honors your devotion to daily spiritual disciplines. You also have the wonderful opportunity to assist in the maturation process in others.

God is the source of growth. You have the privilege of participating and cooperating in the growth process. You join God in your personal spiritual development. You also join God in investing in the spiritual development of other Christ followers. "And the things you have heard me say in the presence of many witnesses entrust to reliable men who will also be qualified to teach others" (2 Tim 2:2 NIV).

Maturation results in multiplication. As you grow, you assist others in their growth. Moses mentored Joshua. Elijah mentored Elisha. Naomi mentored Ruth. Daniel mentored Shadrach, Meshach, and Abednego. Paul mentored Timothy.

Does your life evidence spiritual health? Are you growing? How have you invested in another believer's maturation?

DEVELOPING SPIRITUAL HABITS

Spiritual Habits, Discipleship

"All Scripture is God-breathed and is useful for teaching, rebuking, correcting and training in righteousness, so that the man of God may be thoroughly equipped for every good work." 2 Tim 3:16-17 (NIV)

How do you become all that God has created you to become? What habits are essential to reaching your God-given potential? Over the next five days, let's open the spiritual toolbox and examine five habits necessary for obtaining a lifestyle of Christlikeness.

Habit #1: A daily intake of God's Word

You are what you eat. If you consistently fuel your body with junk food, then your level of energy and performance will be hindered. You will be like a marathoner running with ankle weights.

Soul food is mandatory for spiritual growth. Nourishing your soul requires a daily intake of God's Word. God has revealed Himself through His Word, the Bible. Your Creator has written the owner's manual for your life. "Your word is a lamp to my feet and a light for my path" (Psalm 119:105 NIV).

Let me give you some tracks to run on to assist you in your daily intake: 1) Secure a translation of the Bible that speaks the way you listen. 2) Read four chapters of the Bible per day. In one year, you will have read through the entire Bible. 3) Write down one verse from each of the four chapters that really speaks to your heart. 4) Meditate on the four verses and then write an action step to employ today. Develop this spiritual habit to bring glory to God.

September 7
DAILY COMMUNION THROUGH PRAYER
Spiritual Habits, Daily Disciplines, Prayer

"Very early in the morning, while it was still dark, Jesus got up, left the house and went off to a solitary place, where he prayed." Mark 1:35 (NIV)

How's your prayer life? Are you spending unhurried time alone with God? Your ministry effectiveness will never rise above the level of your daily intimacy with God.

Habit #2: A daily practice of meeting with God in prayer

Jesus is the ultimate model to follow. He demonstrated the daily habit of communing with God in prayer. He exemplified the daily habit of an abiding relationship with God.

Notice that Jesus got up early in the morning to connect with God. When are you at your best? Are you a morning person or a night-owl? Whenever you are at your best is really the best time to have a special meeting with God in prayer.

Where is the best place for you to connect with God in prayer? In his book, *Sacred Pathways*, Gary Thomas identifies nine different ways that people best connect with God. For example, you may best connect with God in solitude, or outdoors, or with worship music playing. Discover what works for you. What environment helps you to focus on God in prayer?

Let me give you some tracks to run on to assist you in your daily practice of meeting with God in prayer: 1) Set up a time. Make a daily appointment with God. 2) Select a place. Find an environment that enables you to focus. 3) Secure a plan. There's nothing like having unbroken fellowship with God.

CONNECTING WITH OTHER BELIEVERS
Spiritual Habits, Daily Disciplines, Fellowship

"And let us consider how we may spur one another on toward love and good deeds." Heb 10:24 (NIV)

The Christian life is not a solo flight. God calls us into a vertical relationship with Himself and a horizontal relationship with other believers and then the lost world. An isolated believer is a disconnected believer. To reach your full redemptive potential requires embracing our next habit from our spiritual toolbox.

Habit #3: A vital connection to other growing believers

Upon the transaction of turning your life over to Jesus Christ, you were adopted into God's family. Now that you are connected to God in Christ, it is time to connect with other growing believers. One of the most effective environments for connecting with other growing believers is through a small group Bible study. This environment enables you to do life with people your age and your life stage. It creates the opportunities to do life with one another.

- *"Be devoted to one another in brotherly love. Honor one another above yourselves."* Romans 12:10 (NIV)
- *"Live in harmony with one another."* Romans 12:16 (NIV)
- *"Accept one another, then, just as Christ accepted you, in order to bring praise to God."* Romans 15:7 (NIV)

Are you connected to other growing believers? If not, why not? Pray right now and make a commitment before to the Lord to get connected to a small group Bible study.

September 9
ACTIVATING YOUR FAITH
Spiritual Habits, Daily Disciplines, Faith

"In the same way, faith by itself, if it is not accompanied by action, is dead."
James 2:17 (NIV)

Habit #4: A practical application of my faith in daily life

Information without application is an abomination. God's Word is to be activated through constant use. Every believer should be a reader, a hearer, and a doer of God's Word. Your faith in Christ is to be expressed through action. How is your faith currently being evidenced through your conversation and conduct? Are you drawing others to Christ or repelling them from Christ by your behavior?

- *"Anyone, then, who knows the good he ought to do and doesn't do it, sins." James 4:17 (NIV)*
- *"Therefore, prepare your minds for action; be self-controlled; set your hope fully on the grace to be given you when Jesus Christ is revealed." 1 Peter 1:13 (NIV)*

We know more than we are doing. We have more information than we are activating. Let's seek to apply what we already know. Sometimes your faith will be tested. Practical application of your faith in the midst of adversity and seasons of uncertainty can intensify your witness. God will put your faith on display. It's all for your good and for His glory.

SERVING OTHERS

Spiritual Habits, Daily Disciplines, Serving

"From him the whole body, joined and held together by every supporting ligament, grows and builds itself up in love, as each part does its work." Eph 4:16 (NIV)

Are you on a path of obtaining Christlikeness? Are you progressing in your faith? Daily spiritual habits enable you to mature spiritually.

Habit #5: The exercise of my faith through ministry and service.

You are never more like Jesus than when you are serving. Jesus is the ultimate example of servitude. If you ever wonder how you should live, how you should conduct your business, and how you should invest your life, just emulate the life of Christ.

- *"For even the Son of Man did not come to be served, but to serve, and to give his life as a ransom for many." Mark 10:45 (NIV)*

Ministry opportunities abound. Be sensitive to the ministry moments God brings into your view. Sometimes the ministry moments are simply an interruption that becomes an opportunity to meet a practical need. Sometimes the ministry opportunities are long term commitments to employ your spiritual gifts in specific ministry environments through the local church.

Your faith is exercised each time you serve others. It is not natural to give your life away. It is not natural to put the needs of others before your own. Service is supernatural and a byproduct of an abiding relationship with Jesus.

What are you giving your life to? Are you living to benefit others?

September 11
BENEFITS OF SERVING
Benefits of Serving, Serving

"Then will I purify the lips of the peoples, that all of them may call on the name of the LORD and serve him shoulder to shoulder." Zeph 3:9 (NIV)

Serving produces spiritual growth.

As you serve God by serving others, you develop spiritual muscles. Spiritual growth produces serving, and serving produces spiritual growth. God does not want you to stay where you are in your spiritual development. God wants you to grow spiritually and to demonstrate your spiritual growth through serving.

Serving involves placing the needs of others before your own (Phil. 2:3-4). To be other-centered is to follow the example of Jesus and to give evidence of spiritual growth. Serving is a process of allowing the life of Christ to be realized through your life to others.

Selfishness is an indication of spiritual immaturity. Selflessness is an indication of spiritual maturity. Do you model selfishness or selflessness? Will you diligently serve others today or persistently seek to be served by others?

Spend a few moments right now expressing your availability to God for His use. Allow Him to have His way in your life today. Even when you don't feel like serving others, faith it until you feel it.

SERVING TO EXPAND THE KINGDOM

Benefits of Serving, Kingdom Growth

"Those who accepted his message were baptized, and about three thousand were added to their number that day." Acts 2:41 (NIV)

Serving produces numerical increase.

As you grow, you serve. As you serve, you grow. In the midst of your serving, God brings others into the equation. He will bring people into your path to give you an opportunity to serve them and to meet their needs. At other times, God will bring people into your life to help meet your needs.

Serving puts feet to your prayer life. Serving gives evidence to a watching world that you are living to benefit others. When you give your life away through selfless service, God multiplies your impact.

Remember, you are never more like Jesus than when you are serving. As you live out the Christ-centered life in our self-absorbed world, God will use you to bring others into the Kingdom. That's right! Heaven's population is multiplied by your faithfulness in serving the Living God.

Keep investing in the lives of others. Continue to shine His light and share His love through serving. God will add to our number. God will draw people to know His love as you serve sacrificially.

September 13
CARRY YOUR CORNER
Benefits of Serving, Responsibility, Unity

"Some men came, bringing to him a paralytic, carried by four of them. Since they could not get him to Jesus because of the crowd, they made an opening in the roof above Jesus and, after digging through it, lowered the mat the paralyzed man was lying on. When Jesus saw their faith, he said to the paralytic, 'Son, your sins are forgiven.'" Mark 2:3-5 (NIV)

Serving produces practical unity.

Are you carrying your corner? What if one of the men decided not to carry his corner? Would the paralytic have made it to Jesus and received healing? Jesus saw their faith and healed the paralytic. Each man was carrying his corner.

When you serve through the ministry of the local church with others, God produces the practical unity to fulfill His plan. God honors the unified body of believers who are committed to being on mission with Him.

Unity is a mark of spiritual maturity. Jesus exemplified unity in His relationship with our Heavenly Father and with His disciples. In His priestly prayer, Jesus prayed that we would demonstrate that same unity (John 17:22-23).

Have you been brought to complete unity with the local expression of the Body of Christ, His Church? Is there anyone you need to make things right with? Don't hesitate to do the right thing in order to honor God and to bring unity to His Body. Do whatever it takes to ensure unity. Serving the one who offended you will produce practical unity.

"From him the whole body, joined and held together by every supporting ligament, grows and builds itself up in love, as each part does its work." Eph 4:16 (NIV)

Serving produces organizational stability.

Who benefits from your serving? The answer to that question changes everything. Once you decide to serve the Lord, your life becomes intentional. You begin to live on purpose. In serving Jesus, you are drawn to connect with His family. Jesus is in charge!

Stability flows from the Head, Jesus, down to the members of His Body, the church. The church is connected and held together by every supporting member. The design is for the church to grow and build itself up as each member does his or her part. Serving together as a team produces organizational stability.

The local church is an organism that God grows as we serve. Stability is the byproduct of a church family serving together in unity. Unity produces stability.

Does that describe the church you are connected to? Are you soaking or serving? Are you a spectator or a participator? Are you a consumer or a contributor?

September 15
PERSONAL REWARD
Benefits of Serving, Reward

"Whatever you do, work at it with all your heart, as working for the Lord, not for men, since you know that you will receive an inheritance from the Lord as a reward. It is the Lord Christ you are serving." Col 3:23-24 (NIV)

Serving produces personal reward.

What motivates you to serve? Do you serve for immediate recognition or eternal reward? Who is calculating your service? Jesus is the Rewarder! As you live to please Him and serve Him, Jesus rewards you personally both now and in the life to come. As Bruce Wilkinson says, "Your belief determines where you spend eternity. Your behavior determines how you will spend eternity."

Jesus rewards your obedience in serving Him. "Behold, I am coming soon! My reward is with me, and I will give to everyone according to what he has done" (Rev. 22:12 NIV). One day you will be rewarded for what you have done for Jesus. None of your service will go unnoticed.

One feature of serving is that you don't serve in order to be rewarded, but as a result of being graced with salvation and the capacity to serve. Serving is an outflow of your gratitude for all that God has done for you. Serving is your way of expressing appreciation to God for His abundant mercy and grace. Yet, God continues to lavish you with blessings even after salvation.

"It was he who gave some to be apostles, some to be prophets, some to be evangelists, and some to be pastors and teachers, to prepare God's people for works of service, so that the body of Christ may be built up until we all reach unity in the faith and in the knowledge of the Son of God and become mature, attaining to the whole measure of the fullness of Christ." Eph 4:11-13 (NIV)

Your identity in Christ propels your mobility for Christ.

Knowing who you are in Christ keeps you living on purpose. Your secure identity in Christ enables you to represent Christ and do works of service that benefit others. Are you being equipped to use your gifts and abilities to serve? Have you found your specific area of service? Have you been mobilized?

Express your faith. If you have not turned your life over to Christ, do so now by expressing your faith in Jesus alone. Once you are saved, you become a child of God and you are graciously adopted into His family.

Explore your options. God loves variety. There are countless ways to serve God through the ministry of the local church. Be sure to explore the options available to you at the local church where you are connected. It is prudent to tryout a ministry opportunity and see if it fits your gift mix. If it does not fit you, then try another one.

As John Maxwell says, "You will be most valuable where you add the most value."

September 17
MULTIPLY MINISTRY EFFECTIVENESS
Ministry, Effectiveness

"...so that the body of Christ may be built up until we all reach unity in the faith and in the knowledge of the Son of God and become mature, attaining to the whole measure of the fullness of Christ." Eph 4:12-13 (NIV)

Multiply your ministry effectiveness.

God's plan is for the body of Christ to connect and grow. Every member of the body matters! Every member is a minister! As you serve through the ministry of the local church, you can multiply your ministry effectiveness by inviting others into the process.

Extend your ministry. Do you have anyone shadowing you in order to do what you do? Are you grooming anyone to participate in the ministry that you are involved in? You can multiply your ministry effectiveness by inviting others to come alongside you for a season. Eventually, your ministry will be extended through them. Do you have someone in mind?

Jesus modeled the ministry of multiplication. He allowed his twelve disciples to shadow Him so that they could do what He did. When Jesus died, rose from the dead, and then ascended to heaven, the ministry of multiplication continued through the disciples. They took the ministry and message of Jesus to the ends of the earth through inviting others into the process. In fact, you have been invited into the process.

HARMONIOUS RELATIONSHIPS

Harmony, Unity, Relationships

"Live in harmony with one another. Do not be proud, but be willing to associate with people of low position. Do not be conceited." Romans 12:16 (NIV)

Harmony moves the heart of God.

God desires that you live in harmony with Him and with others. Live your life rightly related to God through an abiding relationship with Jesus. The byproduct of that relationship is harmony with others. You cannot have a right relationship with God without having a right relationship with others.

Harmony is a choice. You can choose God's way and allow Him to express His life through you. Or you can reject God's path that leads to harmony by embracing the option that Satan presents. The enemy to harmony is disharmony. Satan seeks to poison relationships in order to foster disharmony. But, God calls believers into action. "Finally, all of you, live in harmony with one another; be sympathetic, love as brothers, be compassionate and humble" (1 Peter 3:8 NIV).

What path will you take today? Are you going to ensure harmony with God and with others? Will your conversation and conduct demonstrate a life of harmony? It's your choice!

September 19
WORLDLINESS OR GODLINESS
Worldliness, Righteousness, Godliness

"Religion that God our Father accepts as pure and faultless is this: to look after orphans and widows in their distress and to keep oneself from being polluted by the world." James 1:27 (NIV)

There is a perpetual tug on the believer's life to go back to being a slave to sin instead of a slave to righteousness. Satan seeks to lure you to compromise your convictions and seek pleasure through worldliness.

Staying clean while living in a dirty world becomes your daily challenge. God wants you to keep yourself from being polluted by the world. You cannot pursue godliness and worldliness at the same time. Your divided loyalty will not yield the fruit of righteousness.

Advertisements in our culture are designed to convince you that you need something that you currently don't have. They always over-promise and under-deliver. The products and services advertised never completely satisfy.

Worldliness contaminates our relationships with others as illustrated in Paul's letter to the church at Corinth. They were placed in a seedbed of wordliness.

> • *"Brothers, I could not address you as spiritual but as worldly--mere infants in Christ. I gave you milk, not solid food, for you were not yet ready for it. Indeed, you are still not ready. You are still worldly. For since there is jealousy and quarreling among you, are you not worldly? Are you not acting like mere men?" 1 Cor 3:1-3 (NIV)*

Is your life marked by worldliness or godliness? What kind of life are you portraying to a watching world?

CONVERSION FAITH

Conversion, Faith, Salvation

"You, however, did not come to know Christ that way. Surely you heard of him and were taught in him in accordance with the truth that is in Jesus."
Eph 4:20-21 (NIV)

Have you come to know Christ? When did that eternal transaction take place in your life? Where were you when you recognized your sinfulness and your desperate need for Jesus to come to your rescue?

Conversion is the redemptive work of God in a person's life. Your conversion is the event of being delivered from the kingdom of darkness and brought into the kingdom of light. Your conversion is the event of being adopted into God's family and being filled with the Holy Spirit. "But we ought always to thank God for you, brothers loved by the Lord, because from the beginning God chose you to be saved through the sanctifying work of the Spirit and through belief in the truth" (2 Thess 2:13 NIV).

Have you trusted in Jesus alone for salvation? "That if you confess with your mouth, 'Jesus is Lord,' and believe in your heart that God raised him from the dead, you will be saved. For it is with your heart that you believe and are justified, and it is with your mouth that you confess and are saved" (Romans 10:9-10 NIV). Don't delay the decision to have a right relationship with God through faith in Jesus.

September 21
PUTTING OFF YOUR OLD SELF
Old Self, Sin Nature

"You were taught, with regard to your former way of life, to put off your old self, which is being corrupted by its deceitful desires." Eph 4:22 (NIV)

Does your struggle with sin end at conversion? If so, why do believers sin? The penalty for your sin has been paid in full by the atoning work of Christ on the cross. Yet, the presence of sin is still contaminating our culture and inviting believers to compromise their convictions.

Paul acknowledged that the old self is in a state of decay. The fleshly corruption creates an inner civil war for the child of God.

- *"I know that nothing good lives in me, that is, in my sinful nature. For I have the desire to do what is good, but I cannot carry it out. For what I do is not the good I want to do; no, the evil I do not want to do--this I keep on doing." Romans 7:18-19 (NIV)*
- *"So I say, live by the Spirit, and you will not gratify the desires of the sinful nature. For the sinful nature desires what is contrary to the Spirit, and the Spirit what is contrary to the sinful nature. They are in conflict with each other, so that you do not do what you want." Gal 5:16-17 (NIV)*

What a celebration to behold for your deliverance from your former way of life! Put off the old self. There's a new you in view through the redemptive activity of God. The victory has been won!

PUTTING ON THE NEW SELF

New Self, Sanctification, Holiness

"...and to put on the new self, created to be like God in true righteousness and holiness." Eph 4:24 (NIV)

You are in the process of becoming who you are in Christ.

In Christ, you are a saint, blessed, chosen, adopted, redeemed, forgiven, included, sealed, and secure. Your new self is a spiritual reality in Christ that becomes evident practically as you live out your faith. "Therefore, my dear friends, as you have always obeyed--not only in my presence, but now much more in my absence--continue to work out your salvation with fear and trembling, for it is God who works in you to will and to act according to his good purpose" (Phil 2:12-13 NIV).

God expects you to work out what He has worked in. You are complete in Christ. Your new self in Christ has been given everything you need to embrace the life of Christ in your daily lifestyle. Take off the old and express the new.

What adjustments need to be made in your schedule, your energy allocation, and your financial stewardship to become who you are in Christ? What is keeping you from expressing the life of Christ practically through your daily interactions? Are your current habits helping you to develop and demonstrate your new self?

September 23
BELIEVING RIGHT
Beliefs, Behavior, Spiritual Maturity

"...to be made new in the attitude of your minds;" Eph 4:23 (NIV)

Does it really matter what you believe? To live right, you must believe right. Your behavior is a direct reflection of your beliefs. In order to live to please God, your beliefs must align with God's revelation.

Spiritual growth requires being made new in the attitude of your mind. Nurturing your mind with God's Word informs your beliefs and transforms your behavior (Rm. 12:1-2). "Finally, brothers, whatever is true, whatever is noble, whatever is right, whatever is pure, whatever is lovely, whatever is admirable--if anything is excellent or praiseworthy--think about such things" (Phil 4:8 NIV).

Do you know what you believe and why you believe? Can you articulate with clarity the convictions you hold about life, death, sin, holiness, and eternal life? Are your beliefs in alignment with God's revelation?

Allow God to groom you and grow you. Place yourself in a weekly Christ exalting worship experience with other believers, and then seek to develop your beliefs through a small group Bible study.

THE JERSEY YOU WEAR

Jersey, Identity, Integrity

"You were taught, with regard to your former way of life, to put off your old self, which is being corrupted by its deceitful desires; to be made new in the attitude of your minds; and to put on the new self, created to be like God in true righteousness and holiness." Eph 4:22-24 (NIV)

Live up to the jersey you wear.

Our culture is saturated with a passion for sports. From the stands to the playing field, excitement and anticipation flow like a white water rafting river. The current is swift as fans and players hyper-focus on the game at hand.

It's all about the jersey you wear. There is a team you are pulling for. You sacrifice for that team. You cheer on and promote that team. Your loyalty is lavished on that team. You are an authentic fan.

When you become a child of God, you receive a new jersey. Once you are adopted into God's family you are fitted with the Jesus jersey. Now you are playing to please Jesus. You are representing Jesus on this broken planet. You are robed in His righteousness and blessed with a new identity.

Are you living up to the jersey you wear? Do those closest to you know what team you are on? Is it evident to your neighbors, schoolmates, and co-workers that your loyalty is to Jesus and His game plan?

September 25

SLIPPERY SLOPES

Slippery Slopes, Temptation, Holiness

"For we know that our old self was crucified with him so that the body of sin might be done away with, that we should no longer be slaves to sin--because anyone who has died has been freed from sin." Rom. 6:6-7

Why do we tend to see how close we can get to the edge without falling? What is there about us that is drawn to taking risks? Why do we draw the line in the sand right on the edge of compromise?

God wants us to live a life of holiness and righteousness. His desire is for us to be Christlike. In other words, God wants every believer to be a fully devoted follower of Christ.

Satan has the opposite agenda. He wants you to doubt God's Word and deny God's way. Satan uses deception to try to get you to drift from God and take a shortcut to pleasure and to idolize instant gratification.

What's the key to victory? Avoiding slippery slopes! Don't see how close you can get to the fire without getting burned. Don't flirt with sin and think you will come away unharmed. Draw the line in the sand far from the edge. Sin never delivers what it promises!

Doing Life Together

Body Life, Unity, Forgiveness

"Therefore each of you must put off falsehood and speak truthfully to his neighbor, for we are all members of one body." Eph 4:25 (NIV)

Are you really living or just existing? In our instant-access world, there is a propensity to become robotic and just go through the motions. Information overload anesthetizes us to the daily grind of life. Often we miss opportunities to connect with others on a deeper level. Why? Because we are in a hurry to get to the next item on our "to do" list. We become consumed with maneuvering through the domino line up of tasks and neglect being relational with God and with others.

Jesus gave His life to bring us life. He rose from the dead to usher in our salvation. He saved us from our sin and from ourselves. But it doesn't end there. Jesus is building His Kingdom through His Body, the church. If you are a child of God, then you have been adopted into His family and you are now part of His Body. Together, we are all members of one body, His Body.

Now that we are family, we must learn how to do life together. In his letter to the church at Ephesus, Paul presents some essentials for doing life together. If the Body of Christ is going to function efficiently and effectively in order to affect the nations, then we must learn how to serve Jesus together.

Is there anyone in His Body with whom you are currently at odds with? Is there anyone you need to extend forgiveness to in order to do life together? What are you waiting for? Make things right. Call them. Email them. Text them. Write them. Go visit them. Do whatever it takes to keep a right relationship with Jesus and His Body. You will never go wrong doing right!

September 27
DIFFUSING ANGER
Anger, Devil, Righteous Indignation

"'In your anger do not sin': Do not let the sun go down while you are still angry, and do not give the devil a foothold." Eph 4:26-27 (NIV)

He lost his cool! She flipped! What were they thinking? Can you believe what he said? Did you ever dream we would see this day? What happened?

Anger is either good or bad. If your anger is righteous indignation against sin and immorality, then it is good. If your anger is a reaction to not getting your way or a result of your impatience, then it is bad.

Jesus expressed anger when the Temple had been contaminated by the money changers instead of being a house of prayer for all nations. His anger was righteous indignation exposing their blatant irreverence toward the things of God. Yet, Jesus did not let the sun go down on His anger. In other words, He expressed his anger in a manner that confronted sin and prompted righteousness.

- *"In your anger do not sin; when you are on your beds, search your hearts and be silent." Psalm 4:4 (NIV)*
- *"A fool gives full vent to his anger, but a wise man keeps himself under control." Prov 29:11 (NIV)*

Have you exhibited healthy anger through the avenue of righteous indignation? Or have you fertilized unhealthy anger which grows into bitterness, rage, and envy? Hate what God hates. Love what God loves.

RELEASING THE FOOTHOLD

Foothold, Temptation

"...and do not give the devil a foothold." Eph 4:27 (NIV)

I asked one of my dear pastor friends, Dr. Bob Anderson, this question: Why are so many pastors falling? He responded, "When you have temptation without opportunity, you are safe. When you have opportunity without temptation, you are safe. But when temptation and opportunity meet, you are in trouble."

To give the devil a foothold is to give the devil an opportunity. It is to give the devil an occasion to act. It is giving the devil a platform in your life to propel his agenda. You give the devil a foothold by allowing him room to occupy. When you give him an inch, he takes a mile. His goal is not to make you swim away from God. The devil just wants to get you to drift and to float down a lazy river. He knows that the undercurrent will cause you to subtly drift from God.

In the context of Ephesians, don't allow your anger to simmer. Neutralize your anger before you go to bed. If you allow your anger to swirl, then you have given the devil an opportunity to operate. Don't give him a foothold.

- *"Submit yourselves, then, to God. Resist the devil, and he will flee from you." James 4:7 (NIV)*
- *"Be self-controlled and alert. Your enemy the devil prowls around like a roaring lion looking for someone to devour." 1 Peter 5:8 (NIV)*

Don't give the devil any real estate. Post a sign that says to the devil, "You are trespassing on my Father's territory!"

September 29
MEETING NEEDS
Blessing, Generosity

"He who has been stealing must steal no longer, but must work, doing something useful with his own hands, that he may have something to share with those in need." Eph 4:28 (NIV)

You may have disengaged from this verse since you immediately recognized that you are not a thief. You are not stealing. You, in fact, have a strong work ethic and would never dream of stealing. So what is God trying to say to you through this verse?

God wants you to embrace a strong work ethic so that you can be a blessing to others. His desire is for you to work diligently so that you can share with those in need. You ought to get all the education you can so that you can excel and be the best at what God called you to do. Why? Because God deserves your best!

However, it is not about you! It is about positioning yourself in alignment with God's priorities so that you can be a blessing to others. God does not bless you so that you can funnel the blessings into your self-centered pursuits. God blesses you in order to expand your capacity to bless others.

Do you have anything left to share with those in need? Statistics show that the average American lives on 120% of his or her income. That means we spend more than we make. Maybe it's time to re-think the American dream.

The life God blesses is the life given to being a blessing to those in need. You are blessed to be a blessing!

GRIEVING THE HOLY SPIRIT

Holy Spirit, Grieving

"And do not grieve the Holy Spirit of God, with whom you were sealed for the day of redemption." Eph 4:30 (NIV).

Have you ever wrestled a kinked water hose? You squeeze the nozzle and the water just drips out. You are trying to wash the car, but the water pressure is absent. The kink in the hose restricts the flow of water. The kink inhibits the flow.

That's what resident sin does to the Holy Spirit living in you. Remember, you are the walking tabernacle of God's Presence. Your body is the temple of the Holy Spirit. He lives in you permanently. He took up residence at the moment of your conversion. He indwells you. When you allow sin to enter, you kink the flow of the Holy Spirit.

You know how it feels to grieve. Grief hurts. It causes distress and intense pain. Grief hinders your ability to function at an optimum level. When you give sin an entry to your life at any level, you grieve the Holy Spirit who lives in you.

Sin offends the Holy Spirit. Sin restricts the flow of the Holy Spirit in and through your life. The presence of sin repels the presence of the Holy Spirit. The Bible teaches us to grieve over our sin. The presence of sin in our lives should grieve us to the point of godly sorrow and then repentance (2 Cor 7:10 NIV). Who is grieving, you or the Holy Spirit?

October 1
BENEFICIAL TALK
Speech, Conversation, Edification

"Do not let any unwholesome talk come out of your mouths, but only what is helpful for building others up according to their needs, that it may benefit those who listen." Eph 4:29 (NIV)

Our words are irrevocable. Once spoken, words penetrate like an arrow on the bull's-eye. Our words have immense power. In fact, they carry the power of life and death.

Paul is admonishing the believers at Ephesus to use their conversation to build up each other. He wants them to be mindful of their words. Beneficial words are those which are helpful and build others up according to their needs. Unwholesome talk does not honor God and does not benefit the Body of Christ.

In those times when you speak before you think, God wants you to employ damage control. Yes! You must go to the one you have offended and seek forgiveness. Within the Body of Christ, this is a true mark of spiritual maturity. Be willing to say, "I'm sorry and I was wrong!"

> • *"If you have been trapped by what you said, ensnared by the words of your mouth, then do this, my son, to free yourself, since you have fallen into your neighbor's hands: Go and humble yourself; press your plea with your neighbor!" Prov 6:2-3 (NIV)*

Unity is at stake! It's worth the agony to have a right relationship with God and with others. When words infuse a relational distance between you and someone else, allow God to speak words of healing and restoration through you to bring about reconciliation. Stay broken and humble before God and watch Him accomplish great things through you.

FORGIVING OTHERS

Forgiving Others, Forgiveness, Trust

"Be kind and compassionate to one another, forgiving each other, just as in Christ God forgave you." Eph 4:32 (NIV)

Forgiveness is immediate; trust takes time.

When you have been wounded, the last thing you want to do is extend forgiveness. You naturally want them to pay for the pain they have inflicted. You want them to suffer the consequences of their actions. Somehow you want them to serve a sentence for their wrong doing.

For the follower of Christ, forgiveness is not optional. Extending forgiveness is commanded and modeled by Jesus. In fact, you cannot have a right relationship with God unless you have a right relationship with others. You cannot have a right relationship with others unless you have a right relationship with God.

Read the verse one more time and focus on the words, "just as." How can you be kind and compassionate to someone who has wounded you? How can you forgive someone who has inflicted pain in your life? "Just as" in Christ God forgave you!

Until you forgive, you will be imprisoned. Until you forgive, you will be shackled by the past. Take God at His Word and extend forgiveness "just as" in Christ God extended forgiveness to you.

October 3
RECEIVING FORGIVENESS
Forgiveness, Jesus, God's Forgiveness

"Therefore, there is now no condemnation for those who are in Christ Jesus, because through Christ Jesus the law of the Spirit of life set me free from the law of sin and death." Romans 8:1-2 (NIV)

When Jesus forgives you, you are completely forgiven.

Jesus died to pay your sin debt in full. He provided for the total and comprehensive forgiveness of your sin. As a result, you are now free to live the abundant life that Jesus saved you for.

Through Jesus Christ, the activity of the Holy Spirit has set you free from the activity of sin and death. The operation of the Holy Spirit has set you free from the operation of sin and death. You are free to reign in this life by allowing Jesus to reign in your life.

Have you received God's forgiveness by trusting in Christ alone for salvation? Are you walking in the freedom Christ provides? Pray and ask God to reveal any fraction of sin in your life so that you can immediately confess it and claim His forgiveness. You are forgiven because Christ took God's wrath for your sin. Yes! He loves you that much. And He loves every person you will interact with today that much! Mercy came running like a prisoner set free!

IMITATION

Imitation, Loving Others, Revelation

"Be imitators of God, therefore, as dearly loved children..." Eph 5:1 (NIV)

How do you imitate someone you can't see? Imitation is proportionate to self revelation. You can only imitate God at the level at which God is willing to reveal Himself. The wonderful news is that God has revealed Himself to us in nature, in the Bible, and in Jesus.

- *"For since the creation of the world God's invisible qualities--his eternal power and divine nature--have been clearly seen, being understood from what has been made, so that men are without excuse." Romans 1:20 (NIV)*
- *"Consequently, faith comes from hearing the message, and the message is heard through the word of Christ." Romans 10:17 (NIV)*
- *"Jesus answered: 'Don't you know me, Philip, even after I have been among you such a long time? Anyone who has seen me has seen the Father. How can you say, "Show us the Father"?'" John 14:9 (NIV)*

So what is God like? Jesus! What is Jesus like? God! In fact, Jesus is God. To know Jesus is to know God. In order for us to imitate God, we must know Jesus.

Here's a good start for you. Imitate God by loving others the way God has loved you. Imitate God by being conformed into the likeness of Christ. Imitate God by being holy in all you do.

October 5
FRAGRANT OFFERING
Fragrant Offering, Influence, Obedience

"Be imitators of God, therefore, as dearly loved children and live a life of love, just as Christ loved us and gave himself up for us as a fragrant offering and sacrifice to God." Eph 5:1-2 (NIV)

What kind of fragrance are you emitting? Jesus released an aroma pleasing to God through His life of instant obedience and selfless love. Jesus made God smile. His loyalty to God and to fulfilling God's agenda produced a fragrant offering that moved the heart of God.

- *"For we are to God the aroma of Christ among those who are being saved and those who are perishing." 2 Cor 2:15 (NIV)*

Once you are in Christ, His life is lived through you. As you surrender to His Lordship and allow Him to bear His fruit through your life, you become the aroma of Christ to God. Your life becomes a perpetual offering to God that brings Him joy, honor, and glory.

As the fragrance of Christ emanates from your yielded life, not only does God receive pleasure from your offering, but other people benefit as well. Others are watching you and how you live out the Christian life in the roadways of life. You have the potential to influence others to Christ by your fragrant offering. Who will come to Christ this week because of your instant obedience and selfless love?

PURITY AND POWER

Sin, Holiness, Purity

"But among you there must not be even a hint of sexual immorality, or of any kind of impurity, or of greed, because these are improper for God's holy people." Eph 5:3 (NIV)

How much dirt does it take to contaminate drinking water? At what point would you consider the water improper for consumption? It wouldn't take much, would it?

God takes sin seriously. There is no room in the life of a child of God for sin. Sin is as repulsive to God as a diesel mechanic on a white couch. Sin contaminates.

Some things are simply improper for a follower of Christ.

"The acts of the sinful nature are obvious: sexual immorality, impurity and debauchery; idolatry and witchcraft; hatred, discord, jealousy, fits of rage, selfish ambition, dissensions, factions and envy; drunkenness, orgies, and the like. I warn you, as I did before, that those who live like this will not inherit the kingdom of God." Gal 5:19-21 (NIV)

God calls us to be holy.

"But the fruit of the Spirit is love, joy, peace, patience, kindness, goodness, faithfulness, gentleness and self-control. Against such things there is no law. Those who belong to Christ Jesus have crucified the sinful nature with its passions and desires." Gal 5:22-24 (NIV)

What adjustments do you need to make to remove the improper items from your life? How close are you to being pure? Without purity, there is no power!

October 7
LUMINARIES FOR THE LORD
Influence, Light, Luminaries

"For you were once darkness, but now you are light in the Lord. Live as children of light." Eph 5:8 (NIV)

Salvation is an event, followed by a process. At the moment of your salvation, you are delivered from the kingdom of darkness and placed in the kingdom of light. You instantly become light in the Lord. Instantaneously, you become a child of light. Your new identity in Christ demands a new productivity for Christ.

- *"You are the light of the world. A city on a hill cannot be hidden."* Matt 5:14 (NIV)
- *"Therefore, if your whole body is full of light, and no part of it dark, it will be completely lighted, as when the light of a lamp shines on you." Luke 11:36 (NIV)*

Live as a child of the light. In Christ, you are the light of world. Your whole body is full of light. Shine like stars in the universe. You have become a luminary for the Lord! Your assignment is to shine brightly in this dark world that God strategically placed you in. Regardless of your home environment, school environment, work environment, or recreation environment, God has launched you into those environments to be His luminary.

Are you living as a child of light? Is it evident to those in your sphere of influence that you are a luminary for the Lord?

PLEASING GOD

Pleasing God, Obedience

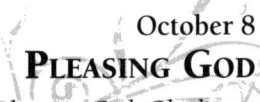

"...and find out what pleases the Lord." Eph 5:10 (NIV)

We tend to live our lives trying to please others. Just about the time we feel as though we have reached the pinnacle of pleasing others, they change their mind. After hosting Dr. Robert Smith of Beeson Divinity School for a few days, he shared with me an amazing concept. He said, "Don't fall in love with the Body (Body of Christ); fall in love with the Head. The Body is fickle. They will be singing 'Hosanna' on Monday and then 'crucify' on Thursday. The Father is faithful."

Does anything else matter more than living to please God? Is there any other pursuit that supersedes that of pleasing God? What are you currently giving your life to?

- *"And we pray this in order that you may live a life worthy of the Lord and may please him in every way: bearing fruit in every good work, growing in the knowledge of God." Col 1:10 (NIV)*
- *"On the contrary, we speak as men approved by God to be entrusted with the gospel. We are not trying to please men but God, who tests our hearts." 1 Thess 2:4 (NIV)*

Make God's smile the goal of your life today. You may want to place a smiley face sticker on your dashboard near the speedometer in your car to serve as a daily reminder of why you exist. You are alive to make God smile.

October 9
LIVING WISELY

Living Wisely, Decisions, Stewardship

"Be very careful, then, how you live--not as unwise but as wise..."
Eph 5:15 (NIV)

Over the years I have experimented with different ways to enhance my daily intimacy with God. The most vital element in my spiritual development has been a consistent intake of God's Word. Sometimes I commit to reading a chapter of Proverbs each day for an entire year. Thus, I read the book of Proverbs all the way through each month. That's been an incredible adventure. The following verses are my favorite from the fourth chapter of Proverbs.

- *"Above all else, guard your heart, for it is the wellspring of life. Put away perversity from your mouth; keep corrupt talk far from your lips. Let your eyes look straight ahead, fix your gaze directly before you. Make level paths for your feet and take only ways that are firm. Do not swerve to the right or the left; keep your foot from evil." Prov 4:23-27 (NIV)*

There are so many options for you to embrace in this world. Countless paths await your selection. Careless living will grant you unlimited choices that will never deliver what they promise. The writer of Proverbs, under the inspiration of the Holy Spirit, alerts us to the higher path of living wisely.

Would you be willing to spend a few moments reflecting on this passage from Proverbs and begin taking inventory of your life? Are you guarding your heart? Is your speech laced with purity? Is your vision focused on the way that brings honor to God? Are you taking paths that are pleasing to God? Do you consistently avoid evil? Live wisely!

INTERRUPTIONS

Interruptions, God's Invitation

"Then Peter said, 'Silver or gold I do not have, but what I have I give you. In the name of Jesus Christ of Nazareth, walk.'" Acts 3:6 (NIV)

An interruption is often God's invitation.

Life can be extremely hectic and chaotic. We are bombarded with snail mail, email, text messages, and cell phone calls. Our lives are marked by perpetual busyness. In the midst of being on the go all the time, we encounter interruptions. Sometimes an interruption occurs when we are on our way to engage in a meaningful experience such as corporate worship. Peter and John had that kind of interruption.

They were about to enter the place of worship. Peter and John were almost stepping through the temple gate when they were interrupted by a beggar. The unnamed beggar snatched the moment by asking them for money. Peter and John could have easily ignored the man, but they chose to turn the interruption into an opportunity to make Jesus known.

Jesus is not asking you to be something you are not. Jesus is not asking you to give something you do not have. He wants you to be who you are in Christ and be willing to give what you have in order to bless others.

Peter and John gave the beggar so much more than money could buy. They were channels of blessing which provided spiritual and physical healing to the man who had been crippled since birth. Because of their willingness to turn an interruption into an opportunity, the man experienced healing and began walking and jumping and praising God in the temple.

Be ready for an interruption today. It just might be God's invitation for you to join Him in His activity.

October 11
MOTIVES MATTER
Motives, Commitment

"When Simon saw that the Spirit was given at the laying on of the apostles' hands, he offered them money and said, 'Give me also this ability so that everyone on whom I lay my hands may receive the Holy Spirit.'" Acts 8:18-19 (NIV)

Motives matter to God.

Simon had practiced sorcery prior to becoming a Christ follower. Simon himself believed and was baptized and then followed Philip everywhere. His motives may have been pure when he gave his life to Christ, but his motives were contaminated soon thereafter. He wanted the power of God without a commitment to purity before God. Simon wanted to purchase the ability to lay hands on people in order for them to receive the Holy Spirit.

> • *"Peter answered: 'May your money perish with you, because you thought you could buy the gift of God with money! You have no part or share in this ministry, because your heart is not right before God. Repent of this wickedness and pray to the Lord. Perhaps he will forgive you for having such a thought in your heart.'"*
> *Acts 8:20-22 (NIV)*

God wants to use you in His redemptive activity. God wants you to permeate His love and radiate His light. However, God does not honor impure motives.

> • *"Religion that God our Father accepts as pure and faultless is this: to look after orphans and widows in their distress and to keep oneself from being polluted by the world." James 1:27 (NIV)*

Stay close and clean!

"Those who had been scattered preached the word wherever they went." Acts 8:4 (NIV)

Bloom where God has planted you.

Are you radiating God's light right where you are? Do those in your sphere of influence know who you are and whose you are?

Maybe you are in a very difficult environment. Maybe you have been placed in a dark and dreadful situation. Instead of asking God why, ask God what He would like to do in you and through you right where you are.

God allowed persecution to come to the church at Jerusalem which scattered them throughout Judea and Samaria. Notice how the spread of the Gospel is directly proportionate to the commission of Acts 1:8.

- *"But you will receive power when the Holy Spirit comes on you; and you will be my witnesses in Jerusalem, and in all Judea and Samaria, and to the ends of the earth."* Acts 1:8 (NIV)

Sometimes God allows difficulties to come into our lives in order for us to move out of our comfort zone. God's passion is for the world to know Jesus personally and intimately. You are His ambassador. You are His missionary.

You are now entering the mission field. Be intentional.

October 13
REVEALING GOD'S GRACE
Reveal, Grace, Witness

"But the Lord said to Ananias, 'Go! This man is my chosen instrument to carry my name before the Gentiles and their kings and before the people of Israel. I will show him how much he must suffer for my name.'" Acts 9:15-16 (NIV)

Light reveals what darkness conceals.

We are finite. God is infinite. We have limited understanding. God is omniscient. We tend to view people as they are. God sees what people can become.

Ananias feared the consequences of engaging a persecutor such as Saul at any level. Yet, God was inviting Ananias to participate in the redemptive process. God was bringing Ananias into the opportunity of bringing light into the darkness of Saul's lifestyle. Ananias was to be the light bearer. However, fear dominated the path.

God knows a person's heart. Nothing is hidden from God's sight. In His grace, God sees what a sinful person can become in Christ. God had chosen the least likely candidate to be His chosen instrument. Saul's life would be radically transformed. Will Ananias be willing to be used of God as light to reveal what darkness conceals? Is Ananias willing to release his fear of Saul and embrace God's power to transform a persecutor into a preacher of the Gospel?

Is there anyone in your life whom you feel is beyond reach? Maybe God wants to use you as His light to reveal what darkness has concealed. Maybe God wants you to participate in the redemptive process. Are you available for God's use? Do you believe that God can use you?

REMOVING SCALES

Obedience, Salvation, Soulwinning

"Then Ananias went to the house and entered it. Placing his hands on Saul, he said, 'Brother Saul, the Lord--Jesus, who appeared to you on the road as you were coming here--has sent me so that you may see again and be filled with the Holy Spirit.'

Immediately, something like scales fell from Saul's eyes, and he could see again. He got up and was baptized, and after taking some food, he regained his strength. Saul spent several days with the disciples in Damascus." Acts 9:17-19 (NIV)

Where Satan puts a period, God puts a comma.

Is there anyone whom God cannot change? Is there a person alive on planet earth without hope? God always has the final say. God is always at work. In fact, God works the night shift. While you were sleeping, God was working.

Saul received both spiritual sight and physical sight. He identified with Christ through baptism, ate, regained his strength, and then reconnected with the disciples in Damascus. Saul experienced the transforming power of God. God now wants Saul to become a transforming agent in the Kingdom of God.

Do you currently have a Saul in your life? Is there someone close to you with whom you have been burdened for? Does someone near you need radical transformation? Are you willing to be involved in God's process of removing the scales?

Place your "yes" on the altar. Make yourself available for God's use. Pray for God to soften the heart of the one you are burdened for. Anticipate God's invitation. Watch God do a redemptive work.

October 15
GOD'S PURPOSE IN SUFFERING
Purpose, Suffering, Sovereignty of God

"But the Lord said to Ananias, 'Go! This man is my chosen instrument to carry my name before the Gentiles and their kings and before the people of Israel. I will show him how much he must suffer for my name.'" Acts 9:15-16 (NIV)

We know that God wants us to permeate His love and radiate His light. We know that God wants us to be holy because He is holy. However, we don't normally get as excited about the thought of suffering.

God's purpose for Paul included suffering. His life was marked by the road of adversity. In his second letter to the church at Corinth, Paul articulated his path of suffering.

- *"Five times I received from the Jews the forty lashes minus one. Three times I was beaten with rods, once I was stoned, three times I was shipwrecked, I spent a night and a day in the open sea, I have been constantly on the move. I have been in danger from rivers, in danger from bandits, in danger from my own countrymen, in danger from Gentiles; in danger in the city, in danger in the country, in danger at sea; and in danger from false brothers. I have labored and toiled and have often gone without sleep; I have known hunger and thirst and have often gone without food; I have been cold and naked."* 2 Cor 11:24-27 (NIV)

Are you in a season of suffering? Are you facing a difficult situation? If God allows something to come into your life, His purpose will prevail. God has the final say.

Let me encourage you to make room in your life for mystery. Trust God with the circumstances in your life that just don't make sense.

SEIZING OPPORTUNITIES

Seizing Opportunities, Wisdom

"Be very careful, then, how you live--not as unwise but as wise, making the most of every opportunity, because the days are evil." Eph 5:15-16 (NIV)

What does the abundant life look like in the 21st Century? How can the follower of Christ maximize the time granted on planet earth?

Step 1: Walk circumspectly. Be alert to the reality of your environment. Be aware of your surroundings. Pay close attention.

> • *"Watch your life and doctrine closely. Persevere in them, because if you do, you will save both yourself and your hearers."*
> *1 Tim 4:16 (NIV)*

Step 2: Detect evil. Recognize that the days are evil. Satan pushes his agenda and mobilizes his demonic activity.

> • *"Be self-controlled and alert. Your enemy the devil prowls around like a roaring lion looking for someone to devour." 1 Peter 5:8 (NIV)*

Step 3: Make the most of every opportunity. Every moment matters. Make every moment count. Sometimes the opportunities we miss are the interruptions God permits.

> • *"His divine power has given us everything we need for life and godliness through our knowledge of him who called us by his own glory and goodness." 2 Peter 1:3 (NIV)*

What adjustments do you need to make in your attitude and in your actions in order to seize the moments God gives you?

October 17
LISTENING TO GOD

Listening to God, Obedience

"Then a cloud appeared and enveloped them, and a voice came from the cloud: 'This is my Son, whom I love. Listen to him!'" Mark 9:7 (NIV)

Are you listening? We have the ability to engage in selective listening. We hear what we want to hear. We choose to tune in or to tune out.

Peter, James, and John had a mountaintop experience with Jesus on Mt. Transfiguration. They were privileged to hear the voice of God affirming His Son and our Savior, Jesus. God's direct word to them was an imperative instructing them to listen to Jesus. Listening is equivalent to obeying. Thus, to listen to Jesus is to obey Him (1 John 2:3).

Can you hear me now? God is a God who speaks. He has revealed Himself to us through His Son and through Scripture. To know Jesus is to know God. To grow in your knowledge of Jesus is to grow in your understanding of His Word. Revelation demands a response. God expects instant obedience.

How do you know if you are really listening to God? Is your life marked by obedience to God's Word? Obedience to God's Word is a clear indicator of your level of listening to God.

Is your life too noisy to hear from God? Is your schedule too busy to hear from God? The men and women who have been greatly used of God have ensured unhurried time alone with God each day. They intentionally carved out time to be still and simply listen for God's voice.

Discerning God's Will
God's Will, Discernment, Obedience

"Therefore do not be foolish, but understand what the Lord's will is."
Eph 5:16-17 (NIV)

Are you wrestling with God's will? Do you want to know what He wants you to do next? So what does it take to know and do God's will? Read the following verses and identify God's revealed will as specifically stated in each verse.

- *"For my Father's will is that everyone who looks to the Son and believes in him shall have eternal life, and I will raise him up at the last day." John 6:40 (NIV)*
- *"It is God's will that you should be sanctified: that you should avoid sexual immorality;" 1 Thess 4:3 (NIV)*
- *"Give thanks in all circumstances, for this is God's will for you in Christ Jesus." 1 Thess 5:18 (NIV)*

From these three verses alone, you can ascertain that it is God's will for you to be saved by placing your faith in Jesus alone for salvation. It is God's will for you to be sanctified and for you to avoid sexual immorality. It is God's will for you to be identified by an attitude of gratitude.

As you read the Bible, take time to personalize Scripture. God has a word specifically for you and your situation. God has a specific plan for your life. God wants you to seek Him daily in relationship and take Him at His Word.

Discerning God's will begins with discovering God's Word. Now walk in the light God gives you and obey what you already know. Watch to see what God does in you and through you. The best is yet to come!

October 19
BEING SPIRIT FILLED
Being Spirit Filled, Control, Surrender

"Do not get drunk on wine, which leads to debauchery. Instead, be filled with the Spirit." Eph 5:18 (NIV)

My eleventh grade Sunday School teacher took three of us boys snow skiing in Keystone, Colorado. We had an adventurous time navigating the slopes and conquering the moguls. One snowy night, we experienced the glide of a sleigh ride pulled by a horse. Once we arrived near the top of the mountain, we entered an old cabin. Inside the cabin awaited a mountaineer cooking juicy steaks over an open fire.

When I ponder the Spirit filled life, I envision giving over the reins of my life to the control of the Holy Spirit. I want God, by the power of His Holy Spirit, to have complete control of my life. The Spirit filled life is all about control. Are you willing to yield to the Spirit's control? Are you willing to give the Holy Spirit the reins to your life?

The baptism of the Holy Spirit is an event. You are baptized in the Holy Spirit at the moment of your conversion. Upon confessing Jesus as Lord of your life, you are simultaneously indwelt by the Holy Spirit. You are sealed by the Holy Spirit and have eternal security.

Being filled with the Holy Spirit is an ongoing process. As you daily yield to the Spirit's control, the fruit of the Spirit is evidenced in your life. At salvation you got all of Him. In sanctification, He gets all of you. Are you Spirit filled?

FINDING HELP

God's Comfort, Assurance, Holy Spirit

"God is our refuge and strength, an ever-present help in trouble."
Psalm 46:1 (NIV)

God never intended for you to walk through adversity alone. Maybe you have heard someone say that God will never put more on you than you can handle. That's not true. God will not put more on you than you can handle with His help.

The Christian life is not a solo flight. God does not launch you out into the world and expect you to live the Christian life on your own. God provides refuge when you need to retreat, strength when you need to endure, and help when you need relief. Your Heavenly Father knows exactly what you need and the exact moment you need it.

> • *"And I will ask the Father, and he will give you another Counselor to be with you forever--the Spirit of truth. The world cannot accept him, because it neither sees him nor knows him. But you know him, for he lives with you and will be in you." John 14:16-17 (NIV)*

God gives you His Holy Spirit at the moment of your conversion. You are inhabited by the Counselor who is the Spirit of truth. You are the walking tabernacle of God's Presence. Your body is His temple. The Holy Spirit is your Comforter.

Are you in need of help? Are you hurting, lonely, or discouraged? Share your heart with God in prayer and anticipate His response.

October 21
SIMPLIFYING LIFE

Simplifying Life, Fearing God, Obedience

"Now all has been heard; here is the conclusion of the matter: Fear God and keep his commandments, for this is the whole duty of man." Eccl 12:13 (NIV)

Are you longing for simplicity in your world of complexity? Solomon understood a life filled with a mosaic of opportunities. His world was lavished with unlimited choices. Solomon enjoyed the pursuit of pleasure, wisdom, and wealth. Yet, he declared that it was all meaningless. He had it all, and yet, it did not deliver at all. At the end of Solomon's pursuit, he discovered simplicity in his world of complexity.

Jesus combated the shroud of legalism propelled by the Scribes and Pharisees. They sought to complicate the Ten Commandments. They inflated the Law of God and inflicted excessive burdens on those seeking to honor God's Law. In His Sermon on the Mount, Jesus brought clarity and simplicity to God's Word.

> • *"So in everything, do to others what you would have them do to you, for this sums up the Law and the Prophets." Matt 7:12 (NIV)*

Assess your world. Are you overwhelmed? Simplify and focus: Revere God, obey God and serve others.

DAY BY DAY

Decay, Renewal, Focus

"Therefore we do not lose heart. Though outwardly we are wasting away, yet inwardly we are being renewed day by day." 2 Cor 4:16 (NIV)

Is it possible to experience renewal in the midst of decay? It depends on your focus. If you spend your life focused on the externals, then discouragement awaits. However, if you intentionally focus on the inner life, renewal and encouragement await.

Paul acknowledges that this body you live in is outwardly wasting away. Even if you ascribe to physical fitness, healthy eating habits, and sufficient rest, your body remains in a state of decay. Applying more skin care products will not halt the deterioration of your body.

Inwardly, you can be renewed. How is that possible? It is possible through your day by day personal love relationship with Jesus.

- *"Let us fix our eyes on Jesus, the author and perfecter of our faith, who for the joy set before him endured the cross, scorning its shame, and sat down at the right hand of the throne of God." Heb 12:2 (NIV)*

Being renewed day by day results from daily intimacy with Jesus. Are you spending unhurried time alone with Jesus? Are you growing in your desire for Him to have full control of your life? Are you hungering and thirsting after His righteousness?

October 23
COMMITMENT AND LORDSHIP
Commitment, Devotion, Lordship

"Then Jesus said to his disciples, 'If anyone would come after me, he must deny himself and take up his cross and follow me.'" Matt 16:24 (NIV)

You become what you are committed to.

Who is the object of your loyalty, passion, and energy? What are you giving your life to? How are you allocating your time? What are you committed to?

To become a fully devoted follower of Christ, your commitment must be to Christ and His agenda. Your disposition is to be that of instant obedience. Wherever He wants you to go, whatever He wants you to do, and whatever He wants you to say, your answer is to be a resounding "yes."

Are you committed to deny yourself daily? Jesus must have first place and top priority in your life. Are you committed to take up His cross daily? Bearing the cross of Christ is to embrace the way of suffering and being misunderstood for your faith. Are you committed to follow Him daily? Following Christ is a moment by moment submission to His authority and His plan. Jesus is Lord!

Does your daily commitment to Christ give evidence to His Lordship in your life? What adjustments do you need to make? Have you substituted anyone or anything else in the place of Christ?

FORGIVENESS AND ETERNAL LIFE

Forgiveness, Heaven, Eternal Life

"In him we have redemption through his blood, the forgiveness of sins..."
Eph 1:7 (NIV)

We cannot have eternal life and heaven without God's forgiveness.

All kinds of records are broken on a daily basis. Just when you thought a particular feat was impossible, someone attempts it and pulls it off. Years ago, I was watching the television show, "That's Incredible." On this particular episode, they featured a young man who proclaimed that he could eat a ten speed bicycle. They showed him at the very beginning of the hour looking over a tray filled with tiny dime-sized pieces of the entire bicycle. You would not believe it, but this young man ate the ten speed bicycle one bite at a time with intervals of drinking Coca-Cola within the hour. Now, "That's Incredible!"

Of all the amazing accomplishments being done on the earth, there is one that we just can't pull off. We cannot have eternal life and heaven without God's forgiveness. It doesn't matter how hard we try. It doesn't matter how wonderful we think we are. It doesn't matter how good we have been today. We just cannot obtain heaven and eternal life without God's forgiveness. It is impossible.

The fact that God takes the initiative to bring us into a right relationship with Himself is incredible. To think that the Creator of the universe would value us to the degree that He would provide redemption and forgiveness of our sins through the shed blood of His Son, Jesus, is incredible.

What is your greatest need? God's forgiveness!

October 25
AVAILABLE FORGIVENESS
Forgiveness, Eternal Life, Salvation

"For God so loved the world that he gave his one and only Son, that whoever believes in him shall not perish but have eternal life." John 3:16 (NIV)

One of my best friends died of cancer two months after we graduated from college. We had studied together, prayed together, and played golf together. He was a fellow pastor who had a deep abiding walk with God and a passion for souls. I preached his funeral.

If I have ever prayed for something, it has been for God to provide a cure for cancer. So many individuals have been directly impacted by cancer. Sometimes, it hits really close to home. Perhaps you can relate.

There is another cancer that flows through our entire family tree all the way back to Adam. It is the cancer of sin. Every person is infected and affected by it. Every person suffers the consequences of it. The cancer of sin prevents us from going to heaven.

There's wonderful news! God has provided the cure. The cure for the cancer of sin is God's forgiveness. And God has made His forgiveness available to all. But, it's not automatic.

IMPOSSIBLE

Impossible, Sin, Heaven

"...for all have sinned and fall short of the glory of God." Romans 3:23 (NIV)

It is impossible for God to allow sin into heaven.

God is perfect; we are imperfect. God is righteous; we are unrighteous. God is pure; we are impure. God is sinless; we are sinful. God is flawless; we are flawed.

- *"But just as he who called you is holy, so be holy in all you do; for it is written: 'Be holy, because I am holy.'" 1 Peter 1:15-16 (NIV)*

God is holy; we are not. So how can a person enter heaven, where God allows no sin? This creates a tremendous dilemma. How can anyone go to heaven? Our fallen nature disqualifies us. We are not fit for heaven. We are insufficient to meet the requirements for entrance into heaven.

Have you come to the end of yourself? Have you realized that you cannot go to heaven based on your own righteous deeds?

October 27
REPENTANCE

Sin, Repentance, Forgiveness

"But unless you repent, you too will all perish." Luke 13:3b (NIV)

What comes to mind when you hear the words "about face?" It means to make a 180 degree turn. It means to turn around in order to go the opposite direction. When Jesus told the woman caught in the act of adultery to go and sin no more, He was telling her to repent. To repent is to have a change of mind which results in a change of behavior.

The most incredible news I have ever embraced took place on March 28, 1979, when I turned from my sin and trusted Christ alone for my salvation. The wonderful news that transformed my life is found in this next verse. Read it slowly.

> • *"That if you confess with your mouth, 'Jesus is Lord,' and believe in your heart that God raised him from the dead, you will be saved. For it is with your heart that you believe and are justified, and it is with your mouth that you confess and are saved."*
> *Romans 10:9-10 (NIV)*

Have you confessed Jesus as Lord? Do you believe that God raised Jesus from the dead? If so, re-visit the event of your salvation and trace the progress of your spiritual maturity. If not, confess your sin and invite Jesus to take over your life from this moment on.

"The thief comes only to steal and kill and destroy; I have come that they may have life, and have it to the full." John 10:10 (NIV)

Jesus has come to bring us abundant life on earth in the here and now. You don't have to delay the reality of heaven on earth. Eternal life can be a present reality in your life.

Jesus has prepared your eternal habitation. You may or may not live in a mansion now, but in heaven, your mansion awaits. But heaven is more than a mansion; heaven is enjoying eternal fellowship with Jesus.

- *"And if I go and prepare a place for you, I will come back and take you to be with me that you also may be where I am."*
  John 14:3 (NIV)

How can you get in on the Good News that God has provided in His son, Jesus?

- *"Whoever believes in the Son has eternal life, but whoever rejects the Son will not see life, for God's wrath remains on him."*
  John 3:36 (NIV)

Would you like to receive God's forgiveness by trusting in Christ as your personal Savior and Lord? If you do not believe, you will not receive. God has done His part to provide eternal life to you. Now, it's your turn to respond by faith to God's provision.

October 29
MUTUAL SUBMISSION
Mutual Submission, Reverence

"Submit to one another out of reverence for Christ." Eph 5:21 (NIV)

Has your relationship to Christ changed the way you relate to fellow believers? If you have been adopted into God's family, then all the Christ followers on the planet are now your family members. You may not be in close proximity to the multitudes of believers around the world. But, you have those in your sphere of influence who would be considered your immediate spiritual family. How are those relationships going? Are there any of your relationships that are under strain? Are there any relationships that need an extra measure of attention?

God's Word teaches us to submit to each other as a result of our love and reverence for Christ. In other words, because we love Jesus and are rightly related to Him, we willingly place the needs of others before our own. Out of reverence for Christ, we choose to live in such a way as to benefit and bless others.

- *"Be devoted to one another in brotherly love. Honor one another above yourselves." Romans 12:10 (NIV)*
- *"Live in harmony with one another." Romans 12:16a (NIV)*
- *"Be completely humble and gentle; be patient, bearing with one another in love." Eph 4:2 (NIV)*

Jesus is the ultimate model of mutual submission. We mutually submit to each other in the family of God just as Christ willingly submitted to the Father's Will. Jesus placed our needs before His own.

Let's demonstrate mutual submission each day. Let's give evidence to our reverence for Christ through how we interact with others within God's family.

"Wives, submit to your husbands as to the Lord." Eph 5:22 (NIV)

Does your husband deserve your submission? Has he earned it? Does he treat you in such a way as to warrant your response of submission? Are you motivated to submit to your husband? These are painful questions if you bypass the intent of God's revealed Word.

In the language of the New Testament, the verb is supplied in verse twenty-one and implied in verse twenty-two. The verb is the word, submit. It means to arrange under. This vital word is not a statement of value or worth, but rather of God's order. God has arranged the home to reflect God's order. Your value has already been established by the completed work of Jesus on the cross.

- *"For the husband is the head of the wife as Christ is the head of the church, his body, of which he is the Savior. Now as the church submits to Christ, so also wives should submit to their husbands in everything." Eph 5:23-24 (NIV)*

God's Word to the wife is that she submit to her husband as to the Lord. Because of your right relationship with God, you are to willingly submit to your husband. Your submission is not based on your husband's behavior but on your growing relationship to Christ. You choose to submit to your husband because you have chosen to revere Christ. Your submission is a direct reflection of your devotion to Christ and your obedience to Him.

God knows your situation. He created the one you are married to. God knows what you need, and He always has your best interest in mind.

October 31
God's Word to Husbands
Love, Marriage, Sacrifice

"Husbands, love your wives, just as Christ loved the church and gave himself up for her to make her holy, cleansing her by the washing with water through the word, and to present her to himself as a radiant church, without stain or wrinkle or any other blemish, but holy and blameless." Eph 5:25-27 (NIV)

How would you define love? Is love a verbal expression, an act of kindness, or a gift extended to another? Is love being willing to do what you do not enjoy in order to benefit someone else? Is love a natural flow from a heart that is full?

God's Word to the husband is for you to love your wife. Jesus is the model to follow. Jesus defined love by His willingness to die for the church and to rise again for the church. He gave His life so that we could live with Him eternally. Jesus is the ultimate portrait of unconditional love.

Husband, do you love your own body and care for it? Just as Jesus loves His Body, the church, you are to love your wife as you love your own body. Loving your wife is not based on her performance. You don't love your wife in response to her meeting your needs. You love your wife intentionally and unconditionally as a result of your love relationship with Jesus.

Any adjustments needed? There's always room for improvement.

HER GREATEST NEED

Marriage, Love, Respect

"So God created man in his own image, in the image of God he created him; male and female he created them." Gen 1:27 (NIV)

Marriage is God's idea. He ordained it. He designed it. God created us in His image. In marriage, the two become one. Satan attacks this spiritual union by seeking to make the two who have become one, two again. Satan's goal is to infuse suspicion, isolation, and insecurity.

God created the woman with the innate need for love and intimacy. Her greatest need is to be loved. The wife needs to know that her husband loves her. Intimate love moves beyond the surface and seeks to communicate understanding and validate feelings. God commands the husband to love his wife unconditionally.

When the wife's greatest need goes unmet, loneliness and resentment begin to germinate. Husband, God expects you to love your wife as you love yourself. God's expects you to prime the pump by taking the initiative to communicate love to your wife.

November 2
HIS GREATEST NEED
Marriage, Love, Respect

"However, each one of you also must love his wife as he loves himself, and the wife must respect her husband." Eph 5:33 (NIV)

The husband's greatest need is respect. God created the man with the innate need to be honored and respected. Wife, your husband needs to know that you respect him. You may be thinking to yourself, "But, I don't respect my husband." Maybe he is not living in a manner deserving a response of respect. Maybe your husband has not earned your respect.

You choose to respect your husband because of your reverence for Christ. You communicate respect to your husband not based on his behavior or based on how he treats you, but in response to your love relationship with Jesus. Whether your husband deserves your respect or not is not the issue. Are you willing to meet your husband's greatest need because you are willing to honor Jesus?

Take the initiative to show respect to your husband out of reverence and obedience to Christ. As you show respect, you will be priming the pump for love to flow from him to you. If your husband refuses to take the initiative to communicate love to you, then be the first to get the love flowing by showing respect.

Ask God to give you the grace you will need to meet your husband's greatest need.

BEING A BLESSING
Giving, Reward, Motive

"'So when you give to the needy, do not announce it with trumpets, as the hypocrites do in the synagogues and on the streets, to be honored by men. I tell you the truth, they have received their reward in full. But when you give to the needy, do not let your left hand know what your right hand is doing, so that your giving may be in secret. Then your Father, who sees what is done in secret, will reward you.'" Matt 6:2-4 (NIV)

What are you currently doing to benefit others? What resources has God made available to you? Are you using what God gives you to benefit others? You are blessed by God to be a blessing to others.

Give secretly and God will reward you. It is not only what you give but how you give that moves the heart of God. God sees everything you do and everything you don't do. God sees and knows. If you give to be seen of men, then that is the extent of your reward. However, when your giving is done in secret, God rewards you.

- *"For we must all appear before the judgment seat of Christ, that each one may receive what is due him for the things done while in the body, whether good or bad." 2 Cor 5:10 (NIV)*

- *"But just as you excel in everything--in faith, in speech, in knowledge, in complete earnestness and in your love for us --see that you also excel in this grace of giving." 2 Cor 8:7 (NIV)*

Motive matters! God sees how much you give and God sees how you give.

November 4
Praying on Purpose
Praying, Daily Disciplines

"But when you pray, go into your room, close the door and pray to your Father, who is unseen. Then your Father, who sees what is done in secret, will reward you." Matt 6:6 (NIV)

It is so easy to neglect prayer. One reason is because praying is such a private experience. Another reason is because we tend to be easily distracted during our times of prayer. Sometimes we have difficulty connecting with an invisible God. Prayer requires faith. Prayer requires patience and discipline. In fact, prayer is hard work.

Jesus nurtured His relationship with our Heavenly Father through the consistent discipline of prayer. Jesus modeled the value of staying connected to the One who created us. In His Sermon on the Mount, Jesus gave some practical steps to developing a meaningful prayer life.

Not "if" we pray, but "when" we pray, we are to embrace an intentional plan. Let me give you a concise action plan that you can plug into your daily routine. Set an appointment to meet with God. Secure a place that ensures privacy. Start praying through Scripture.

FORGIVING OTHERS

Forgiving, God's Love

"For if you forgive men when they sin against you, your heavenly Father will also forgive you. But if you do not forgive men their sins, your Father will not forgive your sins." Matt 6:14-15 (NIV)

You cannot live the Christ-centered life without instant forgiveness. Living in a right relationship with God and with others requires instant forgiveness.

Think about where you would be without God's forgiveness. Think about the alienation and the isolation and the rejection that would be your constant companion. But God came to your rescue by allowing Jesus to die to pay the penalty of your sin.

Now think about forgiving others. Is there anyone in your life whom you haven't forgiven? Are you holding a grudge? Has the poison of bitterness and resentment saturated your life? What is keeping you from extending instant forgiveness?

If you don't forgive instantly, God won't forgive you! That ought to motivate you to do whatever it takes to extend forgiveness to others. They may not deserve it, and you are right. However, you don't deserve God's forgiveness, and yet, He gives it.

Forgiving instantly is not based on how others treat you; it is based on how God has treated you. Extend God's love to others by extending forgiveness instantly.

November 6
FASTING
Fasting, Spiritual Discipline

"When you fast, do not look somber as the hypocrites do, for they disfigure their faces to show men they are fasting. I tell you the truth, they have received their reward in full. But when you fast, put oil on your head and wash your face, so that it will not be obvious to men that you are fasting, but only to your Father, who is unseen; and your Father, who sees what is done in secret, will reward you." Matt 6:16-18 (NIV)

What is fasting? Fasting is conscientiously delaying gratification of your appetite. You have a God-given desire for food. Your body craves the consumption of food. In fasting, you redirect your ambition for food with your pursuit of God's agenda. Fasting allows you to forsake your drive for food in order to focus on your relationship with God.

Sometimes you feel called to fast from an activity that normally consumes much of your attention. You may feel called to fast from coffee, caffeine, golf, or television for a specific period of time. The purpose of the fast is not for you to draw attention to yourself, but to draw near to God.

Why would God reward fasting? Jesus modeled that fasting was as normal to a Christian as eating food and drinking water. God rewards fasting because He is true to His Word. God keeps His promises. God promises to reward your discipline of fasting.

Fast secretly and systematically. I am reminded of a quote by John Piper: "There's a difference in fasting to be seen and being seen fasting."

STORING UP TREASURE

Stewardship, Money

"'Do not store up for yourselves treasures on earth, where moth and rust destroy, and where thieves break in and steal. But store up for yourselves treasures in heaven, where moth and rust do not destroy, and where thieves do not break in and steal. For where your treasure is, there your heart will be also.'" Matt 6:19-21 (NIV)

How much of what you are currently doing will impact eternity? How much of what you are currently acquiring will go with you to heaven? There's more to this life than what you see. There's more to this life than the material and temporal.

Jesus gives such a practical teaching on living for eternity. Jesus points us to the reality of the afterlife in heaven. Our tendency is to place the emphasis on our lives on planet earth. Jesus shows us that we are to live our lives with eternity in mind.

So how do you store up treasures in heaven? You store up treasures by investing in that which makes an eternal difference. For example, when you give financially through the local church, you are storing up treasures in heaven. When you share the plan of salvation with a lost person and lead them to embrace Jesus as Savior and Lord, you are storing up treasures in heaven. When you pray for our missionaries around the world, you are participating in their ministry through prayer and storing up treasures in heaven. When you give, pray, fast, and forgive, you store up treasures in heaven.

Are you consumed with life on this planet? Would you be willing to focus your life and your resources in order to advance the Kingdom of God? Heaven has plenty of room for the treasures you are storing up.

November 8
WORRYING
Worrying, God's Provision

"Therefore I tell you, do not worry about your life, what you will eat or drink; or about your body, what you will wear. Is not life more important than food, and the body more important than clothes? Look at the birds of the air; they do not sow or reap or store away in barns, and yet your heavenly Father feeds them. Are you not much more valuable than they? Who of you by worrying can add a single hour to his life?" Matt 6:25-27 (NIV)

Worry has a way of wearing us down. We fixate on something that we have no control over and invite it to consume our thoughts. Our emotional reserves are taxed as worry siphons our energy. The byproduct of worry is erosion.

Worry is like rocking in a rocking chair; it will keep you busy, but you don't get anywhere. Worry is an indicator of unbelief. Worry is a banner that waves declaring that we don't trust God. Faith and worry cannot co-exist. You can't fully rely upon God and worry at the same time.

Jesus commands us: "Do not worry." Your heavenly Father knows what you need. Do you trust God to do what He says He will do? Do you believe God has the resources necessary to meet your needs? Are you confident that God will meet your needs? You know God is able. Maybe you wonder if God is willing.

Worry is a choice. Trust is a choice. We can choose to worry, or we can choose to take God at His Word and trust Him. Be sensitive to God's invitation for you to join Him in His resolution of your trying circumstances.

FIRST THINGS FIRST

"But seek first his kingdom and his righteousness, and all these things will be given to you as well." Matt 6:33 (NIV)

Take a look at your priorities and assess your life. See where you are allocating your time and energy. One of Satan's most effective tools to diffuse a believer's focus is busyness. Your life becomes consumed with keeping too many plates spinning. Before you know it, you have over-committed and over-scheduled your life. Jesus has the answer.

Jesus offers a promise that is activated upon your obedience. To seek first the Kingdom of God is to align your life with God's agenda. To seek first His Kingdom is to embrace God's priorities. Jesus includes the pursuit of His righteousness. When a person is born again, that person receives the imputed righteousness of Christ. The believer's position is that of being in Christ. In order to seek His righteousness, you allow the righteousness on the inside of you to be worked out. It is the process of working out what God has worked in.

Make it your priority to seek His Kingdom and His righteousness. All the other things that you need will be provided to you as well. Before seeking things, seek God's agenda. Seek to love what He loves and to hate what He hates.

What has first place in your life? Who gets the most of you?

November 10
MAKING YOUR HOUSE A HOME
Home, Harmony, Peace

"'But if serving the LORD seems undesirable to you, then choose for yourselves this day whom you will serve, whether the gods your forefathers served beyond the River, or the gods of the Amorites, in whose land you are living. But as for me and my household, we will serve the LORD.'" Josh 24:15 (NIV)

Do you like to go home?

Think about your current home life. When you have finished up at work or school or running errands, do you like to go home? Is your home an oasis or a war zone? Do you look forward to going home or is it a daily dread?

God wants you to experience His Presence and express His love at school, at work, at church, and at home. Decide today to do your part in making your home a peaceful place. Do your part to generate an atmosphere that is harmonious and joyful. Allow God to have His way in your home. Embrace the passion of Joshua.

Take responsibility for the spiritual climate of your home. Settle in your heart to worship and serve God and to lead your family to do the same. As you extend unconditional love, instant forgiveness, clear expectations, and passionate devotion, your home will become an environment that moves the heart of God.

"Children, obey your parents in the Lord, for this is right. 'Honor your father and mother'--which is the first commandment with a promise--'that it may go well with you and that you may enjoy long life on the earth.'" Eph 6:1-3 (NIV)

God gives a clear word on the essentials for a peaceful home. A home that brings honor to God is a home where children obey their parents. When children respond to their parents with instant obedience, peace permeates the home. When obedience erodes, rebellion erupts.

Children must first be in submission to their parents if they are going to be in submission to God. The horizontal obedience to parents directly affects the vertical allegiance to God. Obedience to parents is the children's God-given role. For a child to live in rebellion to parents is to live out of fellowship with God. Obedience is an indicator of a right relationship with God. Without obedience, there is no blessing.

The first commandment with a promise is that children honor their father and mother. Think of what is means to dishonor. There's no peace in the home when children dishonor their parents. To honor the Lord, children must honor the parents He gave them. Quality of life is based on the fruit of your relationship with your parents and with the Lord.

A peaceful home begins with children and parents being in a right relationship with God. Anger must be diffused. Resentment must be eradicated. Bitterness must be evacuated. Forgiveness must be extended and received.

What needs to happen in your home for peace to permeate?

November 12
CHILD OF GOD
Child of God, Salvation, Eternity

"Dear friends, now we are children of God, and what we will be has not yet been made known. But we know that when he appears, we shall be like him, for we shall see him as he is. Everyone who has this hope in him purifies himself, just as he is pure." 1 John 3:2-3 (NIV)

Are you a child of God? Have you been born into God's family by placing your faith in Jesus alone for salvation? Recall your initial experience with Christ. Before Christ, you were running to sin. Now that you are in Christ, you are running from sin and to Christ.

Now, think about what you are becoming. You know who you are and whose you are. You know that your name is written in the Lamb's Book of Life. You know that there is nothing you can do to cause God to love you any more, and there is nothing you can do to cause God to love you any less. You know that God wants you to progress in your faith and wants you to mature spiritually. You know that one day you will receive your glorified body and be like Christ. You will finally and eternally see Jesus as He is.

Until you cross over to the other side, God wants you to live a life of purity. You are to purify yourself by living a consecrated life.

"Religion that God our Father accepts as pure and faultless is this: to look after orphans and widows in their distress and to keep oneself from being polluted by the world." James 1:27 (NIV)

STAGES OF PARENTING
Parenting, Honoring God

"Fathers, do not exasperate your children; instead, bring them up in the training and instruction of the Lord." Eph 6:4 (NIV)

Parenting is a blessing from the Lord. The opportunity to mold and shape a child into a fully devoted follower of Christ is a high privilege and responsibility. God entrusts parents with the task of rearing children. That role can be appropriated in a way that honors God or in a way that breaks the heart of God.

You can trace every family conflict to one common denominator: selfishness. When there is conflict, someone is being selfish. Selfishness can invade the realm of parenting quickly. Instead of doing what is best for your children, you can embrace what is best for you personally to the neglect of what is best for them.

You can choose to be controlling, driving, demanding, and domineering. Or you can go the other extreme and choose to be distant, detached, and disinterested. Both extremes are unhealthy. Here's a helpful model, developed by Bruce Johnston, to follow:

> Be a Caretaker when your child is Birth to 5 years old.
> Be a Cop when your child is 6 to 11 years old.
> Be a Coach when your child is 12 to 17 years old.
> Be a Consultant when your child is 18 & older.

Think about how you were parented and compare it to the four stages of parenting. Now, examine how you are currently parenting to see where you are in the process. What adjustments do you need to make in your being parented or in your parenting?

November 14
VOCATIONAL VISION
Vision, Vocation, Lordship

"Serve wholeheartedly, as if you were serving the Lord, not men, because you know that the Lord will reward everyone for whatever good he does, whether he is slave or free." Eph 6:7-8 (NIV)

Who do you work for? Your answer to that question will quickly identify your motivation for waking up each morning. What if you decided that you work for Jesus? What if you allowed Jesus to become your boss?

The reality is that Jesus is your boss if you have made Him Lord of your life. His Lordship in your life is a measurement of your followership. If you are following Jesus and serving Him wholeheartedly, then He is your boss. You are not working for an earthly boss. You are not trying to please or appease an earthly boss. Your passion is to please your ultimate boss, Jesus.

Jesus rewards your work. Jesus is keeping up with all you do and all you say. He knows when you have gone the extra mile and He knows when you have not given your best. Jesus sees what no one else sees. You may not receive the compensation from your earthly boss that you desire or deserve. However, Jesus is the one who gives you ultimate compensation for your work. Jesus rewards you!

When you are on your way to work, begin to visualize who you are working for. Now, begin to see that Jesus is the One you are seeking to please. Jesus is the One whom you are working for. Jesus is your boss!

Would you allow your vocational vision to be formed by your boss, Jesus?

SEGMENTED

Segmented, Kingdom of God, Lordship

"I tell you the truth, anyone who will not receive the kingdom of God like a little child will never enter it." Mark 10:15 (NIV)

The Kingdom of God is God's people on mission with God to fulfill God's purposes on earth! Where is the Kingdom of God? Wherever Jesus is King! Is Jesus King of your heart? Is Jesus King of your home? Is Jesus King of your church? Is Jesus King of your work?

Our tendency is to live segmented lives. We have our personal life, our home life, our church life, and our work life. Often believers express their faith through personal devotion to the Lord and through public worship at church. Why do we conceal our faith at home or at work? Why do we segment our Christianity as though we can only express our faith in our personal life and church life?

We come into the Kingdom of God by simple childlike faith in the completed work of Jesus on the cross. The Kingdom of God is wherever Jesus is King. What if we allowed Jesus to be King in our heart, home, church, and work? What if we allowed our relationship with Jesus to be evidenced in every domain of life? Instead of concealing our Christianity, let's reveal our love relationship with Jesus 24.7.365 in every area of life.

November 16
WORKING FOR THE LORD
Work, Lordship, Integrity

"Serve wholeheartedly, as if you were serving the Lord, not men, because you know that the Lord will reward everyone for whatever good he does, whether he is slave or free." Eph 6:7-8 (NIV)

Where do you work? Now think about your workplace and rediscover your ultimate boss, Jesus. Therefore, you are working for Jesus. When you are working, in the workplace, for the Lord, what does that look like?

Snapshot #1: You willingly do what you are asked to do.

When your passion is to please Jesus, you will obey your earthly boss. Your obedience is not based on how your boss treats you; your obedience is based on pleasing your ultimate boss, Jesus.

Snapshot #2: Your attitude will be consistent with your actions.

Your beliefs determine your behavior. If you believe that Jesus is your ultimate boss and if you believe that you are truly working for him, then your actions at work will be consistent with your beliefs. Your actions will reflect the authenticity of your attitude.

Snapshot #3: Your actions are consistent when no one is watching.

Do you give your best when no one is looking? Jesus is watching even when your earthly boss is not in visual contact. What you do when no one is watching is a clear indicator of your caliber of character.

Take a close look at each snapshot of a believer working for the Lord. Identify the snapshot that needs improvement in your life.

LEADING FOR THE LORD

Work, Leadership, Lordship

"And whatever you do, whether in word or deed, do it all in the name of the Lord Jesus, giving thanks to God the Father through him." Col 3:17 (NIV)

Leadership is influence with integrity. Everyone is a leader at some level. Everyone has a God-given sphere of influence. You may not fully comprehend the parameters of your sphere, but God has placed you on this planet to be an irresistible influence for His Glory.

For those serving as an employer, embrace these actions steps:

Action Step #1: Don't threaten your employees.

Action Step #2: Treat your employees with dignity and respect.

Action Step #3: Recognize your employees' value and worth.

What are you doing with the influence God has given you?

November 18
CAREER OR CALLING
Career, Calling, Lordship

"Each one should use whatever gift he has received to serve others, faithfully administering God's grace in its various forms. If anyone speaks, he should do it as one speaking the very words of God. If anyone serves, he should do it with the strength God provides, so that in all things God may be praised through Jesus Christ. To him be the glory and the power for ever and ever. Amen."
1 Peter 4:10-11 (NIV)

Turn your career into a calling. What does God want to accomplish through you right where you are? It's not about you. It's really not about your career. It is all about God being at work in you and through you to accomplish His agenda.

Whatever environment God has placed you in, think about the people you have the opportunity to impact. Think about the interactions and connections that are made possible because of where God has placed you. Your career is a calling from God to represent Him. Now do it with the strength God provides. Do it so that in all things God may be praised. Your career is more than just a career; it is a calling from God. It's not about money or position. It's all about allowing God to have your career so that He can have you.

Let God use you right where you are. Make yourself completely available for His use and watch expectantly.

YOUR MISSION FIELD
Work, Mission field, Influence

"But in your hearts set apart Christ as Lord. Always be prepared to give an answer to everyone who asks you to give the reason for the hope that you have. But do this with gentleness and respect, keeping a clear conscience, so that those who speak maliciously against your good behavior in Christ may be ashamed of their slander." 1 Peter 3:15-16 (NIV)

Turn your workplace into a mission field. From age 18 to 65, if you work 40 hours per week, you will work at total of about 94,000 hours. Wow! Think about that for a moment. You will spend a major portion of your life at work.

What will you do with the 94,000 hours? That's a lot of time to make an eternal difference. It all depends on how you view your workplace. If it is just a place to earn money, then your impact will be greatly limited. If it is just a place to climb the professional ladder, then your impact will fall short. However, if you began to embrace the reality that your workplace is your mission field, then eternity becomes a blessing for those in your sphere of influence who turn their lives over to Christ alone for salvation.

How many people will be in Heaven because of your faithfulness in serving the people in your workplace as your mission field? You are a missionary to your workplace!

November 20

WORK AND WORSHIP

Work, Worship, Lordship

"Ascribe to the LORD the glory due his name; worship the LORD in the splendor of his holiness." Psalm 29:2 (NIV)

Turn your work into an act of worship. Don't worship your work! Let your work be an act of worship. You have a choice. You can treat worship as a noun or a verb. As a noun, worship becomes something you go to on Sunday mornings in a building incorrectly referred to as the church. As a verb, worship becomes something you do twenty-four-seven-three-sixty-five. Worship becomes a lifestyle. Instead of going to church to worship, you become the church worshipping.

What would be different about your workplace if you embraced worship as a verb? What would be different about your attitude and actions related to work if you began to turn your work into an act of worship? The heart of God is moved by how you work just as much as how you express your worship to Him on Sunday mornings in the corporate worship setting. Your work matters to God. Your workplace matters to God. Turning your work into an act of worship will be one of the most important decisions you will make on this side of eternity.

SPIRITUAL WARFARE

Spiritual Warfare, Devil

"For our struggle is not against flesh and blood, but against the rulers, against the authorities, against the powers of this dark world and against the spiritual forces of evil in the heavenly realms." Eph 6:12 (NIV)

The devil actually exists. A passenger on the plane noticed a pastor sitting next to him reading the Bible. The passenger quizzed the pastor about his belief in the Bible. The pastor let the passenger know that he indeed believed every word of the Bible. The passenger frustratingly asked about the pastor's belief in Jonah actually being swallowed by a large fish. The pastor said, "Well, of course I do. In fact, when I get to Heaven, I'll ask Jonah about it."

The passenger inquired, "What if Jonah's not there?"

The pastor responded, "Then you can ask him!"

Friend, there is a Hell and the devil actually exists. The Bible affirms, "Be self-controlled and alert. Your enemy the devil prowls around like a roaring lion looking for someone to devour" (1 Peter 5:8 NIV).

God is for you. The devil is against you. God has an agenda for your life. The devil has an agenda for your life. God is at work. The devil is at work. There is a perpetual war going on in the spiritual realm.

Are you in touch with the reality of the enemy?

November 22

FACING THE ENEMY

Spiritual Warfare, Devil

"The thief comes only to steal and kill and destroy; I have come that they may have life, and have it to the full." John 10:10 (NIV)

The devil always opposes. The devil opposes God and anything of God. Since the devil can't attack God, he seeks to attack that which is closest to God's heart, you! The devil attacks God's children. The devil is the enemy!

The devil seeks to steal what Jesus reveals. Jesus is the devil's greatest threat. Jesus brings you life, meaning, and purpose. Jesus reveals His plan for your life. Jesus gives you a reason to live and a song to sing and a mission to fulfill. The devil can't stand what Jesus has done for you. The devil can't rest until you forsake your loyalty to Christ. The devil can't cease agitating you and attacking you until you give up.

Recognize that the devil is anti-God. Become aware of the devil's strategy. Don't give in to his schemes. Don't compromise your convictions and your commitment to Christ. Let the devil know who you are and whose you are.

BEING AN OVERCOMER

Spiritual Warfare, Devil, Victory

"You, dear children, are from God and have overcome them, because the one who is in you is greater than the one who is in the world." 1 John 4:4 (NIV)

The devil is already defeated.

Jesus lives in you. You are greater than the devil. He has nothing on you. You are a child of the King. Jesus has made your victory over sin, over Satan, and over death, a reality! The devil is already beaten!

- *"Praise be to the God and Father of our Lord Jesus Christ! In his great mercy he has given us new birth into a living hope through the resurrection of Jesus Christ from the dead, and into an inheritance that can never perish, spoil or fade--kept in heaven for you, who through faith are shielded by God's power until the coming of the salvation that is ready to be revealed in the last time." 1 Peter 1:3-5 (NIV)*

The devil's time is limited. He knows that his end is near. Therefore, the devil mobilizes his demonic entourage to distract and discourage believers. Remember, the penalty for your sin has been paid in full by the atoning work of Jesus on the cross. Remember, the same power that raised Jesus from the dead is living in you in the Person of the Holy Spirit who lives in you (I Cor. 6:19-20).

November 24

STAYING CONNECTED

Spiritual Warfare, Intimacy, Prayer

"And pray in the Spirit on all occasions with all kinds of prayers and requests. With this in mind, be alert and always keep on praying for all the saints." Eph 6:18 (NIV)

Stay close to Jesus.

You can live out your positional victory in Christ through practical steps. Step one is to stay close to your commander, Jesus. He is source of life and He alone is your source of victory. Jesus reigns! Does He reign in your life?

Spiritual warfare demands connectivity. To live in positional victory you stay close to Jesus through prayer. Prayer is communication with Jesus. Prayer is nurturing the life of Christ in you. Praying in the Spirit involves praying according to God's will, God's way, and God's Word. One of the most effective ways to allow Jesus to reign in your life is by praying Scripture.

Notice that Paul includes being alert and being persistent. To be alert is to be aware of your surroundings and your standing in Christ. To always keep on praying means to stay connected and stay consistent in your communication with the Lord.

Your level of protection in spiritual warfare is vitally related to your daily connectivity to Christ through prayer. Are you praying? Are you staying connected to Christ and His provision?

THE ARMOR OF GOD

Spiritual Warfare, Armor

"Finally, be strong in the Lord and in his mighty power. Put on the full armor of God so that you can take your stand against the devil's schemes." Eph 6:10-11 (NIV)

Put on your gear. God has provided you with everything you need to engage in the spiritual battle. You must appropriate what God has provided.

How can you be strong in the Lord and be strong in His mighty power? When you take God at His Word, you receive the benefits of His promises. Put on the full armor of God. Gear up for battle. You don't wage war with fleshly weapons. You fight spiritual battles with spiritual armor. God has provided the attire. Are you willing to put it on?

- *"Therefore put on the full armor of God, so that when the day of evil comes, you may be able to stand your ground, and after you have done everything, to stand. Stand firm then, with the belt of truth buckled around your waist, with the breastplate of righteousness in place, and with your feet fitted with the readiness that comes from the gospel of peace. In addition to all this, take up the shield of faith, with which you can extinguish all the flaming arrows of the evil one. Take the helmet of salvation and the sword of the Spirit, which is the word of God."* Eph 6.13-17 (NIV)

The armor of God is for your protection. The weapons are for your use. Stay connected! Stay engaged!

November 26
STANDING YOUR GROUND
Spiritual Warfare, Prayer, Victory

"I pray also that the eyes of your heart may be enlightened in order that you may know the hope to which he has called you, the riches of his glorious inheritance in the saints, and his incomparably great power for us who believe. That power is like the working of his mighty strength, which he exerted in Christ when he raised him from the dead and seated him at his right hand in the heavenly realms, far above all rule and authority, power and dominion, and every title that can be given, not only in the present age but also in the one to come."
Eph 1:18-21 (NIV)

Stand your ground. You don't have to be a victim of spiritual warfare; you can be victorious in spiritual warfare. You don't have to be a victim of the devil's schemes; you can be victorious in spite of his schemes.

Take your stand! Stand your ground! In order to stand your ground you must be grounded. Are you grounded in Christ? Have you embraced your new identity in Christ? You don't have to retreat; you can defeat the enemy. The devil has already been defeated by the cross and empty tomb. Now stand in light of the crucifixion and resurrection of Jesus.

We are fighting from victory, not for victory.

Activate these steps to live out your positional victory in practical ways: Stay close to Jesus, put on your gear, and stand your ground. Remember that kneeling keeps you standing.

THE BREAD OF LIFE
I am sayings, Bread of Life

"Then Jesus declared, 'I am the bread of life. He who comes to me will never go hungry, and he who believes in me will never be thirsty.'" John 6:35 (NIV)

Because He is the bread of life, I am nourished.

Jesus had fed the multitudes with a boy's lunch consisting of two small fish and fives loaves of bread. As S.M. Lockridge used to say, "God is the only One who can multiply two times five and get five-thousand." The people were fixated on the miracle of multiplication and bypassed the miracle worker, Jesus. Instead of believing in the One who provided the bread, they were content to have their appetites fulfilled with earthly bread.

Jesus is the true bread from heaven. He has come to give life to the world. Jesus is the bread of life. Because He is the bread of life, I am nourished. My soul is satisfied. The hole in my heart has been filled. My life is now complete. My life now makes sense. As John Piper says, "God is most glorified when we are most satisfied in Him." Have you come to that place of recognizing Jesus as the bread of life? Has Jesus become your Source for life? Are you most satisfied in Him?

Because Jesus is the bread of life, you are nourished. By placing your faith in the atoning work of Christ on the cross, you become a child of God. Your new identity includes that of Jesus becoming the bread of your life. Jesus is now your nourishment. He is now your reason for living. Jesus is your Source!

November 28

THE LIGHT OF THE WORLD

I am sayings, Light of the World

"When Jesus spoke again to the people, he said, 'I am the light of the world. Whoever follows me will never walk in darkness, but will have the light of life.'"
John 8:12 (NIV)

Because He is the light of the world, I am illuminated.

Everything changed on March 28, 1979, when I received God's gift of eternal life. Jesus, the light of the world, took up residence in my heart and has illuminated my life both inwardly and outwardly. My ambitions, my desires, and my outlook took on a new perspective. The character of Christ has been daily formed in me. Throughout the years, His light has informed me of areas that need to be brought under His Lordship.

Jesus wants to not only shine in you but also to shine through you. His light through your life alters the world around you. Every interaction becomes intentional. Each conversation becomes an opportunity to allow Jesus to shine His light through you. Just as light influences darkness, Jesus has saved you and set you apart to influence others.

Because He is the light of the world, you are illuminated. Now, illuminate the environments that God places you in. Allow the light of Jesus to shine brightly through your life today. Eternity is at stake!

JESUS IS THE GATE

I am sayings, Gate, Security of the Believer

"Therefore Jesus said again, 'I tell you the truth, I am the gate for the sheep.'"
John 10:7 (NIV)

Because He is the gate, I am secure.

My security in Christ is not based on my feelings. There are days when my emotional security may be threatened. There are days when I just don't feel safe and secure. Fortunately, my security is not anchored to my feelings. My eternal security is found in Jesus completely.

Because He is the gate, you are secure. After placing your trust in the completed work of Jesus on the cross, you are completely saved. Your eternal security is not based on your daily performance, but on the finished work of Jesus on the cross. You didn't earn salvation and you cannot lose your salvation. The same One who saved you is the One who keeps you.

As a believer, if you choose to sin, you will face consequences. You don't lose your salvation, but your fellowship with Jesus will be strained and your ability to bear the fruit of the Spirit will be inhibited. Confess your sin now. Specifically agree with God concerning your sin. Remember what you were saved from!

Now walk with Jesus and He will help you find pasture. Jesus will help you develop authentic relationships with other believers, and He will help you develop spiritual disciplines to nurture His life in you. Jesus will help you build intentional relationships with unsaved people so that you can shine His light and share His love with them.

November 30
THE GOOD SHEPHERD
I am sayings, Good Shepherd

"'I am the good shepherd. The good shepherd lays down his life for the sheep.'"
John 10:11 (NIV)

Because He is the Good Shepherd, I am valued.

Your value is not determined by your portfolio. Your value is not determined by your performance. Your value is not determined by your personality. Your value is determined by what God has done on your behalf. Before you could do anything with God or for God, in His mercy and grace, God decided what to do with you and for you.

Your value was established before you were born. Then, God provided a tangible demonstration and validation of your value when He became man.

Is the Lord your shepherd? Have you allowed Him to be the Shepherd and Overseer of your soul? Now think about your value in God's economy. You are the apple of God's eye. You are His treasure. Look around! Do you see other people in your weekly routine? Guess what? God values them, too.

BELIEVE AND RECEIVE
I am sayings, Resurrection and Life, Eternity

"Jesus said to her, 'I am the resurrection and the life. He who believes in me will live, even though he dies; and whoever lives and believes in me will never die. Do you believe this?'" John 11:25-26 (NIV)

You are born, you live, you die, and then you go to heaven or hell. There's more to this life than the here and now. There's more to this life than what is visible.

In light of eternity, life on planet earth is brief. Yet, there is life on the other side of the grave. Everyone will face God and acknowledge that Jesus is Lord. Those who make that confession before death will go to heaven. Those who fail to make that declaration before death will face God, confess that Jesus is Lord, and then spend eternity separated from God in the literal place called hell.

There's hope! Because Jesus is the resurrection and the life, you are invited to spend eternity in heaven. You are invited to respond to God's offer of salvation by placing your faith in the redemptive act of Jesus dying on the cross to pay the penalty for your sin. You are invited to receive the gift of eternal life and then spend your remaining days upon the earth inviting others to receive the gift of eternal life. How many people will be in heaven because of you?

December 2
THE ONLY WAY
I am sayings, Way, Truth, Life, Salvation, Jesus

"Jesus answered, 'I am the way and the truth and the life. No one comes to the Father except through me.'" John 14:6 (NIV)

Often I have heard people insert their belief that "we are all trying to get to the same place, just taking different paths to get there." Scripture does not affirm that belief. In fact, there is only one way to get to heaven. Jesus is the only way! Now that is both exclusive and inclusive. Those who reject Jesus as the only way don't receive the benefit of eternal life in heaven. They are excluded from heaven for failing to accept Jesus as their personal Lord and Savior.

Be informed. Since Jesus is the only way to heaven, you can know for certain that you have the gift of eternal life. Everyone who trusts in Jesus alone for salvation is included in the eternal benefits of that decision.

- *"That if you confess with your mouth, 'Jesus is Lord,' and believe in your heart that God raised him from the dead, you will be saved." Romans 10:9 (NIV)*
- *"Salvation is found in no one else, for there is no other name under heaven given to men by which we must be saved." Acts 4:12 (NIV)*

Have you met the way? Have you embraced the truth? Have you experienced the life? Be informed and be transformed by the only One who can make an eternal difference in your life, Jesus.

ABIDING IN CHRIST

I am sayings, Vine, Abiding in Christ

"'I am the vine; you are the branches. If a man remains in me and I in him, he will bear much fruit; apart from me you can do nothing.'" John 15:5 (NIV)

God will never ask you to do anything without equipping you to do it. God has an assignment for you to complete during your time on this blue and green planet called earth. God's assignment requires His empowerment. You cannot fulfill God's agenda without God provision. God's assignment for your life flows out of your abiding relationship with Christ. God's command is not for you to bear fruit, but rather to focus your energy on abiding in Christ.

Your fruitfulness will be proportionate to your level of intimacy with Christ. Don't bypass your love relationship with Christ in order to seek to bear fruit. Your passion is not to be channeled in the area of bearing fruit. As you stay connected to Christ and allow His energy, His strength, and His life to flow through you, you will bear much fruit.

Because He is the vine, you are fruitful. Jesus is the source! Stay connected to Him. Guard your love relationship with Him. Protect your daily walk with Christ. Don't allow anything or anyone to rob your relationship with Him. Ensure that your abiding relationship with Christ gets your best and not your leftovers. Don't give Jesus your crumbs. He deserves your passionate pursuit.

Are you connected? Are you abiding? You are the branch. Remain in Him and He will bear His fruit through you. Focus on abiding!

December 4
THE REASON FOR THE SEASON
On Mission, Missions, Christmas

"But after he had considered this, an angel of the Lord appeared to him in a dream and said, 'Joseph son of David, do not be afraid to take Mary home as your wife, because what is conceived in her is from the Holy Spirit. She will give birth to a son, and you are to give him the name Jesus, because he will save his people from their sins.'" Matt 1:20-21 (NIV)

Joseph received the heavenly news that Mary would give birth to the Son of God and that He was to be named Jesus. The name Jesus is the Greek form of the Hebrew name, Joshua, which means, "Yahweh is salvation." Jesus came on mission to bring forth salvation. The Christmas mission is the story of redemption. The reason for this season is to celebrate and articulate the wonderful news that Jesus saves!

God initiated reconciliation. The Creator of the universe has sought to redeem His fallen creation. In His infinite mercy and grace, God demonstrated the ultimate portrait of compassion by allowing His Son to pay the penalty for our sin. God gave us His best so that we could have unbroken fellowship with Him for all eternity.

> • *"God made him who had no sin to be sin for us, so that in him we might become the righteousness of God." 2 Cor 5:21 (NIV)*

There is a reason to sing this season. There is a reason to serve this season. Jesus is the reason!

December 5
GOD WITH US

On Mission, Missions, Christmas

"All this took place to fulfill what the Lord had said through the prophet: 'The virgin will be with child and will give birth to a son, and they will call him Immanuel' --which means, 'God with us.'" Matt 1:22-23 (NIV)

Whenever you go through a difficult experience, having someone with you brings comfort. Whether it is related to grieving the death of a loved one, waiting for the doctor's report at the end of a surgical procedure, or being a primary caregiver to a family member, there is comfort in having someone with you. Why is that? Why do we long to have someone share our sorrows and our joys with us?

God has made you for relationship. God has placed within you the deep abiding desire for relationship. He could have made you to be robotic. Instead, God has created you to be relational. You will never know true peace until you have a right relationship with God through faith in His Son, Jesus. God made the Christmas transaction possible. You can be the recipient of the Christmas mission of God becoming flesh and choosing to be born as a baby in a manger.

God is with us. God created you and the earth upon which you are living out your life. It was not enough to just create human beings to occupy the earth. God wanted to give you the capacity to enjoy the most profound relationship in this life. The ultimate relationship is that of being in a right relationship with God.

December 6
RESPONDING TO THE INCARNATION
On Mission, Mission, Missions, Christmas

"In the beginning was the Word, and the Word was with God, and the Word was God. He was with God in the beginning." John 1:1-2 (NIV)

Do you see it? God became like us so that we could become like Him. The miracle of Christmas is that God became like us. God's mission was to shine His light and to share His love by giving us a visible demonstration of His holiness, His compassion, and His grace.

- *"The Word became flesh and made his dwelling among us. We have seen his glory, the glory of the One and Only, who came from the Father, full of grace and truth." John 1:14 (NIV)*
- *"Jesus answered: 'Don't you know me, Philip, even after I have been among you such a long time? Anyone who has seen me has seen the Father. How can you say, "Show us the Father"?'" John 14:9 (NIV)*

What will you do with the Christmas Mission? God has made Himself known to you so that you could know Him personally and intimately through a saving relationship with Jesus. Now that you know Him, your mission is to make Him known.

RECEIVING THE ULTIMATE GIFT
On Mission, Salvation, Love

"For God so loved the world that he gave his one and only Son, that whoever believes in him shall not perish but have eternal life." John 3:16 (NIV)

Travel down memory lane with me for a moment. Think about your Christmas experiences as a child. What do you remember as the most meaningful gift you received? Can you still feel the excitement of the anticipation of the gift? That experience is locked in your memory because it was special to you.

The ultimate gift in this life is the gift of eternal life. There is no greater gift and there is no greater demonstration of God's love. The moment you recognized your sin and accepted God's provision for your forgiveness through your faith in Jesus, you received the ultimate gift. Let me ask you a question. Do you know that God is for you?

- *"But God demonstrates his own love for us in this: While we were still sinners, Christ died for us." Romans 5:8 (NIV)*
- *"For the wages of sin is death, but the gift of God is eternal life in Christ Jesus our Lord." Romans 6:23 (NIV)*

Consider the individuals currently in your sphere of influence. Have they received the ultimate gift? Have you responded to the Christmas Mission by sharing your salvation story with them? Are you willing to be used of God to make Jesus known to those God places in your path?

December 8
LIVING ON MISSION
On Mission, Soulwinning, Discipleship

"'Come, follow me,' Jesus said, 'and I will make you fishers of men.'"
Mark 1:17 (NIV)

There's no place like being in the center of God's will. Living outside of God's will is like trying to sprint with ankle weights on. When you live each day in the center of God's will, there is tremendous freedom, joy, peace, and meaning. You move from success to significance. You begin to live in light of eternity.

You are called by Jesus to come into relationship with Him. As you abide in Christ and grow in Him, He develops you into His fully devoted follower. Think in terms of a journey instead of a destination. Your eternal destination is secure. Now focus on the journey of knowing Jesus, growing in Him, and going for Him into the world. Through your intimate relationship with Jesus, He grooms you to become a fisher of men. Your life becomes devoted to bringing others into the Kingdom of God. You embrace the Christmas Mission of sharing the salvation story with others.

You are called to make an eternal difference in the lives of those God brings into your path. God's will is for you to know Jesus personally and to make Him known locally and globally. Your Christmas Mission is to share God's love 365 days a year. There's never a moment for you to not be on mission.

Embracing The Great Commission

On Mission, Great Commission

"'Therefore go and make disciples of all nations, baptizing them in the name of the Father and of the Son and of the Holy Spirit, and teaching them to obey everything I have commanded you. And surely I am with you always, to the very end of the age.'" Matt 28:19-20 (NIV)

You cannot spell God without "go." You cannot spell gospel without "go." You are commissioned by God to go for Him. In this powerful passage we call the Great Commission, Jesus gives clear marching orders for the church of the living God. His commission is your mission. You are not on earth to occupy space and convert oxygen into carbon dioxide. There's more in store for you than simply existing on this broken planet called earth. God has an assignment for you that is bigger than you and beyond your ability to fulfill on your own. God's plan for your life demands His supernatural provision.

God loves variety and created diversity. What moves the heart of God is for the body of Christ to come together in unity to fulfill the Great Commission. The command is for you to make disciples of all people groups. How can you pull off an assignment of that magnitude? God never calls you without equipping you. His commission includes His provision. As you go, you make disciples of all people groups by relying on God's power. When you were born again, God empowered you by indwelling you with His Holy Spirit. You have a choice to operate in your own strength or in His strength.

Are you willing to become a Great Commission Christian? God's power is awaiting your response!

December 10
BEING AN IRRESISTIBLE INFLUENCE
On Mission, Influence, Soulwinning

"But you will receive power when the Holy Spirit comes on you; and you will be my witnesses in Jerusalem, and in all Judea and Samaria, and to the ends of the earth." Acts 1:8 (NIV)

Have you ever witnessed a wedding ceremony? As a pastor, I usually conduct the wedding ceremony, but there are occasions when I get to simply sit with my family and witness a ceremony. Recently, we attended an outdoor wedding that was as close to a dream wedding as you can imagine. The weather was perfect, the outdoor decorations were captivating, and the ceremony was Christ exalting. The love the bride and groom had for each other permeated like a breeze in a field of wild flowers.

I can share details with you about the wedding ceremony because I experienced it for myself. I was there and I can testify of every element featured in the ceremony. Did you realize that you are commanded by God to be His witness? You are to testify of His saving power. You are to testify of His redeeming love. You are to be His witness to this lost and dying world that Jesus died for.

As a witness of the transforming love of God, you are to be an irresistible influence in your city, your state, your country, and the world. You have been placed on earth with the most incredible and the most important mission to employ. Your mission is to be a witness for Jesus. Your purpose is to represent Jesus in every conversation, every interaction, and every connection He provides.

What kind of witness are you? Your life, as a witness, will either draw people to Christ or repel them from Christ.

THE PEOPLE GOD USES

Available, People God Uses, Lordship, Availability

"'I am the Lord's servant,' Mary answered. 'May it be to me as you have said.' Then the angel left her." Luke 1:38 (NIV)

Why did God choose Mary to give birth to the Son of God? In His perfect wisdom, God chose Mary because He knew she would willingly make herself available for His use. Mary affirmed her availability by saying, "I am the Lord's servant." She honored God by her posture of availability. She demonstrated such a beautiful portrait of being receptive and responsive to God's will. Mary declared, "May it be to me as you have said." In other words, she was acknowledging that she belonged to God for His glory.

God uses people who are available. What is your level of availability for God's use? Often our lives become so cluttered and overextended that there's little room for availability. Can you relate? God wants to use you. God is more concerned about your availability than your ability.

What needs to change in your life? What adjustments need to be made in your daily schedule to make room for God? Your availability matters to God. Would you be willing to say, "Lord, I'm Yours?"

December 12
BEING INTENTIONAL
People God Uses, Intentional, John the Baptist

"The people were waiting expectantly and were all wondering in their hearts if John might possibly be the Christ. John answered them all, 'I baptize you with water. But one more powerful than I will come, the thongs of whose sandals I am not worthy to untie. He will baptize you with the Holy Spirit and with fire. His winnowing fork is in his hand to clear his threshing floor and to gather the wheat into his barn, but he will burn up the chaff with unquenchable fire.' And with many other words John exhorted the people and preached the good news to them." Luke 3:15-18 (NIV)

Knowing who you are "not" is just as important as knowing who you "are." God has designed you with a specific personality type. He formed you to be His image bearer. God saved you to fulfill His assignment for your life. It's not about your story that God plays a part in. It is all about God's story that you get to play a part in. God invites you to join Him in His story.

John the Baptist was clear about his identity. He understood that he was not the Christ. John understood and embraced his role as the one who would point others to Jesus. John the Baptist lived a focused life. He was intentional about preparing the way for others to encounter Jesus.

There is tremendous freedom in fulfilling God's purpose according to your unique design. Giving your life to something bigger than you, and to something that will impact others for eternity, is worth your focus. God uses people who are intentional. Are you intentionally on mission with God? Have you fully surrendered your life to God's agenda?

GIVING SACRIFICIALLY

People God Uses, Selfless

"Another of his disciples, Andrew, Simon Peter's brother, spoke up, 'Here is a boy with five small barley loaves and two small fish, but how far will they go among so many?'" John 6:8-9 (NIV)

The first question people ask during times of transition is, "How will this affect me?" If you have experienced the transition of a child moving onto a college campus, or taking on a new job assignment, or moving into a new neighborhood, or helping a loved one get acclimated to an assisted living center, you have probably asked the question, "How will this affect me?" We are by nature self-centered and self-absorbed. Often we act as though the earth rotates around our axis. It is so easy to become self-consumed.

Maybe that's why this encounter that Andrew had with a boy and his sack lunch means so much to me. Here's a boy who places the needs of others before his own. Here's a boy who has an aggressively developing appetite, yet selflessly gives up his lunch so that others can eat.

There is a valuable lesson for us to consider. It is not how much you have, but what you are willing to selflessly give in order to bless others. Jesus does not bless you based on what you have, but on how you give. Being selfish comes naturally. Being selfless is a result of walking in the Spirit. Being selfless is the product of an abiding relationship with Jesus.

Maybe there is a better question for us to ask: "How will this affect Jesus?"

December 14
COMPASSION IN ACTION

People God Uses, Compassionate, Good Samaritan

"But a Samaritan, as he traveled, came where the man was; and when he saw him, he took pity on him. He went to him and bandaged his wounds, pouring on oil and wine. Then he put the man on his own donkey, took him to an inn and took care of him. The next day he took out two silver coins and gave them to the innkeeper. 'Look after him,' he said, 'and when I return, I will reimburse you for any extra expense you may have.'" Luke 10:33-35 (NIV)

Has your day ever been interrupted by tragedy? How did you respond? The Good Samaritan responded to tragedy by getting involved in the resolution. He demonstrated compassion in action by seeking to meet the needs of the one who had been violated and wounded. While others walked on by as to keep their distance, the Good Samaritan walked directly to the man in desperate need to extend a helping hand.

Life is full of opportunities to ignore or meet needs. You can easily become apathetic and slip into a numb state of existence whereby the needs of others no longer tug at your heart strings. What if God wants you to get involved? What if God wants to use you to make an eternal difference in the life of someone in need? How will you respond?

- "When Jesus landed and saw a large crowd, he had compassion on them and healed their sick." Matt 14:14 (NIV)
- "When Jesus landed and saw a large crowd, he had compassion on them, because they were like sheep without a shepherd. So he began teaching them many things." Mark 6:34 (NIV)

Jesus is our model of compassion. Choose to be like Jesus!

GOD'S SPECIALTY

People God Uses, Paul, Brokenness

"But the Lord said to Ananias, 'Go! This man is my chosen instrument to carry my name before the Gentiles and their kings and before the people of Israel. I will show him how much he must suffer for my name.'" Acts 9:15-16 (NIV)

God specializes in using broken people. His love shines brightly through the cracks of broken vessels. Paul understood brokenness. Though he was God's chosen instrument to bring the gospel to the Gentiles, he traveled the way of suffering. As you read Paul's writings in the New Testament, you quickly detect that Paul's journey was filled with adversity. Here's a snapshot of some of his experiences.

> "Five times I received from the Jews the forty lashes minus one. Three times I was beaten with rods, once I was stoned, three times I was shipwrecked, I spent a night and a day in the open sea, I have been constantly on the move. I have been in danger from rivers, in danger from bandits, in danger from my own countrymen, in danger from Gentiles; in danger in the city, in danger in the country, in danger at sea; and in danger from false brothers. I have labored and toiled and have often gone without sleep, I have known hunger and thirst and have often gone without food; I have been cold and naked. Besides everything else, I face daily the pressure of my concern for all the churches." 2 Cor 11:24-28 (NIV)

Are you broken before the Lord? Anything that breaks the heart of God should break your heart. Often God will allow you to go through difficult circumstances to form the character of Christ in you. In your brokenness, you have a wonderful opportunity to know Christ more intimately and to make Him known more effectively.

December 16
HELPING OTHERS
People God Uses, Barnabas, Sensitive

"When he came to Jerusalem, he tried to join the disciples, but they were all afraid of him, not believing that he really was a disciple. But Barnabas took him and brought him to the apostles. He told them how Saul on his journey had seen the Lord and that the Lord had spoken to him, and how in Damascus he had preached fearlessly in the name of Jesus." Acts 9:26-27 (NIV)

Where would you be without someone believing in you? Everybody needs a Barnabas! Saul would have never become the Apostle Paul without a Barnabas in his life. Barnabas was sensitive to the activity of God. He recognized God at work in Saul's life and willingly stood in the gap for him when others wanted to reject him. Barnabas was sensitive enough to detect the person behind the murderous past. He identified what Saul could become as the Apostle Paul and thoughtfully worked behind the scenes to help Paul reach his God-given potential.

Spend some time reflecting on your spiritual journey. Identify the people God brought into your life who became like a Barnabas to you and helped you develop in your faith. Write their names down and pray over each name. Thank God for their influence in your life.

Are you willing to be a Barnabas to someone this week? Would you be willing to be sensitive to the activity of God in someone's life and allow God to use you to be a blessing?

EXTENDING HOSPITALITY

People God Uses, Lydia, Hospitable

"When she and the members of her household were baptized, she invited us to her home. 'If you consider me a believer in the Lord,' she said, 'come and stay at my house.' And she persuaded us." Acts 16:15 (NIV)

Have you ever been to someone's house and you felt right at home? After being there, you experienced a special touch of love and encouragement. You left feeling better than when you arrived! Now that's hospitality. When someone rolls out the red carpet on your behalf, you feel valued.

After Lydia became a Christ follower, she extended gracious hospitality to Paul and his traveling companions. Lydia rolled out the red carpet to make them feel right at home. She sought to meet their needs and to provide an atmosphere where they could be refreshed. Her ministry of hospitality did not end there. God blessed Lydia's hospitality and allowed her home to become the meeting place for the church at Philippi.

- *"After Paul and Silas came out of the prison, they went to Lydia's house, where they met with the brothers and encouraged them. Then they left." Acts 16:40 (NIV)*

During Paul's imprisonment in Rome, he wrote a beautiful love letter to the church at Philippi. You can read it now by opening the Bible and turning to the book of Philippians. God used Lydia to touch our lives even today through her willingness to be hospitable.

December 18
LIVING FOR THE GLOBAL GLORY OF GOD
Missions, Global Missions, Ends of the Earth

"Suddenly a great company of the heavenly host appeared with the angel, praising God and saying, 'Glory to God in the highest, and on earth peace to men on whom his favor rests.'" Luke 2:13-14 (NIV)

You are here to bring glory to God. You have been created by God to fulfill His agenda. God's agenda is global and your purpose is to live for His global glory. Don't waste your life. You are too valuable to God. Don't wade in the pool of apathy. Time is too short.

> • *"Why, you do not even know what will happen tomorrow. What is your life? You are a mist that appears for a little while and then vanishes." James 4:14 (NIV)*

The brevity of life and certainty of death are realities that should motivate us to passionately bring God glory every moment of each day. What are you doing for the global glory of God? It is impossible to be self-consumed and live for the global glory of God. It is impossible to be self-centered and live for the global glory of God.

The angels got it. They demonstrated at Jesus' birth that their focus was to bring glory to God. God alone is worthy of our adoration. God alone is worthy of a life focused on bringing Him glory. Are you willing to reorient your life around living for the global glory of God?

THE ULTIMATE PROMISE KEEPER
Missions, Global Missions, God

"He told them, 'This is what is written: The Christ will suffer and rise from the dead on the third day, and repentance and forgiveness of sins will be preached in his name to all nations, beginning at Jerusalem. You are witnesses of these things. I am going to send you what my Father has promised; but stay in the city until you have been clothed with power from on high." Luke 24:46-49 (NIV)

Jesus developed His disciples by investing time with them. He modeled what He wanted to multiply in them and through them. Jesus commissioned His followers to preach in His name to all nations. Then Jesus affirmed that He would send them what His Father had promised. He instructed them to stay in Jerusalem until they received the impartation of the promise.

God is the promise giver and He is a promise keeper. The promise He gave to the followers of Christ was the Person of the Holy Spirit. The promise He gives to every person who receives the gift of eternal life is the Holy Spirit.

> • *"We know that we live in him and he in us, because he has given us of his Spirit."* 1 John 4:13 (NIV)

Are you a child of the promise? Have you been born into God's family? God's glory lives in you in the Person of the Holy Spirit. Will you live for the global glory of God by sharing His promise with all nations beginning with your neighbors?

December 20
UNIFIED PRAYER
Prayer, Global Missions, Unity

"They all joined together constantly in prayer, along with the women and Mary the mother of Jesus, and with his brothers." Acts 1:14 (NIV)

Anticipating Christmas generates major excitement and energy. You can feel it in the air as people saturate their flower beds, yards, and homes with decorative lights. The traffic heightens as shoppers strategically complete their Christmas lists. Travelers prepare to make their rounds among the family traditions. Anticipation of celebrating the birth of Christ brings out the best in us.

Following the ascension of Christ, a hundred and twenty believers were gathered in the upper room anticipating the arrival of the Holy Spirit. They were anticipating the fulfillment of the Father's promise. They all joined together. They continued with one accord in prayer. The Greek word is "homothumadon" which means with one mind, one accord, and one passion. In the language of the New Testament, it means to have the same mind and to rush along in unison.

God honored their unity as demonstrated in their continual praying together. God allowed them to express their unity through a ten day prayer meeting of anticipation. Unified prayer was their preparation for the impartation of the Holy Spirit on the Day of Pentecost.

Do you pray in anticipation of God's answer? Have you experienced unified prayer with other believers? What if you brought unified prayer into your Christmas experience?

December 21
THE LANGUAGE OF LOVE
Missions, Global Missions, Ends of the Earth

"When the day of Pentecost came, they were all together in one place. Suddenly a sound like the blowing of a violent wind came from heaven and filled the whole house where they were sitting. They saw what seemed to be tongues of fire that separated and came to rest on each of them. All of them were filled with the Holy Spirit and began to speak in other tongues as the Spirit enabled them."
Acts 2:1-4 (NIV)

The joy of Christmas is celebrating the birth of Jesus and giving meaningful gifts to those we love. Jesus came to give us the ultimate gift, eternal life. As we exchange gifts this Christmas, it is an expression of valuing others. As you shop for that perfect gift to bless someone dear to you, you thoughtfully consider what they need and what they like. You consider their tastes, interests, and desires. You focus your gift on their uniqueness.

God speaks your love language in that He meets you at your greatest point of need. Salvation has come in the miracle of the manger, Jesus, born to bring life everlasting. On the Day of Pentecost, God demonstrated that the Gospel is for everyone. He broke through the ethnic and language barriers by allowing those present in Jerusalem to hear the Gospel in their own language. As the people groups represented in Jerusalem on the Day of Pentecost returned to their homeland, the Gospel spread.

God's love language is universal. The miracle of Christmas is that, in Christ, God's glory may be revealed to all nations. Are you available for God's use?

December 22
ANNOUNCING GOOD NEWS
Christmas, Awareness, Shepherds

"And there were shepherds living out in the fields nearby, keeping watch over their flocks at night. An angel of the Lord appeared to them, and the glory of the Lord shone around them, and they were terrified. But the angel said to them, 'Do not be afraid. I bring you good news of great joy that will be for all the people. Today in the town of David a Savior has been born to you; he is Christ the Lord. This will be a sign to you: You will find a baby wrapped in cloths and lying in a manger.'" Luke 2:8-12 (NIV)

God is always at work. He never sleeps and never takes a power nap. God's activity is redemptive. In His redemptive activity, God chose to announce His good news of great joy to shepherds. Shepherds were considered unclean in their day. They were not honored for their vocational choice. Though despised by people, they were loved by God. God allowed the shepherds to participate in His redemptive activity.

Is there anyone you have been praying for lately who is in need of salvation? Have you had moments of doubt? Maybe you have wondered if it is even possible for God to convince them of their need for salvation. You may have felt that they are beyond God's reach. The good news of great joy is that there is not a person on planet earth beyond God's reach. For Christmas, be reminded of God's activity. Ask God to heighten your awareness of His activity. Make yourself available for the redemptive activity of God in the one you have been praying for. God is working!

RESPONDING TO GOD'S INVITATION

Christmas, Response, Obedience

"When the angels had left them and gone into heaven, the shepherds said to one another, 'Let's go to Bethlehem and see this thing that has happened, which the Lord has told us about.' So they hurried off and found Mary and Joseph, and the baby, who was lying in the manger. When they had seen him, they spread the word concerning what had been told them about this child, and all who heard it were amazed at what the shepherds said to them." Luke 2:15-18 (NIV)

God speaks. God reveals Himself so that we may know Him and serve Him. God invites us to join Him in His redemptive activity. He includes us in the redemptive process. Yes! God could accomplish His mission without us. He doesn't need us. God chooses to use us in communicating His love to a lost and drifting world.

The shepherds responded to God's invitation through instant obedience. They hurried off to find Jesus! There wasn't a delay to calculate the cost of obedience. They passionately sought the Lord and responded to God's offer instantly. The shepherds are examples of how God's revelation demands a response. They could have responded in apathy or in resolve.

What has God revealed to you? Have you responded to God's revelation by obeying instantly? What is keeping you from walking in the light God has given you? Imagine responding to God with a resolute, "Yes, Lord!" For Christmas, consider what God has been speaking into your life. Make a decision to trust God and His perfect timing. Decide to obey Him instantly. Leave the results up to God!

December 24
REFLECTING ON SPIRITUAL MARKERS
Christmas, Spiritual Markers

"But Mary treasured up all these things and pondered them in her heart."
Luke 2:19 (NIV)

Think back to a Christmas experience you had in which you were deeply moved. Do you remember the specifics of the event that made it so touching? With our modern day affinity for technology, you probably captured the experience with a camera or a video recorder. Special moments are worth capturing and worth sharing.

Mary's experience was beyond words. Though cameras were nonexistent at that time, God gave Mary the wonderful capacity to treasure up all the things that the shepherds had shared with her concerning Jesus. She pondered them in her heart. Mary gathered all the information coming her way about Jesus, and she embraced God's activity. Can you imagine how she felt? Mary was chosen by God to bring the Savior into our world.

Have you recognized the value God places on you? Retrace the spiritual markers in your life. Spend time reflecting on each one. Treasure each one and ponder them in your heart. Consider how God is at work in you, around you, and through you to bring His light and His love into our world of desperation.

Our Savior Is Born

Christmas, Incarnation, Soulwinning

"All this took place to fulfill what the Lord had said through the prophet: 'The virgin will be with child and will give birth to a son, and they will call him Immanuel' --which means, 'God with us.'" Matt 1:22-23 (NIV)

Merry Christmas to you and your family!

The day we have been anticipating all year is finally here. We have the wonderful privilege of celebrating the birth that changed our past, present, and future. Jesus is born!

God is with us. God is for us. God is in us. This day of celebration goes far beyond simply a day of exchanging gifts and seeing our loved ones. This day marks the day when God became like us so that we could become like Him. Have you received the ultimate gift made available to you by God? Have you received God's gift of eternal life? If so, then say so!

- *"The shepherds returned, glorifying and praising God for all the things they had heard and seen, which were just as they had been told."* Luke 2:20 (NIV)
- *"I pray that you may be active in sharing your faith, so that you will have a full understanding of every good thing we have in Christ."* Philem 1:6 (NIV)

Are you willing to share the ultimate gift that you have received with others? Jesus came to earth, lived, died, rose from the dead, and ascended back to heaven so that we could have eternal life and share it with others. Now that's what Christmas is all about!

December 26
DECLARING YOUR FAITH
Christmas, Faith, Witnessing

"The shepherds returned, glorifying and praising God for all the things they had heard and seen, which were just as they had been told." Luke 2:20 (NIV)

The Christmas story is rooted in God's nature and character.

God's story is the story of redemption. In His grace and mercy, God has come to us in order to rescue us from our sin and our eternal damnation. God's redemptive activity is an outflow of His holiness and compassion.

The shepherds responded to God's invitation by going into Bethlehem to see Jesus lying in a manger. They shared their angelic experience with Joseph and Mary to affirm their belief in Jesus as the savior of the world. The shepherds returned with an attitude of praise and adoration for all that God had done in their midst. They identified that their personal experience lined up with God's revelation.

God keeps His word. When God speaks, you will know that His activity is just as He said. The shepherds anchored their faith in the certainty of God's revelation. You can trust God to do what He says He will do. There isn't a fraction of error. God speaks so that we can know Him, serve Him, and make Him known throughout the earth.

THE TESTING OF YOUR FAITH
Faith, Doing Life, Trials, Perseverance

"Consider it pure joy, my brothers, whenever you face trials of many kinds, because you know that the testing of your faith develops perseverance. Perseverance must finish its work so that you may be mature and complete, not lacking anything."
James 1:2-4 (NIV)

My dad has had a life of trials. His parents were alcoholics, and a few years into his marriage to my mom, he became an alcoholic. My mom and dad divorced when I was about seven. My dad spent most of his adult life in and out of prison and combating the ferocious enemy, alcohol. The last few years have been tranquil as he has aged.

Today, I took my dad to visit the nursing home he has picked out for his next place of residence. I met with the administrator and signed the paperwork. It's hard to believe that I would be helping my dad prepare for this type of transition. I think it has been a day of facing this trial and allowing God to test our faith and develop perseverance.

Walking with God for the past three decades, I have learned that God is serious about spiritual maturity. God uses all kinds of situations and circumstances in our lives to bring us into maturity. He does not want us to lack anything. God also allows us to experience trials in order to reveal His heart of compassion. God cares about you and everything you go through.

Doing life requires trusting in God's provision. Doing life in a fallen world creates opportunities for us to experience joy in the midst of adversity. God's character does not shift. He is the Rock. Consider your circumstances, and then consider it pure joy. God is up to something special in your life.

December 28
PUTTING FEET TO YOUR FAITH
Trust, Faith, Obedience

"Was not our ancestor Abraham considered righteous for what he did when he offered his son Isaac on the altar? You see that his faith and his actions were working together, and his faith was made complete by what he did."
James 2:21-22 (NIV)

Doing life requires faith. As a follower of Jesus Christ, you are in the minority on this planet. You are doing life on the narrow path in the midst of a fallen world. Your beliefs will be challenged. Living the Christian life will be marked by opposition and resistance. However, your faith in Christ and His provision will be authenticated by your actions.

Are you putting feet to your faith? Are you allowing your faith to hit the pavement of real life in the real world? Abraham serves as a wonderful example of trusting in God's provision no matter the cost. He was willing to sacrifice his only son in order to be obedient to God. As you know, God came to the rescue in the fourth quarter with a few seconds left on the clock. God provided the substitute. Why did God allow Abraham to go through such a trying experience? God was testing Abraham's faith.

Do you fully trust God to do what He says He will do? Do you fully trust God to empower you to do life His way during your short stay upon the earth? God wants to reveal His glory in you and through you as you live out your faith. Allow your faith to be expressed to a watching world by your actions. As you are doing life, your faith will either attract others to Christ or distract them from Christ. Will your actions give evidence to a vibrant faith in God?

MAKING THINGS RIGHT

Life, Reconciliation, Forgiveness

"All kinds of animals, birds, reptiles and creatures of the sea are being tamed and have been tamed by man, but no man can tame the tongue. It is a restless evil, full of deadly poison." James 3:7-8 (NIV)

Doing life requires restraint. There are countless temptations used of Satan to entice us to compromise our Christianity. His goal is to get us to drift from our devotion to God. One of Satan's favorite tools is an unbridled tongue. He knows that our words can do more damage than our actions alone.

Have you ever said something you deeply regretted? Have you had one of those moments when you spoke before you had time to really think through and process what you were going to say? Ouch! It is impossible to retrieve words once spoken. If only we could snatch them out of the air before they made contact with the tympanic membrane of someone's ear. If you have ever allowed words to slip and wound someone, then embrace this great word from God on how to respond.

- *"If you have been trapped by what you said, ensnared by the words of your mouth, then do this, my son, to free yourself, since you have fallen into your neighbor's hands: Go and humble yourself; press your plea with your neighbor!" Prov 6:2-3 (NIV)*

Has God placed someone on your heart that you have wounded with your words? Are you willing to go to them in humility in order to apologize and ask for their forgiveness? God will honor your obedience to His word. God will make a way for you to experience restoration. Restoration is God's specialty! Don't delay. Make things right!

December 30
SUBMITTING TO GOD'S AGENDA
Life, Submission, God's Will

"Submit yourselves, then, to God. Resist the devil, and he will flee from you."
James 4:7 (NIV)

Doing life involves submission and opposition readiness. God is at work and the devil is at work. Anytime you choose to join God in His activity, Satan will oppose. You can walk in victory by submitting to God. Submission is a conscious choice to surrender your agenda to God's agenda. Moment by moment surrender allows God to have His way in your life. Your usefulness to God will be proportionate to your willful submission to God.

It is not enough to submit to God's agenda; you must also resist the devil. Opposition readiness is not optional for the follower of Christ. If you are going to reign victorious in this life, you must consciously resist the lure of the enemy. Satan is the master of disguise. He seeks to get you to drift into his path and to get you to neglect your devotion to God.

Will you submit to God? Will you resist the devil?

ANTICIPATING THE LORD'S RETURN
Life, Second Coming, Anticipation

"Be patient, then, brothers, until the Lord's coming. See how the farmer waits for the land to yield its valuable crop and how patient he is for the autumn and spring rains. You too, be patient and stand firm, because the Lord's coming is near." James 5:7-8 (NIV)

In our society of instant coffee, microwavable breakfast, and fast food, we don't wait well. We want what we want right now. When it comes to the return of Christ, patience is required.

Jesus came to the earth, lived, died a sacrificial death, rose from the dead, and ascended to the Father in heaven. Jesus is coming again. In His second coming, Jesus will come like a thief in the night.

We tend to get so comfortable in this life that we forget about the reality of the Lord's return. Just as a farmer waits patiently for the rain and the fruition of his crops, we are to wait patiently for the Lord's return. That means to live in anticipation of the visible return of the Lord. We are to stand firm by obeying God's Word with the expectation of the soon coming of Christ.

Could Jesus come back today? Are you ready for His return? Turn your eyes upon the Lord and anticipate His return.

NOTES

NOTES

NOTES

INDEX

374